THE ENSIGN LEAVING YARMOUTH ON HER FIRST VOYAGE.

Frontispiece.

"NOR'ARD OF THE DOGGER"

OR

Deep Sea Trials and Gospel Triumphs.

*BEING THE STORY OF THE INITIATION, STRUGGLES,
AND SUCCESSES OF THE MISSION TO
DEEP SEA FISHERMEN.*

BY

E. J. MATHER,

FOUNDER AND DIRECTOR.

With Illustrations

BY J. R. WELLS AND C. J. STANILAND, R.I.

Antony Rowe
Publishing Services

This book has been printed digitally and produced in a standard
specification in order to ensure its continuing availability

Published by Antony Rowe Publishing Services in 2005
2 Whittle Drive
Highfield Industrial Estate
Eastbourne
East Sussex
BN23 6QT
England

ISBN 1-905200-14-5

Printed and bound by Antony Rowe Ltd, Eastbourne

To the Queen.

MADAM,

Conscious of the many literary failings of the narrative, yet confident of your gracious interest, I dedicate to Your Majesty this Story of successful effort to better the condition of those thousands of your subjects whose lives are spent upon the wild North Sea.

Permit me to subscribe myself,

MADAM,

Your Majesty's most obedient

and very humble Servant,

E. J. MATHER.

ST. ANDREW'S DAY,
1887.

FOREWARD
The Countess of Euston, High Sheriff of Suffolk 2004-5

In this reprinting of E J Mather's book, we celebrate 125 years of service to fishing people throughout the United Kingdom. Mather's association with the Fishermen's Mission is best shown by his book telling of the initiation, struggles and successes of a work carried out among fishermen and their families since 1881.

Nor'ard of the Dogger was first published in 1887 and was dedicated, by permission, to Queen Victoria, who read it with interest at Balmoral. She not only sent £50 to the funds of the Mission but also became Patron, and in other ways showed her sympathy with a work of which she saw the far reaching possibilities for good.

My own family links with the Mission go back to 1886 when the then Duchess of Grafton supplied the sixth Mission ship "Euston" in memory of her late husband. The vessel was 80 tons and joined the Lowestoft fleet under Skipper Snell. Her war years were spent under Admiralty orders in Scapa Flow providing care and comforts for the hundreds of crews of minesweepers and patrol boats.

Today , 125 years later, that good work among our fishing communities continues. It began by the insight, dedication and Christian motivation of Ebenezer Mather. A work that still has "far reaching possibilities for good" among those who carry our 'peacetime's most dangerous job" - bringing in the harvest of the sea.

With all best wishes

Ann Euston

The Countess of Euston
Euston
Suffolk

PREFACE.

BEING associated with Mr. Mather in the good work carried on by the Mission to Deep Sea Fishermen, I have acceded to his request to write a few remarks by way of preface to this interesting book. If I were now to deal with the subject of this Mission, as I hope to do some day, I should have to dwell at great length on its social, moral, sanitary, and national aspects. On every one of these there is almost as much to be said as upon the subjects embraced in the following pages. It is possible that there are many earnest and good people who, though they may not have zeal for the religious element of our Mission, may nevertheless desire an opportunity of helping us for other reasons. The Mission is as well for the body as the soul, and in order to enlist sympathy for our work in its philanthropic aspect I cannot do better than reproduce here a letter which I wrote to Mr. Mather on the occasion of the dedication of the smack *Euston* :—

"BOARD OF TRADE, WHITEHALL, *May* 28, 1886.

"DEAR MR. MATHER,—It is as I feared it would be. I have a press of work, both official and private, and I am none too well. I cannot be with you to-morrow, but all my good wishes will be there. I have no doubt that many speakers will put before the meeting the aspect of your Mission from the religious point of view, and will point to its success in that field with satisfaction. This they are well entitled to do. But I had intended, could I have been present, to refer to another aspect of the case, and to confine my remarks to that. I mean the work-a-day useful work of the Mission in its bearings on the physical and social well-being of the men. There are people who may not take an interest in matters solely religious, but who will take an interest in the physical well-being of the masses. Now, what I wanted to point out was, that for this sort of people, as well as for the other, there is grand work in the support of the Mission-ships. The giving of surgical and medical aid to the wounded or sick, the distribution of healthy literature to minds that would otherwise for a time be unemployed, the cheery home influence brought to crews of the trawlers by the presence of the Mission-smacks, the self-respect engendered by inducing the men to keep away from the floating grog-ships, the safety to property and to life that is a constant attendant on the successful work of the Mission-ships—all these things, even if they stood by themselves, are objects which the general public ought to appreciate, and which every one desiring to give to Fisherman Jack and his wife and bairns a lift up and a helping hand should subscribe to.—Wishing you every success in your useful and therefore good work, believe me, ever yours sincerely, "THOMAS GRAY."

I will not, by any further remarks, stand between the reader and Mr. Mather's enthusiastic and charming narrative.

THOMAS GRAY.

CONTENTS.

—◆◆—

viii   CONTENTS.

NOR'ARD OF THE DOGGER.

—◆—

CHAPTER I.

A NEW CRUSADE.

"Darkness was upon the face of the deep, and the Spirit of God moved upon the face of the waters."

"Don't you think something might be done for our men in the North Sea?" This enquiry was addressed to me in the autumn of 1881 by a gentleman who was largely interested in the fleet known as the "Short Blue," nearly all the vessels in which are either owned by or mortgaged to Messrs. Hewett & Co., the pioneers of "fleeting," as now extensively carried on.

The question puzzled me. The questioner was evidently quite serious, but my ignorance of the very existence of "our men in the North Sea" prevented my grasping his full meaning; so I innocently replied, "Yes, I might send them some parcels of tracts." My friend exclaimed, laughing heartily—(I have laughed myself many times since,

A

when thinking of the answer in the light of knowledge subsequently acquired)—"You cannot have much notion of who and what our men are if you consider that sending parcels of tracts would be 'doing' anything in the sense in which I intended it."

Until then my information on the important question of our national fish supply had been of the most meagre character. Fish appeared on my table. I was aware that it came from the fishmonger's, but beyond that I had not troubled to inquire. For aught I knew, it might have grown on the fishmonger's slab; or at any rate, it was caught by men who went out at night from the towns and villages on the coast, and returned with the dawn to be welcomed by watchful wife and bairns. At all events, there could be no question of claim upon me in respect of the fish consumed at my table, for were not my housekeeping accounts settled weekly?

I now know that, although so far as concerned my fish bills I had punctually paid the price demanded by the fishmonger, there is another price, rigorously exacted and duly paid away in the North Sea, of the items of which I had never even heard.

No notion had I until that day of a floating population, numbering upwards of twelve thousand, being found, year in, year out, tossed upon the wild

North Sea, between 54° and 56° N. latitude, too far from land to run for shelter, and compelled to ride out the heaviest gales or founder. For the deep-sea trawler spends only a few days ashore between those eight weeks' voyages which succeed each other through all seasons, and year after year, from the time he first ships as a boy until premature old age incapacitates him for further labour, or—as is, alas! too often the case—he falls a prey to the furious winter storms which rage in the German Ocean.

My friend's remarks excited my interest in a novel subject; the interview was prolonged, for every question I put to him elicited some fresh and startling information, until presently I became not interested merely, but intensely pained and shocked at the condition of things revealed, and eager to ascertain by personal investigation whether or no "something could be done," some remedy be devised and applied.

To be actively interested in missionary effort both at home and abroad, and yet live for many years in absolute ignorance of a "field white already to harvest" lying unreaped at our very doors, is a humiliating discovery, and I confess to having been at first somewhat sceptical; but facts, cited by one who was in a position to speak positively, convinced me that here indeed was work of an unique

and possibly perilous character, and, in the result,
I sought and obtained permission to visit the " Short
Blue " fleet in one of the fish-carrying steamers.

Since first, by God's grace, I learned to know
the Saviour, and perhaps more especially since a
long and serious illness, some twelve years ago, I
have sought to cultivate the habit of turning instinctively to God, realising and enjoying the child's
privilege of bringing to the Father every circumstance of the daily path, and seeking His guidance
and blessing. So, when my friend had gone, I
thought quietly and prayerfully over all he had told
me, and came to the conclusion that his visit had
not been a mere accident, but that the Master
had fresh work to be done, and was leading in this
matter for the accomplishment of His own purposes.
Little did I then think how much lay ahead for
the glory of God, and the blessing, temporal and
spiritual, of thousands of deserving yet neglected
men.

Our blessed Lord, when on earth, sent forth His
disciples by two and two, and I was happy in
securing the companionship of a friend and fellow-
worker, the Rev. R. B. Thompson, now the Vicar of
a Yorkshire parish, and, moreover, *a good sailor*.

This latter qualification is a *sine qua non* for
missioners on the high seas, and no one should
attempt the work who is not only a good sailor, but

prepared to face both discomfort and danger in the service of his Divine Master.

For several days before we started there had been strong winds ashore, and it was likely to prove rough outside ; but our time was so very fully occupied, that there was no chance of postponing the trip until the return of more favourable weather. Taking train at 7.30 A.M. from Fenchurch Street to Rainham, my friend the Vicar and I walked across the marshes which extend from the station to the river-side. Here we were ferried on board the *Supply*, an iron steamer 100 feet long, 24 feet beam, and built especially for the fish-carrying trade. We found her lying alongside the coal-hulk, the captain and crew already on board, forty-five tons of coal stowed in the bunkers, thirty tons of ice in the ice-room, and 3000 empty fish trunks in the hold.

The captain, a quiet, determined-looking man, bade us welcome, and within half an hour of our arrival we had cast off from the hulk, and waved our adieux to old Charlie Bull, the ship-keeper, who, notwithstanding the bustle of departure, had found time to say to us, " Bless the Lord, gentlemen, I've been agoin' the road to glory these thirty years, and I'm right down glad to see yer a-goin' where you are, for there's a many of 'em never thinks o' nothin' beyond this life, and God knows it's a precious hard life for 'em at the best o' times. God bless ye, gentlemen! God bless ye!"

As we steamed past Gravesend and onwards towards the Nore, I inquired from the captain where he expected to find the "Short Blue" fleet.

"Somewheres to the *Nor'ard of the Dawger*," he replied; "they've just crossed over." He might as well have told me the middle of the Atlantic!

But my object in making this cruise was to obtain information, and as the skipper was quite ready to answer questions, although singularly silent and taciturn when not actually addressed, I managed while standing at his side that day to store my mind with a vast amount of knowledge not usually found in books, but, all the same, of great value.

The good skipper must have thought me rather a bore, but he was most patient under the infliction, and explained very clearly the nature and extent of the vast submarine field from which a harvest approaching 400,000 tons of excellent human food is annually reaped—a yield, in proportion to the acreage, greatly in excess of that produced under cultivation on shore. I learned that the Dogger Bank extends some 170 miles north and south, by 65 miles east and west, and that by the expression "just crossed over" he meant that the "Short Blues" had been trawling for four months on "the other side," *i.e.*, off the coast of Holland and North Germany, but had now changed their ground for the season, and would probably work gradually down to the south'ard of the Bank, so as to escape the tremendous seas which roll in along its northern edge during the winter.

This and much more I gleaned from my informant, and then was gratified to find that he himself was a Christian, and he manifested the deepest interest in my story, and especially on learning that I was going out with a view to ascertaining what could be done towards organising permanent missionary effort, and armed with 1000 portions of the New Testament, freely granted by the British and Foreign Bible Society, and more than that number of illustrated periodicals given by the Religious Tract Society, for free distribution amongst the smacksmen.

As not only the captain of the *Supply*, but several of his crew were Christian men, and heartily in sympathy, some meetings for prayer and Bible-reading were held during the trip out and home. We came up with the "Short Blues" about 300 miles from the Thames, and though I had frequently passed through fleets of herring, mackerel, and pilchard fishing craft, I was not prepared for the imposing sight of 220 fine smacks of from fifty to eighty tons burden, their tanned sails reflecting the most brilliant scarlet in the rays of the setting sun, and extending for several miles east and west of the admiral's vessel.

Our arrival was the signal for a wild scramble to gain possession of the empty fish trunks which the steamer had taken out from London. Boats manned by crews as rough, unkempt, and boisterous in manners as appearance, put off from all the smacks, and our deck soon swarmed with some 400 of the wildest fellows I had ever seen.

Amongst the 1 500 hands in the fleet there were perhaps twenty-five or thirty professing Christians, but the great majority were utterly careless and godless, and on that afternoon some of them appeared to indulge in language more coarse, profane, and disgusting than usual. As soon as all the boxes were out, the delivery of the fish commenced, but the crush of boats around the steamer was so great as to become a source of danger, each crew endeavouring to seize the first turn and circumvent their neighbours; the painters were soon hopelessly entangled, and there seemed every prospect of a free fight on the deck of the cutter, when the captain settled the matter in a rough and ready fashion by casting off the ropes and steaming ahead for fully a mile. This gave a little breathing space to the men engaged in stowing the fish in the carrier's hold, and allowed time for the angry

FETCHING BOXES FROM THE CARRIER.

passions of the boats' crews to expend themselves in a spell of hard rowing!

Now was our opportunity for dispensing the store of books, and they were thankfully—even greedily—accepted. One after another the burly smacksmen edged their way towards us and begged for "a bit o' reading," and the few words spoken for the Master were in most cases respectfully listened to.

Here and there an insulting or threatening word was spoken, but if one man appeared anxious to "capsize" us and our books, there were a dozen ready to defend us from attack; for the work of distribution proved a famous means of introduction, and many a quiet yarn was secured with men who at first fought shy of the "nobs from London;" while, best of all, we were cordially greeted by several who boldly declared themselves "on the Lord's side." To these I confided my desires and hopes with regard to some permanent work in the fleets, and warm were the expressions of gratitude, loud and fervent the exclamations of "Praise the Lord!" when they learnt that something was to be done for them. One dear old fellow, whose bright heavenly smile spoke more eloquently than his words, told me he had been praying for thirty years that the Lord would in His mercy look down upon them and furnish them with some place of worship where they could gather together without

fear of being discharged by their employers. I
learned that Messrs. Hewett had no objection to
men observing the Lord's day, but that several of
the smaller owners not only insisted upon the
trawling being carried on seven days a week, but
also objected to their smacks being used for the
purpose of a prayer-meeting, one owner dismissing
a skipper from his employ with the remark, " I'll
have no hallelujah aboard my vessel ! "

In another case I was told of a small fleet, all
the skippers in which were anxious to keep their
trawls on board on Sunday, and accordingly sent
home a " round robin " to the owners, praying for this
concession.   They waited anxiously for the return
of the cutter with the owners' reply, and when at
length it reached them, their hopes were utterly
dashed, for the employers, while saying that they
would not forbid their skippers to keep the gear on
board, gave them clearly to understand that any
skipper doing so would run the risk of losing his
berth at the close of the voyage.   The matter was
quietly and prayerfully discussed, and eventually
all but one agreed " we ought to serve God rather
than man," and so Sunday after Sunday this solitary dissentient laboured with his gear while all the
other vessels in the fleet were lying-to.   As each
skipper's voyage expired, he ran home for the bi-
monthly refit, yet not a word was said about dis-

charging him, and as this happened to every skipper in turn, they made up their minds that the threat was an empty one.

However, at Christmas the secret came out, for the owner, according to custom, read aloud to his assembled crews the list of the different vessels' earnings during the year. At last he stopped, and put down the paper.

"Oh, but, sir," exclaimed several skippers, "you haven't read what so and so made" (the skipper who had fished seven days a week).

"Why, what is that to you? I've read what *you've* made; doesn't that satisfy you?"

"Why, no, sir; 'cause don't you see he's fished every Sunday while we've kept our trawls aboard."

"Well, well," muttered the owner, "I suppose it's sure to come out, so I may as well tell you. He's at the bottom of the list!"

The man who related this story added reverently, "*Them that honour Me I will honour, but he that despiseth Me shall be lightly esteemed.*" To which I could but respond, "Amen!"

Here were men, loyal to their Saviour, true-hearted earnest Christians, longing for facilities for Divine worship and increased opportunities of public testimony to the hundreds of unconverted men around them, and yet almost entirely debarred from either. True, they frequently proved that

"where there's a will there's a way," hoisting a
Bethel-flag on board some fishing-smack, and sending up to the Throne of Grace and forth over the
sea around the vessel the joyous and inspiriting
sounds of united prayer and praise, but an ordinary
fishing-smack was not the place in which Divine
service could be conducted with any degree of
comfort; the tiny cabin was too confined to admit
more than a dozen occupants, while the space in the
hold was devoted to the stowage of gear. These
good men might truthfully say—

> "*What various hindrances we meet*
> When we approach the mercy-seat!"

Yet, spite of all the hindrances and annoyances,
the jeers of certain of their mates, the open opposition of others, the positive persecution by some of
the employers—spite of all this, the faithful band
held on, trusting with simple confidence in their
Heavenly Father, that He would in His own good
time and way send them "some better thing."

Most interesting were the conversations I held
with these men, gleaning much valuable information as to their mode of life and the many
hardships they were compelled to endure, until
presently we were reminded that all things must
have an end, even a smacksman's day of toil.

The last streak of daylight disappeared, the

last boat pulled away from the carrier, the Admiral's rocket signalled " Down trawl ; " the great fleet fell into open order on the starboard tack, and, as night finally closed in upon us, the twinkling of the numerous masthead lights—with now and again the song of some solitary watcher borne faintly down on the breeze—was the only evidence of our being in the midst of a vast floating town. Then, supper over, some of those whose hearts God had touched, met together in the skipper's cabin for prayer and thanksgiving ; my friend the Vicar gave a powerful address upon the passage " And there was no more sea " (Rev. xxi. 1) ; and very solemn was the hour thus spent at the Throne of Grace.

CHAPTER II.

CLOSER INSPECTION.

" Love kindles as I gaze.   I feel desires
That give assurance of their own success,
And that, infused from Heaven, must thither tend."

WITH the first streak of dawn up went our rockets, and the animated scene of the previous evening was re-enacted, for the fish caught during the night must be ferried from smack to steamer, and no one dreams of rest or breakfast until the fish is iced, the last trunk safely stowed below, the hatches battened down, and the steamer on her way to market.

Soon after three o'clock I was on the bridge surveying the lovely seascape spread around me. In every direction the smacks were lying, with the foresail down, engaged in hauling the trawl. There was still a heavy swell, and the wind suddenly freshened as the sun burst upwards from the eastern sea, a glorious golden ball, not as yet too dazzling to allow of a steady gaze, but momentarily increasing in power and driving away the mists through whose medium it had at first been seen.

"What do you think of the weather, captain?" I asked, as the skipper joined me on the bridge.

"The morning's too proud, sir. I shouldn't be surprised if it turned to rain, with a spell of that old breeze back again." And so indeed it proved before the day was many hours older.

Just then the skipper drew my attention to a smack running round our stern, and said, "He's a hailing you, sir."

"Hailing *me?* Why I don't know any one out here."

"May be not, but that's H——, who sent his boat alongside us the second time last night to get some more books from you. He couldn't leave his wessel, and now he's running round us to thank you."

I looked in the direction indicated, and replied to the peculiar fling of the right hand, and the shout, "What cheer! what cheer, O!" by pointing upwards with my finger.

"Ay, ay! bless the Lord!" came back across the waters as the smack dashed onwards.

The delivery of the fish was now in full swing. Smack after smack bore down towards us, their boats towing alongside, and I watched with a keen and growing interest the process of "ferrying." As each smack arrived in a suitable position to windward of the carrier, the boat's painter was cast off, and the crew took to the oars, facing the bows, and standing to their work.   For more than twenty years I had been accustomed to boating, had pulled my 'thirty-three miles a day against stream, had taken an oar in a rough sea in quest of a capsized boat's crew, but never had I seen such rowing as this. I have witnessed the ferrying or "boarding" of the fish many times since, but the conviction rather increases than diminishes that it is one of the most remarkable and thrilling sights the world can show. Cool intrepidity, the keenest watchfulness, and withal unusual muscular power, are the essentials for this. labour; but, given all these requisites, boarding fish in the open sea must ever remain the most perilous part of a smacksman's calling.

"We lose, on an average, thirty-five men every year in boarding fish," said the owner of a large fleet, to whom I was speaking on the subject.

"But don't you think many lives could be save if life-belts were worn?"

"No doubt, but the men won't wear them; they are afraid of being laughed at and called cowards."

"In other words, they won't wear them because they *are* cowards," I suggested.

The owner smiled and said, "Yes, I suppose that is the truth."

It was indeed the truth.   Here were men of

FERRYING THE FISH—BAD WEATHER.

P. 16.

splendid physique, of proved physical courage, prepared to face without flinching the many dangers incidental to their calling, yet utterly deficient in that moral courage which could face the chaff and ridicule of their mates! However, I made a mental note of the owner's words, and when in due time vessels came under my own control, instructed the ship's husband to make it a *sine qua non*, when engaging a new man, that he should agree to wear a life-jacket whenever engaged in small-boat work. The example thus set has proved contagious; many fishing-smacks have been supplied with life-jackets at the owner's cost. Messrs. Hewett & Co. have not only placed life-jackets of an improved type on board every vessel in their large fleet, but presented a number for the use of the Mission, and news has just reached me, while preparing these sheets for the press, of three men being rescued in the "Short Blue" fleet entirely through wearing these invaluable protections.

There is much to be said upon this subject, and it is referred to in a later chapter. But after every argument has been adduced in favour of "catching the market," the hard, incontrovertible fact remains, that while the market is caught in the interests of trade, it is too frequently caught at the cost of human life.

The smacksman may be rough and unrefined,

B

yet we agree—at any rate in theory—that his life
equals in value the life of the millionaire upon
whose table appears the product of his toil. This
is undoubtedly so in the eyes of Him who is the
Maker of us all.

We are, then, bound to agree further, that to needlessly risk that valuable life in order to secure a good
market is a distinct wrong to the man himself, to
those dependent on him, to the State, and to God.

To put this theoretical agreement in practice
means that measures shall be taken to prevent—if
needs be by legal enactment—the boarding of fish
in bad weather.

But I am anticipating, and must return to that
early morning six years ago.

Hour by hour the work progressed. As each
boat came alongside, one of the crew poised for a
moment on the bow thwart; then, as the boat rose
on the crest of a wave to the level of the steamer's
rail, he gripped the end of the long painter firmly
in his teeth (an easy matter for men accustomed to
masticating sea-biscuits), and leaped on our deck.
Instantly turning, he made fast the painter, and
then received, one by one, from his mates below,
the heavy trunks of fish with which their boat was
laden. In every case the same operation is repeated.
The trunks have a handle—or rather hand-hole—
at either end, and with a mighty heave they are

deposited on the rail of the carrier, as each succeeding wave enables the acrobats to perform the feat. More than once from my coign of vantage on the bridge I saw slight accidents. Either the men in the boat were a moment too soon or too late in heaving, or the man on deck not smart enough in seizing the trunk from their hands. The result in either case was the same; overboard went trunk and fish, the consequent exclamations varying in force according to the value of the particular fish; for "prime" and "offal" were rigorously kept apart.* It struck me at once that, with such incessant heavy labour, carried on amid conditions so unfavourable, there must be many serious cases of fracture and contusion, apart altogether from the loss of life through drowning.

The skipper more than confirmed my impression, and in answer to my startled inquiry, "But what can you do out here for the poor fellows?" promptly replied—

"Do for them! Why, nothing, sir—nothing whatever. We take 'em up to the orspital."

"Do you mean to say that a man, however seriously he may be injured, however grave his illness, has no resource but to be taken to London

* The "prime" fish are soles, turbot, halibut, and brill. Plaice, haddock, cod, ling, conger eel, whiting, gurnet, and skate come under the technical head of "offal."

in one of these carriers, tossed about for at least two days, in all his agony, before medical or surgical aid can be reached ? "

" That's so," responded the skipper. " You understand it wouldn't pay a doctor to come and live out here ; and even if it would, I reckon there's precious few doctors would care to run the risk."

" Why so, skipper ? "

" Because, don't you see, sir, although it's bad enough even at this time of year, it's in the long winter that the accidents mostly happen, and then it would mean the doctor would have to go his rounds among his patients in one o' them small boats, and I guess one day's work of that kind would about settle him."

" Perhaps you are right; but it makes one's heart ache to think of the sufferings of these poor fellows, away three hundred miles from all skilled assistance or careful nursing. Why, it must mean certain death in many cases."

" Very true, sir. I've known scores, myself, during the years I've been in the trade, who've been took home ill or badly hurt, and have either died on the way or after they've reached the orspital ; and the doctors up in London have said—I've heerd 'em myself—that many a life might have been saved if they could have been treated at once, instead of having the long delay. But what's the good o' talkin'? Folks ashore want fish in the winter as well as the summer, and so long as they say 'We must have fish,' so long must men be out here to catch it for 'em. It's true they're earning their living by it, but bless you, sir, there's many a hundred loses their living and their lives to boot over this job, and who cares, ashore, so long as the fish is brought regular to the table?"

"Come, come; that won't do."

"Won't do, sir! Ain't it a fact? There's thousands of hurts and hundreds of lives lost in this 'ere North Sea, and how many folks on shore either knows or cares anything at all about it?"

"Now, skipper, I believe you are coming to the point. It is just that, people on shore don't *know* of these things. You must not accuse them of heartlessness. Until a few days ago I had never myself heard of these great trawling fleets; so how could I *care* for people of whose very existence I was ignorant? And I'm absolutely certain that mine is not a solitary case."

"Well, sir, perhaps you're correct; at any rate, I hope so, but you'll find that the smacksmen out here are of my opinion. They think the folks on shore despise 'em, and look on 'em as so many dogs, not fit to keep company with Christian people."

"I have already found that," I replied; "for several of the men last night expressed the utmost amazement at gentlemen coming out here merely with the object of inquiring for themselves into the conditions of life in the North Sea, and in the hope of benefiting them and brightening their existence."

"Well, sir, I wish you success, with all my heart; but you'll have a mighty hard task, and all the goodwill in the world won't make the sea any smoother nor the winter's cold less freezing."

"I agree with you, skipper, to some extent—indeed, to a great extent; but already I begin to see one or two ways in which very material help might be rendered. What would you say, for example, to some dispensary work being done out here?"

"Grand, sir, grand, if it could be managed, but I can't see how it's possible."

Here the skipper was called away, and our conversation ended for the time, but fresh food for reflection had been given to me, and presently two accidents occurred which brought very forcibly home to my mind the risks to which these men are constantly exposed in their hazardous calling.

In the first instance a man had the end of his finger jammed in a steam-winch. He bore the pain like a Spartan, and pluckily wrapping the injured member in his handkerchief, went back to his own vessel. The next case was more serious.

A fine young fellow, whom I had previously noticed
delivering his fish, incautiously grasped the gunwale
of his boat just as she sheered alongside the smack
on his return from the carrier. Instantly the hand
was crushed and mangled, and the poor fellow was
brought back in all haste to the steamer for conveyance to London. All that could be done was
to bandage the smashed hand, and then place the
arm in a carefully adjusted sling; but alas! the
man had not been many minutes on board before
a heavy sea struck us, pouring over the bows and
dashing right aft, and instantly the patient was
drenched from head to foot, and the bandage
saturated with salt water, of course adding greatly
to the already acute pain; and for two whole days
and one terrible sleepless night that smacksman
bore his agony in silence, only an occasional groan
betraying to those around him the severity of his
suffering.

Meanwhile I had opportunities for conversation
with many of our visitors, and found in their tales
of accident, illness, and loss of life abundant confirmation of all I had learned from the skipper of
the steam-carrier. Left at last to my own medita-
tions, I pondered carefully over the sad story, and
came to the conclusion, not only that, in the words
of my friend, " something *might* be done," but something *must*, and, by God's help, *should* be done to

mitigate the hardships of what at the best must ever be a toilsome, dangerous life. But the question naturally arose, what form shall the assistance take, and how is it to be accomplished ? This indeed was an initial difficulty ; but what are difficulties to the living God ? And I felt absolutely certain that He had guided thus far, and would Himself sweep away every hindrance and plainly indicate the future path.

I had myself known what it is to suffer excruciating pain for many months, though, through God's mercy, I was surrounded by every comfort which medical and skilled nursing could minister. This very fact, however, made me more keenly alive to the needs of the poor smacksman, with neither doctor nor nurse at hand to succour him in his anguish, suffering, and it may be dying, with no other help than the rough though kindly ministrations of his shipmates.

Ay ! and all the while, away over the sea to the westward, there.is a fond wife, or may be a mother, going about her household duties and counting the days until the voyage will be over, and the beloved bread-winner be home again, unconscious, poor soul, that he lies that moment at the hour of his utmost need, his life ebbing away without the comfort of one tender word or the touch of a loving hand.

'Tis no fancy picture this, but the stern reality; and as my mind dwelt upon the facts before me I exclaimed, " No, indeed! I have never paid my fish bill; I have never even understood the cost before."

CHAPTER III.

THE COPER.

" There's no time for idle scorning,
      While the days are going by ;
Let your face be like the morning,
      While the days are going by ;
Oh, the world is full of sighs,
Full of sad and weeping eyes ;
Help your fallen brother rise,
      While the days are going by ! "

" SKIPPER, what is that Dutchman doing in the fleet ? See, away there on the lee quarter, there's a yawl flying the Dutch flag. I didn't know you had any Dutch craft fishing with you. Does he run home with his catch or send it to London ? "

The skipper appeared to be mightily amused, and with a sly chuckle replied, " Ay, sir, he runs home with *his* catch, but it ain't a catch of fish. Look again, sir ; take a good look through the glass, and you'll see he ain't got no trawl aboard."

" Explain yourself. You said he runs home with his catch, but that it isn't a catch of fish. What is he, then ? "

"Why, sir, he ain't a proper fisherman at all; he's a *coper*."

"A *coper!* What's a *coper?* I've heard of a *coper* on shore—a horse-*coper*—but what is a *coper* out here?"

"Well," said the skipper, "I don't rightly know what the word *coper* means, but, bless you, that's the grog-shop."

The good skipper had himself been a total abstainer and an earnest member of a church for many years (though he confided to me that he had only spent one Sunday ashore since the previous Christmas), yet the fervour with which he uttered those last five words might have implied to a stranger that he was a devoted adherent of the "grog-shop," and desired by his tone both to impress me with that fact, and also with his sense of my utter ignorance.

"Why, skipper, surely *you* don't regard yonder Dutchman with friendly feelings?"

"Friendly feelins, sir! I'd like to see every one of them wessels at the bottom of the sea, if, please God, it might be managed without loss of life. All I meant was that I was main surprised as you'd never heard of 'em. I calls 'em the curse of the fleets."

"You forget what I have already told you, that until a few days ago I knew absolutely nothing

of the deep-sea trawlers ; thus of necessity I am
ignorant of their special temptations; but now I'm
here to make up for lost time, so go ahead and tell
me all about these *copers*."

And thus I learned that for upwards of fifty
years these foreign vessels have infested the English
trawling fleets. They appear to have come in the
first instance from the Dutch ports nearest to the
fishing - grounds, and to have dealt fairly and
honestly with the English smacksmen in various
articles of clothing; but gradually, as trade increased, the spirit of evil became more and more
manifest, and sale was in many cases discontinued
in favour of barter—first of fish, such as skate,
which, though fetching a poor price in England, is
over there regarded as " prime ; " then little by little
the wedge was driven home, until there was no
length within the reach of men, on the one hand
greedy of gain, on the other thirsting for strong
drink, to which they would not go.

These Dutch *copers* ostensibly cruised with the
English fleets for the purpose of selling tobacco,
but, once on board, the customers were within
sight of the drink, the odour of which pervaded the
atmosphere; and although a high-principled and
stout-hearted minority resolutely and successfully
resisted, the majority were unable to withstand the
insidious attack of their worst enemy, posing in the

guise of their one and only friend. But still, even the minority must visit the *coper* in order to obtain their supply of tobacco.

" Why *must* they visit the *coper?* " it may be asked. " Why could they not purchase tobacco on shore before leaving England? " Simply because tobacco on shore was four shillings per pound; the same article on the high seas was only eighteenpence, therefore small blame to them if they saved the extra half-crown.

Tobacco purchased at Hull, Grimsby, Great Yarmouth, or Lowestoft had paid a heavy duty; tobacco sold on the *coper* was brought from Holland, or Belgium, or Germany at the mere cost of the article. Doubtless hundreds of English smacksmen frequented the *copers* for the sake of the drink, but, on the other hand, there were many who had no desire to drink, and who, before visiting the *coper*, had fully determined that they would expend just eighteenpence in a pound of " Rising Hope," but not one penny in fire-water. Alas, alas! it was the old story — temptation, seductive, plausible, attractive temptation; the fear of ridicule; the desire to stand well with their mates. Various influences were brought to bear, and, in the end, failure and sin, remorse and fresh resolution— only to go through precisely the same process again and again.

A sturdy skipper, with a wife and children dependent upon his earnings, would go to the grog-
shop for his " weed." When the tobacco transaction
was concluded, the master of the *coper* would appeal
to his customer to " take von leetle drop."

The skipper replies, " Not I, indeed! I've quite
enough to do with my money when I gets ashore,
without spending it here on your cursed liquor."

But the foreigner knew his man, and, assuming
an air of virtuous indignation, he retorted, " Spend
your monish, indeed! I did not ask you to *buy*
I ask you take von leetle drop vid me, just for goot
vellowship."

The tempter succeeded; the " leetle drop " was
taken. As the foreigner anticipated, it created a
desire for more, and the man of good resolutions
went ahead unrestrained. Vows and promises of
amendment were forgotten; money which should
have benefited his family was squandered in the
purchase of aniseed brandy, until by and bye the
purse was empty, while the craving for spirits was
more powerful than ever. What was now to be
done? The foreigner is equal to the occasion.

" Want more prandy, mine frend? Got no more
shillins, did you say? Ah vell, I vill take your fish;
I vill take your spare sails, your ropes, your nets—
dat is all good as monish to me."

The miserable bargain is soon concluded; a boat

loaded with smack's gear passes from the English
to the foreign vessel, and presently returns bearing
abundance of fire-water for consumption by the crew.

Is it an abuse of language to style that foreigner
"the devil's mission-ship?" If any of my readers
think so, it can only be because they do not know
all the evil the *copers* have wrought. By that one
transaction the devil gained several important ends,
e.g., the skipper robbed his employer of valuable
property; robbed his own wife and little ones and
the relatives of his crew of food and clothing; robbed
himself of health and of a good conscience; robbed
the State by converting six sober hardworking
citizens into dissolute drunken wrecks; robbed God
of the service of those who *should* have been on
the Lord's side—not "serving divers lusts and
pleasures," but living "for Him who died for them
and rose again." Yes, the *copers* are indeed "the
devil's mission-ships," and most efficiently and successfully have they conducted their mission.

It does not require a nautical mind to grasp
the fact that although a smack might be well found
in every respect when she left port, she would be
entirely at the mercy of the first gale that swept
over the fleet if both skipper and crew were lying
hopelessly drunk on the cabin floor. Thus a fine
vessel would founder and five to seven precious lives
be sacrificed.

Again, through the incompetency of a drunken steersman there have been constant instances of collision, resulting frequently in loss of both life and property. Scores of men under the influence of liquor have fallen overboard and been drowned; and beyond this I have personally inquired into and verified cases of suicide in the North Sea through men becoming maddened by the fiery aniseed spirit, and in their drunken frenzy leaping overboard.

Then there is a final charge against the *copers*, and, to my own mind, perhaps the most terrible, viz., the impoverishing of cottage homes on shore, which once had been, and which might still have been, bright and happy and prosperous, but for the fact that the bread-winner had been converted on board the devil's mission-ship, and had now finally and literally gone to the devil himself.

Think of the anguish of a woman's broken heart which mourns without a ray of hope! I have myself sat beside a newly made widow, and pointed her and her weeping little ones to the Lamb of God for comfort and peace ; but in what terms could I refer to him who was gone ? The only possible course was to omit all reference to him, for I knew, and the stricken ones around me knew, that he had been drinking incessantly for a week, and at the last had leaped overboard in delirium tremens, with oaths and curses upon his dying lips.

Oh, the sickening horror of that darkened room! Not the mere effect of closed windows and drawn blinds, but the indescribable gloom which no ray of light could pierce—the "horror of great darkness." That figure sitting with clenched hands, drawn and haggard face—mute—the image of utter despair, leaving her wee babe to cry unheeded, and, when at last roused by a neighbour, uttering one wild shriek, "Oh, my husband, my poor husband! he's lost for ever!" and then relapsing into insensibility. And but seven years before that poor woman thought herself the proudest, happiest of wives!

Reader, can you wonder that I call the *copers* the devil's mission-ships?

A grand-looking fisherman, tall, well-built, and weighing, he told me, "somewhere about seventeen stone," gave me some interesting, though sad, details of the *coper* traffic. This man, at the time I first met him, was mate of a smack, and appeared to know so much of the floating grog-shops, that I inquired whether he was in the habit of going on board them himself.

"No, sir, not now; but some years ago I was one of the hands aboard a *coper*."

"'One of the hands!' but surely you could not, as a Christian man, be there with a good conscience."

"No, indeed. I don't see how a Christian man could possibly serve aboard one o' them vessels.

c

But as for myself, I wasn't a Christian in those days—more's the pity!"

"But can you speak German or Dutch? How came you to be one of the crew of a foreign vessel?"

"She wasn't a foreigner. She was a Yarmouth smack and fished in the 'Short Blues.'"

"You surprise me. I thought the *copers* were all foreign craft."

"Well, they are mostly, sir. There's been a many of 'em from Ostend, and Nieudiep, and the Texel, and Bremen, and Cuxhaven. There's one as we call the *Greensider* from Nieudiep, the *Long Betsy* from Copenhagen, the *Nettle* from the Texel, the *Kenan* from Ostend, and lots more; but several Englishmen tried the same game."

"Do you mind telling me the names of the English vessels?"

"Mind! not I. There was one called the *Annie* as used to come out of the Humber, and the *Dora* and the *Angelina* of Yarmouth. I served aboard the *Angelina* myself·for well nigh three years."

"But now I'm puzzled to know how this could be done. How did these English *copers* get their cargo?"

"Well, sir, I can only speak for one of 'em, the *Angelina*. We sailed out o' Yarmouth harbour with our gear aboard just like an ordinary trawler, and then made straight for Nieudiep. When we got there, we took in about £500 worth o' grog and tobacco, and then joined our fleet, an' sold it so as to clear another £500 profit."

" And how long did it take to secure that sum?"

" Just one voyage, sir. We'd clear out the whole cargo in two months, selling the bottles of rum at eighteenpence, gin at a shillin', raw brandy two shillin's, and aniseed brandy two an' threepence. You see, sir, we daren't run home to Yarmouth with any of the stuff aboard, or else the Customs 'ud a nabbed us, but they couldn't touch the thousand pounds in hard cash as the skipper had got locked up down below."

" Quite true ; but now tell me, is that vessel still a *coper ?* "

" No, sir ; she's a fishin' in this very fleet this minit."

" Why is that ? Surely fishing doesn't pay as well as the trade you mentioned just now."

" Quite true, that it don't. But yer see, sir, the insurance clubs stepped in at last and put a stop to it."

" How so ? "

" Why, easy enough ; by just sayin' as they wouldn't insure the vessel any longer unless she gave up the *coperin.*"

" I see ! Then it was Hobson's choice with the

owner. He must either abandon the trade in spirits or sail uninsured. But what reason had the insurance club for taking such action ? "

"Well, I don't know as I can tell that. But I've heerd as Mr. Robert Hewett and the other owners put their oar in, and insisted on the club takin' action. The owners 'ud be glad enough to stop *all* the *copers* if they could, but they can't touch these 'ere foreigners—wuss luck ! "

"Why are the owners so anxious to stop the *coper* trade ? "

"Why, sir, they've every cause to want to do it. They've lost hundred's o' pounds by them *copers*, what with the men a drinkin' themselves stupid so as they couldn't do their work, not to mention the loss of property."

"Ah ! tell me what you mean. Am I really to understand that these *copers* receive the owner's property in exchange for drink ? I've been told that it is so ; but, as you have served on board one, you can speak positively."

"Why, sir, I've seen smacksmen pull the very clothes off their backs, and barter 'em away for liquor when their money was all gone."

"That is surely bad enough, but in that case they are merely *fools*. I want to know if you confirm what I have been hearing as to smacks' nets and gear going to the *coper*."

"Confirm it! of course I can. I've seen scores of nets *coped* away for brandy."

"If that be so, I can quite understand the anxiety of the owners to put a stop to the traffic; there is not only the indirect loss through the drinking, but the positive theft of gear."

"I don't quite know, sir, why you call it an *indirect* loss. I guess it's a pretty direct 'un. When men gets on the drink, whole crews, skipper an' all, don't attend to their business. I've knowed men come fresh out from port when they were flush o' cash, and they'd set to an' drink for days an' days right straight on end, until all the money was gone; an' whar's the owner's interest all that time, I'd like to know?"

"You're right, my friend; it is indeed a direct loss, and I'm not surprised at the owners' making a firm stand against this English vessel you speak of. But now, tell me how you came to leave the *coper*."

"It was 'cause I was driven off; I couldn't stop aboard her any longer."

"What do you mean? Did you fall out with the skipper?"

"No, sir; it was my conscience drove me away, not the skipper."

"Tell me all about it."

"Well, it came about in this way. The weather

was very calm, and one fine mornin' six skippers an' their boats' crews came aboard early and spent the hours drinking spirits. By about mid-day several of 'em were lyin' about the deck dead drunk; others were muddled and stupid, but some of 'em seemed as if the drink had all gone to their brain, and turned 'em raving mad."

"Well, is that the end of the story?" I asked, seeing the man hesitate.

"I wish it had been," he replied, "but it always makes me stop an' think it over, an' collect myself when I tells this 'ere yarn, for I'll never forget the awfulness of it as long as I live."

After waiting a few moments he continued :—

"I was a sayin' as they were some of 'em just like maniacs with the drink they'd stowed aboard, and presently one of 'em goes tearin' and swearin' about the deck, an' then tuk a leap straight bang over into the sea."

"Did he struggle in the water, so as to give you a chance of saving him?"

"Struggle, sir! We all of us—all as were sober —rushed to the side the very moment he jumped overboard, but quick as we were, we were only just in time to see him right away down in the clear blue water, just like a tiny speck far below us, an' in another second he was gone out o' sight for ever. He just went clean down to the bottom like a stone."

" And was it that incident that so deeply affected
you ? "

" It was. I'd heerd of the same sort o' thing
before, but never been eye-witness of it, and that
night when I was in my bunk, I thought how that
man's life was lost all along of our havin' sold him
the liquor, and I made up my mind then and there
as I'd chuck up the berth an' go trawlin'."

" And did this solemn occurrence lead to your
becoming a changed man ? "

" Well, it made me very serious, but it wasn't
till six months afterwards that I was led to the
Saviour, through the death of my brother."

" Was he with you ? "

" No ; he was mate of a smack in another fleet."

" Let me hear the story."

" It was in the big October gale in 1880. Me
an' the skipper was lyin' on the lockers tryin' to
get a bit o' sleep, when all of a sudden I thought
I heard a shout. I started up and listened, and
hearin' nothin' more, I laid down again ; but
presently—I don't know whether I was asleep or
not—I saw my brother's smack struck by a tremendous sea, that hove her down, an' then a second sea
struck her, and she went under with all hands. In
my mind I could see her sinking down, down, till
she rested on the bottom, and then the whole of
her deck seemed to become white, just like snow,

and I saw quite plain an' distinct, written right
across the deck, the words, ' BE YE ALSO READY.'
With that I sprang up and shook myself together,
but the whole thing seemed quite real, an' I couldn't
get rid of it."

" Well, what was the sequel ? "

" Why, just this, sir.   Our vessel, like a great
many others, had been damaged in the gale, an' we
had to run to Yarmouth for repairs.   Just as we
were goin' in between the piers, another smack
belonging to the same owner as my brother's was
towing out.   I hailed 'em, ' Any news of the
Petition ? ' an' the answer came back, ' She's lost
with all hands.'   It was that, sir, that brought me
up all standin', and was the means of my conversion to God."

.   .   .   .   .

No ; I had never heard of the *copers* until I saw
one that morning in the fleet ; but several days
after the conversation with the skipper, when seated
in my own house, I recalled his inability to explain
the meaning of the word *coper*, and taking down
the English dictionary, I found, " *Coper*, one who
barters."   Of course we have the German word
kaufen, to buy, the Dutch *kopen*, and the Danish or
Norse *köpa*, but these latter all clearly refer to
honest trade ; whereas the floating grog-shops in the
North Sea flourished on the frailty of the English

smacksmen, pandering to their appetites and lusts, plying them with temptation, and encouraging by every mean device the craving for drink, thus alluring their victims, until, once within the toils, there needed no further blandishment; the devil's mission-ship had gained another convert, and there was no stopping the headlong course down the steep, broad road of unrestrained self-indulgence. Whatever of good, of moral worth, of natural affection there might have been, speedily disappears before the in-roads of hideous lust. Faster, ever faster speeds the wretched victim, until the work the devil's mission-ship has so well begun finds its fruition in the hopeless wail of a lost soul.

" *The drunkard shall not inherit the kingdom of God* " is the solemn assertion of the Divine Word; but, praise be to His grace, the pages of Holy Writ, while expressing God's hatred of *sin*, teem with offers of pardon, promises of acceptance, and pledges of eternal love to the *sinner*.

It was in the year 1859, immediately after my first apprehension of the Saviour's love to myself, that I was privileged to invite another—a school-fellow—to " taste and see that the Lord is good," and since that day it has been my lot to see many persons, of various ages and social grades, learn the blessedness of putting their trust in Him; yet never, until I visited the North Sea, did I realise or appre-

ciate the force and significance of many passages of
Holy Scripture. On shore, I had seen much of the
bright side of sin, so to speak—the gaiety, the
attractiveness of the world's pleasures; and I have
never agreed with the statement one hears some
Christians rashly make, and which must trip and
hinder those whom they are seeking to help—
that "the world has no pleasures." It is absolutely, ridiculously false. The world abounds in
attractions. But one who sees the crucified Son of
God, and learns to say from his heart, " He loved
me, and gave Himself for me," soon learns very
much more, and can honestly assert, " I have found
not only a Saviour for my sins, a solace and
comfort in times of disappointment and sorrow,
but have been brought into personal and eternal
intimacy with One Who, when everything around me
is brightest, is *Himself* incomparably brighter and
better and more precious to me than all beside."

Away in the North Sea, I saw sin shorn of its
attractions and revealed in all its naked hideous-
ness. Not only the degrading, damning drink
traffic, but other forms of sin only to be mentioned
with bated breath, and for which the Divine writings
reserve the most scathing rebuke—sins for which
is reserved the consuming wrath of Almighty God.
I cannot write of these things, nor have I sufficient command of language to describe the effect

upon myself of all I learned. The evil was more loathsome, more utterly degrading and disgusting, than aught I had ever heard of.

But what of the other side? It was only when at home again in the privacy of my own study that I could calmly consider in all its bearings the mass of knowledge gained in that brief voyage. What perils by reason of the elements! What distressing, excruciating agony from accidents, unrelieved by surgical aid! What loss of life at sea! What broken hearts on shore! What rampant, unchecked riot of evil! *What vast possibilities for good!*

.   .   .   .   .

And if all this terrible picture was so appalling to me, a poor weak sinner like themselves, what must it be to the heart of that Blessed One who loved and died for seamèn as much as landsmen? While I pondered this, and was still uncertain and perplexed, my eye fell upon the second verse of the hymn, " One there is above all others ; " and as I read again the well-known words—

"'Tis eternal life to know Him,"

my heart responded, " Yes, Lord ! eternal life—a present possession ; and I thank Thee for the peace and the joy it brings."

But then came the next line—

" Think, O think, how much we owe Him,'

and I was compelled to cry, " Lord, write that second line indelibly upon my memory ; let me never forget it ; and if it be Thy will that I should do aught for these smacksmen, *show me now Thy way !* "

And then there flashed upon me for the first time the thought, " If the devil has his mission-ship, if men can be found to brave the storms for the sake of fattening upon the weakness and vice of their fellows, shall the servants of Christ be less in earnest than they ? Shall not God, the living God, have *His* mission-ship ? Shall there not be a vessel with every fleet in those wild waters—a vessel whose flag should proclaim her a Witness against sin and impurity, a Champion of good and right, a Herald of mercy and love from God our Father and our Lord Jesus Christ ? "

I accepted this thought as an answer to my prayer for guidance, and, taking it as the gracious indication of the Divine Will revealed to my mind by the Holy Spirit, I never from that moment entertained a doubt of ultimate success.

CHAPTER IV.

DIGESTING THE FACTS.

All that I feel of pity thou hast known
Before I was ; my best is all thine own.
From Thy great heart of goodness mine but drew
Wishes and prayers ; but Thou, O Lord, will do,
In thine own time, by ways I cannot see,
All that I feel when I am nearest Thee !

  .   .   .   .

BUT I have been anticipating, and must return to
the bridge of the carrier. The mate was busily
engaged, with a band of active helpers, in stowing
away in the hold the trunks of fish which had been
piled upon deck, each layer of trunks being in
turn covered by a layer of ice, and so on, layer
upon layer, until the hold had received no fewer
than 3007 trunks.

Meanwhile the admiral had signalled his instructions that the fleet were to " sail." In other words,
they were to move some thirty miles to the westward before shooting their trawls. The consequence
to the steamer of this decision on the part of the
admiral was to leave us with an ever-diminishing
crowd of attendant smacks and boats, until presently
the last laggard had put her fish on board, and the

mate came on the bridge and reported the number
of trunks shipped. Without waiting another instant,
the skipper, who for the previous half hour had been
fidgeting with his watch, telegraphed to the engine-
room "Full speed ahead," and by 9.30 A.M. we were
ploughing our way towards the Thames in the teeth
of a strong south-westerly breeze, the hatches battened down, the companion-ways all closed, every
movable article secured, and the heavily laden
steamer burying herself to such an extent, as she
forced her way through each succeeding billow, as
to give the bridge and smoke-stack the appearance
of an island, the hull being at times entirely sub-
merged. But having spent six hours on the bridge
with a cup of coffee as my only refreshment, I was
determined not to be baulked of my breakfast, and
with the steward's assistance I managed, by judi-
ciously dodging the waves, to reach the cabin in
safety. The mate was not so fortunate. Six hours
of hard labour had naturally been accompanied by
profuse perspiration, and he had seized the earliest
chance to rush below and array himself from head
to foot in warm flannels. He now emerged from
the cabin, and passing me on the deck, exclaimed
in a tone of huge satisfaction, while he complacently
slapped his thigh, "Ah! sir, there's nothing like a
dry change. *Now* I feels right down comfortable—
fit for anything."

And he had need be, for the captain was waiting
on the bridge to be relieved, and there was another
six hours' spell before him in the biting wind.   But
alas for his calculations ! He had barely placed
his foot on the ladder, when an unusually heavy sea
broke aboard, thundered aft along the decks, and
left the poor mate clinging to the rail the picture
of misery, his pride effectually humbled, and his
" dry flannels " hanging bedraggled about his limbs.
As soon as he recovered his breath, he replied to
my inquiring hail as to what he would do now, by
assuring me that it was " all in the day's work,"
and he " must just grin and abide it."   So leaving
the good-natured fellow to his solitary watch, I
joined the skipper below, and was far too hungry
to find fault with the appointments of our *déjeûner
à la fourchette.*

. It was now nearly 10 A.M., and since 3.30 I had
been astir ; and what with intently watching the
hurly-burly on deck and listening to North Sea
yarns for so many hours, I had a violent appetite,
though I found that the meals were substantial
enough to satisfy the most voracious.

Breakfast over, the skipper entertained me for
half an hour with some more gruesome stories of
life and death on the Dogger Bank, and then,
with one consent, we lay down upon the lockers to
sleep.   The skipper speedily gave audible evidence

of being in a sound slumber, but I was unable for
some time to follow his example. My heart was
very full—filled with distress by reason of the sin
and blasphemy I had witnessed, and the tales of
suffering, privation, and peril related to me—filled
with thankfulness for having been permitted to tell
the story of the Saviour's love to men, some of whom
had possibly never heard it before, or heard but to
scoff at and despise it—thankfulness for the testimony maintained by a faithful few in spite of constant opposition, and for the warm welcome they
had given to one going out in the Master's name—
and filled, too, with faith and hope that God would,
in His infinite mercy, answer the many prayers
which had ascended to His throne from these poor
fellows, who were entirely debarred from the many
precious opportunities which are the common privilege of landsmen.

Beyond the fact that the weather was very
stormy, our voyage home was uneventful, and after
thirty-two hours' hard running, the carrier sheered
alongside Billingsgate Market, and my five days on
the Dogger Bank had ended.

Can the reader sympathise with the sinking
sensation in the region of the heart which I ex-
perienced that afternoon?

It was not until I stepped ashore that the
vast responsibility attaching to my newly-acquired

knowledge fully impressed me. Out at sea, all was *couleur de rose*. I was in the presence of the men whose circumstances cried aloud for help and amelioration; and viewed at that distance, and with such a powerful appeal to my own sympathies actually before my eyes, I could not doubt that Christian folk on shore—people with tender hearts and active philanthropic views—would without delay come to the aid of their practically expatriated fellow-countrymen. But there was something painfully depressing in the appearance of the city on that September evening.

The vast warehouses, the offices, banks, churches, glowing in the brightness of an unusually glorious sunset—the busy hum of the thousands of foot-passengers, each one intent upon his own concerns —the general air of material prosperity palpably stamped upon everything around—all these things conspired to chill my hopes. To this day I am unable fully to explain the feeling. It may have been exceedingly weak and foolish, but the fact remains that I was overwhelmed by the many evidences of teeming riches and unlimited comfort and luxury, while sadly conscious that, spite of it all, my new friends the smacksmen were toiling, only three hundred miles away at sea, to supply food to the tables of the wealthy, yet themselves un-cared for and unaided, because so utterly unknown.

From that time forward the needs of the deep-sea fishermen became an absorbing thought and the subject of constant prayer. Though unaware how or when help would be forthcoming, the conviction deepened daily that God Himself was leading, and many circumstances—trivial, perhaps, in themselves—when considered in relation to each other and to the end in view, tended to confirm this assurance, and to fill my heart with hope for the future.

The close of the preceding chapter relates how the sight of the foreign *coper* first gave definite shape to my crude plans for the benefit of the smacksmen. Should not the awful storms, instead of deterring, prove rather an incentive to missionary enterprise? If the fish *must* be caught, and each recurring gale must claim its quota of precious lives —lives of husbands and fathers, of brothers and sons—had not the Master Himself said, " This Gospel of the kingdom *must* be preached " ?

While kneeling in church on the first Sunday after my return to London, my whole heart went out with the petition, " *O God, the Creator and Preserver of all mankind, we humbly beseech Thee for all sorts and conditions of men, ... that it may please Thee to comfort and relieve them, according to their several necessities, giving them patience under their sufferings, and a happy issue out of*

all their afflictions." But when we came to the
words in the " General Thanksgiving," " *We bless
Thee . . . for the means of grace, and for the hope
of glory,*" my thoughts very naturally wandered
away from the crowded London church to the
twelve thousand men tossing upon the North Sea,
with no church to attend, who could not give
thanks for a " means of grace " which they had
never possessed, nor for " the hope of glory " of
which the great majority were entirely ignorant.

Then, too, how the hymns seemed to speak to
my heart that day as we sang—

> " We give Thee but Thine own,
>   Whate'er the gift may be :
> All that we have is Thine alone,
>   A trust, O Lord, from Thee.
>
> May we Thy bounties thus
>   As stewards true receive,
> And gladly, as Thou blessest us,
>   To thee our first-fruits give.
>
> Oh ! hearts are bruised and dead,
>   And homes are bare and cold,
> And lambs for whom the Shepherd bled
>   Are straying from the fold."

And again—

> " Come, labour on !
> Away with gloomy doubts and faithless fear !
> No arm so weak but may do service here :
> By feeblest agents can our God fulfil
>   His righteous will.

Come, labour on !
No time for rest till glows the western sky,
While the long shadows o'er our pathway lie,
And a glad sound comes with the setting sun—
Servants, well done ! "

Shortly afterwards I was visiting in a village in the Midland Counties, and, out of mere curiosity, inquired the population.

" Fifteen hundred," was the reply.

" Ah ! " I thought, " that is precisely the population of one of the great floating villages in the North Sea."

But there the similarity ceased. The inland village lay snugly at the foot of a range of hills, with a river flowing placidly by. The North Sea village was constantly tossed to and fro upon " the grey wilderness of a foaming ocean, swept by winds as pitiless as the hand of death." The stationary village boasted, for its fifteen hundred inhabitants, two churches, two chapels, four doctors, a dispensary, a town-hall, a mechanic's institute, and a lending library. The cruising village possessed absolutely none of these various advantages.

Here then was a *raison d'être* for the suggested mission-vessel—to be not only a rendezvous for Christian fishermen, but a help and a boon to every man in the fleet—at once a church, chapel, temperance hall, library, and dispensary. This was something tangible, at all events in theory; but how was it to be tested practically ?

At a drawing-room meeting I told the whole story —what I had seen and heard during my trip to sea, the inferences I had drawn, and the resolve to put my ideas to a practical test as soon as possible.

" Let an ordinary fishing-smack be equipped for missionary purposes, with a medicine-chest, a Christian skipper and crew, and a special cabin for any missioner, clerical or lay, who may be prepared to volunteer his services."

This was the suggestion, and it was greeted with applause, though rather because of its bold novelty than from its commending itself to the audience as a feasible project.

However, I consulted several of the largest smack-owners, who, smarting under the depredations of the *copers*, eagerly seized upon any plan, which appeared likely to improve the well-nigh intolerable condition of things then existing. These counsellors strongly advised that the scheme be proceeded with ; but as yet the way was not clear, nor did there appear to be the slightest indication of further light upon the subject.

Under these circumstances, the interest which had at first been awakened began to wane, and several people said, " Oh, give up the idea ! "

To such I replied, " Never ! It is no mere per-

sonal idea. One of those skippers told me that he
and others had been praying for thirty years that
God would send a Gospel-ship into the North Sea,
and I believe He will answer these prayers. I cannot
doubt it. The need is so great and so urgent, the
good which would result from the presence of a
mission-vessel is so obvious, that I am persuaded
God has providentially allowed this subject to come·
thus to the front, in order that people on land
may be stirred up to succour their brethren on
the sea. It is a glorious thing for Christians in
England to send the Bible and missionaries to the
heathen; but it will be monstrous to neglect our
fellow-countrymen, living and dying in ignorance
on the seas which wash our own shores. I doubt
whether more than one person in every thousand
among the inhabitants of this land ever heard of the
deep-sea fishermen; but, please God, they *shall*
hear, and beyond question, when once the case is
understood, the requisite remedy will be promptly
and ungrudgingly applied.

CHAPTER V.

THE PROMISE FULFILLED.

I may not see
My hopes for them take form in fact;
But God will give the victory
In due time; in that faith I act.
And he who sees the future sure
The baffling present may endure,
And bless, meanwhile, the unseen Hand that leads
The heart's desires beyond the halting step of deeds.

THE months rolled by, and my faith was sorely tried as one friend after another joined the opposition, and told me my views were chimerical, that the scheme was utterly impracticable, and could only end in a miserable fiasco. But one night, early in June 1882, while kneeling in my room interceding for the smacksmen, there came to me, as though a voice had spoken at my side, the words, "He that cometh to God must believe that He is, and that He is a rewarder of them that *diligently* seek Him." I rose refreshed and inspirited, with the assurance that God was guiding, and would presently make manifest His good pleasure.

The following afternoon the door of my room

opened, and "Skipper Budd" was announced. In strode the skipper, his clean-shaven visage looking as round and jolly as when we had met nine months before "to the nor'ard of the Dawger," and with a beaming cheery smile upon his face, although a glance sufficed to show he had met with an accident, for his left arm was carried in a sling.

"Why, Budd, what's the matter?" I cried.

"Oh, bless the Lord, I've lost the tip of my finger."

For the moment I had great difficulty in repressing a smile. I detest "cant;" but from my slight knowledge of the man I felt quite sure there was no cant in his reply. God forbid, therefore, that I should grieve this simple-minded Christian by even appearing to make light of his words.

"That is a remarkable answer, skipper. It isn't every man who would bless the Lord for such a mishap."

"Perhaps not, sir, but all the same I *do* bless Him; for I've learned since I was converted that 'all things work together for good to them that love Him;' and besides, I should bless Him if only because the hurt to my finger had been the means of bringing me to London to see you, and thank you for sending me out the parcels of books and tracts, and for your cheering letters. And, too, I want to talk to you about what you were saying as to a Bethel-ship."

" Well, Budd, I shall be very pleased to hear all you have to say; but not to-day. You must go right away to the doctor now, and have the smashed finger attended to before the inflammation spreads, —here's an order for the dispensary,—then you can spend a quiet Sunday with your friends, and look in here at ten o'clock on Monday, when we will have a chat about my friends in the 'Short Blue' fleet."

When the skipper was gone, I prayed that the proposed interview might, in the hands of God, prove to be the beginning of that new epoch upon which I believed the smacksmen were about to enter, and I was much encouraged on the following day, both in my private reading of Holy Scripture and by the utterances of God's servants.

My mind—my heart—must ever retain the memory of the next day's events. It was my birthday, and I was greatly cheered at the outset by the texts upon the " Scripture Roll " suspended on the wall of my room. Each text dealt with faith :— " Without faith it is impossible to please Him." " Whatsoever ye shall ask in prayer, believing, ye shall receive." " If ye ask anything in My name, I will do it," &c., &c.

These passages of God's Word were indeed full of comfort and encouragement, well calculated to inspire absolute confidence with regard to the matter which especially weighed upon my mind. What a relief to anxiety is simple trust in the living God!

Budd arrived punctually at ten o'clock, and he had not been with me many minutes when another North-Sea skipper entered. This proved to be none other than the one who had sailed round the carrier at half-past four on that memorable September morning, on purpose to shout a hearty, "What cheer? what cheer?" to the visitor from London.

It was a remarkable coincidence. No North-Sea skipper had ever called on me before, and now, within a few minutes of one another, came two of them, and both bound upon the same errand; for skipper No. 2 was also anxious to hear about a Bethel-ship. "And," he added, "ever since that morning when I saw you on the bridge of the *Supply*, I've had a longing to bow the knee with you at the Throne of Grace."

"And now, sir," said Budd, "won't you tell us whether you have been able to do anything towards that plan you wrote to me about, of having a mission-ship out at sea?"

"Yes, Budd. I've done a great deal; I have prayed unceasingly to Him who knows what is needed infinitely better than you or I can know. Others have prayed too; in fact, many Christian people who have heard the story of my visit to your

fleet are praying daily for an outpouring of Divine
grace upon the North-Sea smacksmen."

"Well, sir, and are we to have a Bethel-ship
sent to us?"

"My friends, you should have one to-morrow if
it were in my power to send her. But have you
considered the cost of such a vessel? Even a second-
hand fishing-smack would cost £1000; then would
come the necessary alterations to fit her for the
purposes of Divine worship and to carry missioners;
and when all that was completed and paid for, how
would she be maintained? for the annual cost of
keeping up the vessel would be very heavy."

The faces of the two men were a study. The
poor fellows had evidently both been expecting
great things from their interview with me, and now,
forsooth, I did nothing but suggest difficulties. It
was impossible to witness their keen disappointment
without feeling sincere sympathy, and I roused
them by exclaiming, "Look there, skippers! what
do you say to those texts on the wall? Do you
think those exhortations and promises are for us
and for to-day, or were they only intended for the
people to whom they were originally addressed?"
With that I read the texts aloud, and had not long
to wait for an answer to my question.

"Why, of course the blessed Bible is *for us, now*."

"Then, if that be so, don't you think we three

might just take God at His word, and kneel down here and plead for a mission-vessel, and all the benefits and blessings which she would mean for the smacksmen ?"

So there we knelt and poured out our hearts before our God, reminding Him that His Blessed Son had chosen fishermen to be His disciples and companions, telling Him how terribly urgent was the case of these nineteenth-century fishermen, and claiming the fulfilment of His "exceeding great and precious promises" on their behalf.

Each of the three offered prayer, and when at length we rose from our knees, it was with that sense of peace in heart and mind which ever results from "casting all your care upon Him."

"Good-bye, sir," exclaimed Budd. "I wouldn't have missed that for anything. I'm right glad I came."

"And so am I," said the other skipper. "It has been a wonderful lift up for us. It seems as if the blessing *must* come soon."

And so we parted—*they* to return to their life of toil and isolation, *I* to ponder over all that had passed, and to seek renewal of strength by continuous waiting upon the Lord.

Having occasion during the day to call on a friend who had heard the story at the drawing-room meeting already mentioned, I told him of the occurrences of the morning.

"Well," said he, "if you think of starting a subscription, here's a guinea for you."

"No, I'm not going to do anything of the kind. If you give your guinea, nine hundred and ninety-nine more would still be needed; and even were these forthcoming, the question of maintenance would remain to be faced. I am not yet clear upon the matter, though firmly persuaded that God is about to do something for those poor smacksmen, and until I see very distinctly what course to take, I shall not make a move."

"Well, let me know when you *are* clear, for I should like to help."

"If you want to help, you can do so most effectively by prayer; that is the great desideratum just now."

Two days later I met this friend in the train when coming to the city.

"What have you done about your mission-smack?" he inquired.

"Just what I asked you to do. I have prayed about it."

"So have I," said he, "and I have also thought the matter over very carefully. I can't afford to *give* you a vessel, but I incline to think with you that a fishing-smack might be employed as an experiment, to test the practicability of your idea. Now, if you are willing, for the sake of the object you have in view, to undertake the entire responsibility and risk of managing a fishing-smack, I don't mind finding the money. Do just as you suggested. Let her fish to cover her expenses ; and if the scheme succeeds, why then you will have made out, as you explained at the meeting, a strong case upon which to go to the public, and you will be able to get sufficient funds to repay me, and to start your proposed mission upon a firm basis. If you will agree to those terms, and not allow my name to appear in the matter, you can call at my office this afternoon, and I'll hand you a cheque for a thousand pounds."

Can the reader imagine my feelings of intense thankfulness on receiving this generous offer ? Only forty-eight hours had elapsed since the two skippers knelt with me and claimed the fulfilment of Divine promises. Here was indeed a speedy answer, and the words instantly recurred to my mind, " *He is, and He is a rewarder of them that diligently seek Him.*"

The cheque was given to me, and I hastened down to Yarmouth and took possession of a fine 56-ton yawl-rigged smack, the *Ensign*, very kindly selected from their fleet and placed at my disposal by Messrs. Hewett & Co. That firm also in the most handsome manner, through their courteous agent, Mr. Harvey-George, offered me *carte blanche* to their stores, workshops, and dry dock, and gave every assistance and advice in effecting the neces-

sary alterations of the vessel, merely charging actual
cost of material and labour.

Within three weeks the first mission-vessel was
ready for sea. An extra bulkhead in the hold
partitioned off a small cabin for the accommodation
of a missionary. The *British and Foreign Bible
Society* presented a handsome family Bible, and
fifty smaller copies for use at the services; the
Religious Tract Society, the *S.P.C.K.*, the *Church of
England Book Society*, and the *Society for Distributing Scripture Truth* all made grants of
volumes; a number of lady friends contributed
a supply of woollen mufflers and mittens; and
finally, a large ship's medicine-chest was presented
to the vessel by a lady who had herself recently
recovered from a long and very dangerous illness.

The chest was complete in every respect, with
medicines, simple surgical instruments, bandages,
splints, ointments, manuals of treatment, &c., &c.,
and the whole was placed in the skipper's charge
by the lady above mentioned, " as a thank-offering
for God's great mercies to me in my illness, and
with the earnest prayer that it may prove a means
of healing to many poor sick and wounded smacksmen." How abundantly has that prayer been
answered!

But who was the skipper? Could the choice
fall more appropriately upon any one than on the

man who said, " Bless the Lord ! I've lost the tip
of my finger " ? So when, after careful inquiry, it
appeared that Budd was not only an earnest Christian, but a smart and successful fisherman, I offered
him the berth, and he thankfully accepted it.

Meanwhile, however, during the period of altera-
tion and outfit for sea, it was not by any means all
smooth-sailing, so far as I was concerned. Several
of the owners did not hesitate to throw cold water
on the scheme. One said to me, " Our men are
sent to sea to catch fish, not to waste their time
shouting hallelujah." Another, with sundry strong
expletives, scoffingly remarked, "Mission to the
fishermen, indeed ! We'll give you just two
months—just one voyage—and we shall hear the
last of *that* whim." Other owners, though not
openly opposed, were cynical and politely sarcastic ;
while many of the smacksmen did not hesitate to
call me hard and ugly names, with which it will
not do to pollute these pages or shock my readers'
ears.

As the news spread at Yarmouth that a " Bethel-
ship," as they termed it, was being fitted out, the
excitement increased daily, and grew at last to such
a pitch as to induce me to hurry the vessel away to
sea, in order that she might enter forthwith upon
the work to which she was commissioned ; and after
a prayer-meeting in the little cabin, commending

the smack and her crew to the care and blessing of Almighty God, this pioneer Mission-vessel started upon her first voyage on a Friday,—a proceeding almost universally regarded amongst seamen as being fraught with certain ill-luck and disaster, yet, in this case, inaugurating what has proved to be, in the words of a recent independent observer, " one of the most remarkable social revolutions of modern times."

When the little *Ensign* cast off her moorings, and, in tow of a steam-tug, passed rapidly down the Yare and out into the open sea, a large crowd collected to witness the departure of the strangest craft the harbour had seen since the launch of the Moravian mission-ships *Harmony* from Messrs. Fellows & Son's yard in 1832 and 1861.

As the great 20-foot Mission-flag shook out its folds under the influence of the increasing breeze, a shout of derision rose from the greater portion of the crowd upon the pier-head. For my own part, when I heard of it afterwards—for I had been obliged to hasten back to London a few hours before—the words of Holy Scripture came to my mind, " Thou hast given a banner to them that fear Thee, that it may be *displayed* because of the truth." Yet there were some in the throng not afraid to wave hats and handkerchiefs and cry " God speed ye ! " though, as the steward of the *Ensign* told me afterwards,

E

" Why, they jeered, yer see, sir, and they cheered too ; but there was a lot more jeerin' than cheerin' ! "

Jeer ! ay, let them jeer.   The adage holds true, " Let those laugh who win ; " and the little craft which was laughed at that day received the warmest of welcomes when she ran in between the piers just four months later ; for had not her reputation been made, and preceded her ?   And so, grateful converts, grateful dispensary patients, grateful wives, inte-rested friends and neighbours, who had heard the wondrous tale—all these gathered to cry, " What cheer, O ? what cheer ?   God bless ye ! "   And as for the jeering, why it has never been heard again.

CHAPTER VI.

ILLNESS AND ACCIDENT.

" O my brothers ! O my sisters !
  Would to God that ye were near,
Gazing with me down the vistas
  Of a sorrow strange and drear ;
Would to God that ye were listeners
  To the voice I seem to hear ! "

THE following story, which I had from the lips of
a smack-owner, fairly illustrates the state of things
thirty years ago. On the one hand, the entire
absence of medical or surgical aid ; on the other,
the droll devices to which uneducated men had
recourse in times of emergency.

Bill Jinks was one of a boat's crew engaged on
a rough morning in ferrying fish to the attendant
carrier. He had just passed up a trunk of soles
to his mate on the steamer's deck, when the mate
slipped on a loose fish, and, to save himself, relaxed
his hold on the trunk, which immediately crashed
down into the boat, striking Bill Jinks on the thigh.
Tough as are these sons of toil, a blow from a de-
scending weight of 100 lbs. will disable even a North-

Sea smacksman, and poor Bill found himself a few minutes afterwards lying on one of the lockers in the steamer's cabin, and two days later he was landed in London and reported himself to the club doctor. The doctor handed him a substantial bottle bearing on a red label the words, " *For external use only.*" That was before the School Board period, and Bill didn't know what *external* meant. The doctor explained that he must rub it on outside the injured limb. Bill rubbed with such force and frequency that in a very few days he was sufficiently convalescent to think of returning to his vessel; but with the spirit of a true philanthropist, he was anxious that others should reap the benefit of this marvellous cure. He accordingly presented himself at the surgery, and begged for two more bottles of " that 'ere physic."

" Why," said the doctor, " you don't need any more now, Bill—you're better."

" Yes, sir, I know as I'm better ; but then, you see, sir, I'm agoin' back to sea to-morrow, and I thought as 'ow it might come in useful among the men. You see, sir, we're all of us a-gettin' a bit of a rap now and agin, in our rough life, and whether the hurt kills us outright or only lames us like, is all accordin' as 'ow it 'appens."

The doctor quite agreed with Bill that it was " all accordin'," and to appease the worthy fellow,

he supplied him with two large bottles of liniment
—red label and all—consoling himself that, even
if there were a mistake made, strong turpentine
wouldn't kill a North-Sea smacksman.

Now it happened that on the very day Bill re-
joined his vessel a poor man was lying ill in another
smack with what I was told was *brownchitis*. There
was no medicine on board. The boat was sent
away to the *coper*, but the only medicine there was
ardent spirits. Then they tried the carrier newly
arrived from London.

" No," said the skipper of the carrier, " I've
no physic, but I've just brought Bill Jinks back—
him as was hurt, yer know—and Bill's got two big
bottles o' physic; you'd best go an' borrow one."

The boat's crew arrived alongside Bill's smack,
and shouted " What cheer, old Bill! What cheer!
'Ull yer let's have the loan o' a bottle o' your
physic? Ned Price is tuk awful bad of the brownchitis."

Now here was, ready to hand, precisely the sort
of emergency on which kind-hearted Bill had
counted, and he promptly passed over a bottle of
liniment into the boat. Away they hied in great
delight, and only a short quarter of an hour elapsed
before the one large iron gravy spoon which the
smack possessed was filled with liniment, and—
spite of the warning label — poured down the

patient's throat.   He seemed to like it.   They
accordingly repeated the dose.   And dose followed
dose, until before very long the big bottle was
empty.

The whole crew, with the exception of the man
at the tiller, had gathered round the patient, and
one, a chum of the poor invalid, who was anxious
for his recovery, observed—

" He's finished that lot, skipper; hadn't we
better go and borrow that 'ere other bottle ? "

" Well, no," said the skipper; " let's see how this
'un works first."

How it worked!   It simply worked *wonders*, for
before the day was over the patient was sitting up,
and the next day saw him on deck.

So much for the red label!   I only know that
this remarkable cure had a thrilling effect on many
skippers and men in the fleet, and they never went
to sea afterwards without being provided with
bottles of " that 'ere physic," which they used for
everything, external and internal !

.   .   .   .   .   .

The " Expeerience Meetin' " is full of novelty to
any landsman visiting the fleets.   To myself it has
often proved both interesting and useful.

The smacksman's notion of an " expeerience
meetin' " is the singing of numerous hymns, inter-
spersed with the narration of incidents in the

spiritual life and experience of the various speakers. On one of these occasions we had thirteen hymns right off, hymn after hymn—each with its chorus again and again repeated—before the " expeeriences " began.

But it occurred to me from the first that the principle might be utilised with advantage in the collecting and collating of facts regarding the dangers, perils, privations, and temptations of these smacksmen. I have therefore to thank what may be termed the *secular* " expeerience meetin' " for having furnished me with a vast amount of information bearing upon the conditions of life in the trawling fleets. Given the particular subject of inquiry, it has merely been necessary to start the theme, and one might quietly lean back and take notes while, one after another, brawny fellows in the prime of hardy manhood, and grizzled old veterans near the end of life's voyage, would spin out their yarns— true narratives, told in simple manly fashion, of illness, accident, and death, without the alleviation of medical aid—of brave men in dire extremity, struggling on amid darkness and storm without reasonable hope of succour—tale upon tale so full of thrilling, absorbing interest, that one was apt to forget the flight of time, and prolong the " expeerience meetin' " many hours beyond the prearranged limit.

The following stories, suitable to my present
purpose, are culled from a mass of notes lying
before me at the moment, and will serve to bring
home to the reader's mind, at all events, some idea
of what forced itself upon my notice six years ago,
and determined me to leave no means untried of
securing the attention of the fish-eating population
on land to the condition of the fish-catching population away on the high seas.

H. B———, third hand of a trawling smack in
the " Short Blues," said :—" It was in the winter-
time, when I was seventeen years of age, I had a
severe attack of measles, from which I've never
properly recovered. There were no mission-ships
in those days—it was long before such a blessing
for us smacksmen was even thought of. We'd been
out from Yarmouth about a fortnight when a heavy
gale o' wind set in, lasting twenty-four hours. Then
it fell a calm, but, as is often the case, it tuk to
blowin' harder than ever towards night. Four of
us were below, an' I'd turned into my bunk, feelin'
very bad an' queer, when suddenly the skipper
shouted, ' Rouse out here, O ! ' On went oilskins
and sea-boots, every man on deck, leaving the boy
below just serving the dinner. There was no time
to think of dinner then.

" ' Pull your jib a-weather, lower the foresail, down
mizen,' roared the skipper, and this done, came the

next order, 'Down with that reef in the mainsail.'
The vessel was plunging and tossing about like a
wild horse, so as we could scarcely stand; the icy
wind was shrieking awful; but, spite of the bitter
cold, I was feeling that hot I could scarce abear
myself. The vessel reefed, we went below for
dinner, which was as cold as charity by this time.
I tuk a bit, but the meat seemed tasteless and just
like fire in my throat. I had the watch on deck
till midnight, and then turned in, but couldn't sleep.

" 'What's the matter, Bill?' said the skipper
when he saw I wasn't eatin' any breakfast the next
morning.

" 'I don't know, skipper; I feel very queer!'

The skipper sent for a saucepan and told the
boy to make me some gruel. The gruel was flour
an' water with a bit o' butter and sugar. I managed
a little, and lay down till I had to take the night
watch again. I could scarce stand, but there must
be no skulkin' aboard a smack. About ten o'clock
the weather fined a bit, and the admiral showed
his signals for shootin' the gear. I didn't feel up
to haulin' ropes about, and when helping to hoist
the big foresail, it seemed as if hot and cold needles
was a bein' run through me. 'It's no good,
skipper,' said I; 'I must go below.'

"Next mornin' I had to turn out an' help clean
an' pack the catch. It was a keen frost, an' the

fish was lying about as hard as bits o' wood; but all the same I was that burnin' hot I felt nigh faintin'. It was my work to go away in charge of the boat to the carrier, but the mate kindly said he'd go instead o' me, and the skipper told me to get away below an' turn in. There I stopped, gettin' worse an' worse, till next mornin', when I was too bad to go on deck, and again the boat went away without me.

"It was the steamer *Hewett* that morning, an' the skipper of her was a good Christian man. Says he, 'Where's Bill to-day?'

"'Oh,' says the mate, 'he's aboard, not well. Our skipper thinks as he's got measles.'

"'Ain't you goin' to send him home?'

"'No, I guess not,' says the mate.

"'Well,' says the cap'n of the *Hewett*, 'you'd better hurry back, an' wrap him up warm an' bring him aboard here, an' I'll take him to London. Measles ain't no joke at his age, an' in a North Sea winter.'

"This was done. We had 240 miles to run in the carrier, an' reached Billingsgate at ten o'clock the next night. At four o'clock the followin' mornin' I was taken out of the cabin, through the cold, wet, and slushy market, an' off to Fenchurch Street Station. It was snowin' heavily all the time, an' we were six hours and a half gettin' to Yarmouth.

Then, bad as I was, I managed somehow to walk four miles in the thick snow to my home, where at last I got a doctor an' proper nursin'; but it was months afore I got over that illness; indeed, I don't know as ever I shall. Now, I put it to you, sir, if we'd had a mission-ship in them days, what a deal o' sufferin' I'd a bin spared; an' there's scores, ay, hundreds of us as ha' bin in just the same fix as me, an' lots of 'em has died right off, 'cause in the first place, they didn't rightly know what was amiss with 'em, an' if they did, they was between two an' three hundred miles from the doctor."

Skipper W—— told of a case, similar to the foregoing, in which the poor patient died through want of proper treatment, and then he proceeded, " B—— has talked about being *ill* in the winter. I'd just like the ladies and gentlemen ashore to see some of the terrible things I've seen in the shape of accidents in the winter-time; they'd precious soon do something to help the smacksmen if they was to see the horrors with their own eyes. Why, I've seen a poor man struck over the head with a piece of a spar, as seemed reg'lar to take the whole scalp right off, and there he lay on the deck bleeding. Well, do you know, sir, the cold was that intense, as by the time we'd picked the poor chap up, and carried him below, the frost had froze the wound and stopped the bleedin'."

" Do you really mean that ? " I inquired.

" Mean it !   Of course I do, sir ; I'm only tellin' you gospel truth."

" Ay," chimed in another, " the cold's the worst part of it when you get hurt out here in the winter-time.   The cuts an' bruises and smashes is bad enough, but when salt water an' frost come to get into them—well, it's a caution."

This final expression seemed to the good men sitting round to be the very strongest epithet applicable to the painful subject, and with one accord they endorsed and repeated the remark, " Ay, it's a caution."   I thought so too.

Skipper P—— said :—" Eleven years ago, when I was working out of Hull in the smack *Superb*, we were caught in very squally weather.   One dark night, with strong wind and the sea running high all around us, all of a sudden a barque scudding along before the wind ran right against us, carrying away both our masts.   I was at the tiller when it happened, and the mizen-boom fell on me, dislocating my knee and breaking the small bone of my leg.   Then, as if that wasn't enough, the mizen mast-head fell on the top of the boom, pinning me down to the deck.   It was twenty-four hours before any help came to us.   There we lay tossing and washing about in the rough seas with everything gone clean by the board.   The next evening one of Mr. Holmes' smacks bore down to our assistance ; a line was hove aboard, a warp made fast, and so we were towed home to Hull. But, sir, *we were five days over the job*, and that, added to the day that passed before help came to us made six days for me to be shipmates with that smashed leg down in the cabin, and by the time the doctor got hold of me, the leg was all stiffened up again, and didn't he make me sing out when he began to haul it about ! Now there's another case for you, sir, to tell your friends ashore. I'd just like to know what *they'd* think if they had to lie like that for six days, lashed on a locker in a rough sea. Why, they've only just to send next door or round the corner, and there's the doctor all handy. Then, besides my own case, I've been aboard with one man who had his leg broken twice. My mate had his eyes so bad I was obliged to send him home ; the poor chap was in great suffering. Another mate was sent home with rheumatism ; but, dear me, if I were to tell all the cases of salt-water boils, crushed hands and fingers, scalds and gashes and smashes, I could make a terrible long list. There's just one, however, I'll mention. W——— was telling of a poor chap with a bad scalp-wound. I saw one case of that kind I'll never forget. One of the hands was helping to get out the boat when the boom suddenly jibed over, struck the back of his head, and peeled the whole entire skin and hair right off from back to front; and there the poor man lay on the deck, stunned by the blow and with his face completely covered by the scalp."

"Horrible!" I exclaimed. "What did you do?"

"What did we do! Why, we drew the whole lot right tight back into its place, and bound up the poor chap's head, and sent him up to the hospital."

Skipper G——, one of the ancient type of smacksman, here remarked, "Well, sir, you've heerd a lot o' yarns, an' I make no doubt they're all right down true, but I've been listening a long time, an' though you've been told about broken legs an' all that, the men as was hurt seems to have been tuk home in their own wessels. Now, sir, you'll b'lieve me being tuk ashore like that 'ere ain't a patch upon the privilege I enjyed in havin' a ride to London for two hundred an' ninety miles aboard the steamboat."

"Well, G——," I replied, "when I say I would like to hear your story, you will please understand I do *not* relish listening to all these blood-curdling details, but I *do* like to know to the full what you poor smacksmen are exposed to, and the different casualties to which your hard rough life renders you liable. I should like to know all, the very worst, and then I can present a faithful picture to my friends on shore, in order that they may become *your* friends and help you in your need."

"Right you are, guv'nor. An' if so be you'll do that, why then I guess we'll run some chance o' gettin' help."

"My friend, you will be absolutely certain of help if it please God to spare my life to tell your story. There are thousands of people willing and ready to support any good cause, and if ever in this world there has been need to extend a helping hand, it is now and to you."

"Well, God bless you for sayin' so," heartily responded old G——, "an' may He send the help along quick!"

"Now, G——, we are waiting for your story."

"It's a very or'nary story," said G——, "an' p'raps you won't think as there's much in it, but there was a sight more in it than I cared for at the time. It was eighteen years ago come next December, an' I was third hand o' the *D*—— at the time. It had been blowin' 'ard, with a lot o' snow, for nigh upon a fortnight, an' we'd three steamboats with the fleet, all waitin' for the chance of a cargo for market. Well, the weather fined a bit, an up goes the admiral's signal for puttin'-to. It was hardly the sort o' weather you'd choose for makin' a haul, but then what was we to do? we'd bin idle so long, don't yer see. Anyhow, we shot

the gear, an' the first haul at midnight we brought
up among the fish a poor fellow as 'ad bin washed
overboard from another smack. We had to throw
him into the sea agin, and then we down trawl on
the other tack. Well, how it come to happen I've
never rightly knowed; but what with the frost an'
the fish lyin' about, the deck was slippery, an' I got
knocked clean off my pins, an' fell with my right
leg all twisted like under me. They helped me
up, but I well nigh screamed with the pain, and
sure enough, my leg was broke in two places.
My shipmates lowered me down into the cabin, an'
there I lay on the floor till mornin', every jerk o'
the little wessel makin' me groan with the pain.
The wind had fallen more during the night; but
lor, sir, there was a sea runnin' as was enough to
knock all the pluck out o' yer. Presently our
skipper comes below, an' says, 'Now, G——, there's
some o' the vessels sendin' their fish aboard the
cutter; will yer stay here an' see if it's finer to-
morrow, or will yer take yer chance this mornin'?'
Well, sir, it were a puzzler. However, thinks I,
it *may* be finer to-morrow, but, as likely as not,
another twenty-four hours 'll see a stronger wind
than ever, so I up an' says, 'I'll go now, skipper,
if it's all the same to you.'

"The skipper called two o' the others, an' between
'em they managed to push an' haul me on deck, but,

oh my! the pain was dreadful, a-runnin' right up
my body. Well, the boat was a-lyin' on the lee side,
an' they spread some o' the trawl-warp tier-boards
along the thwarts, an' a rug on the top of 'em for me
to lie on; but, oh dear! it was the gettin' into that
boat as was the job, an' when at last they dropped
me in, I fainted dead off. With that they thought
it better to clear out all the bed sort o' business, as
they'd rigged up, an' away went the boat with me
all heaped up a top o' the boxes o' fish. I come to
myself afore they fetched alongside the steamboat,
an' I've thought many a time since, as if I hadn't,
the bump o' the boat agin the carrier 'ud a brought
me to my senses. Well, well, it's no use makin'
the story longer nor it need be, but them few
minutes alongside that steamer I'll never forget as
long as I live. Bang, crash, bump; one minit our
boat was up above the cutter's rail, the next we
could see her keel, an' every time we struck her I
seemed as if I must faint again with the torture o'
them broken bones. But it was all over at last.
After tryin' time after time to get me out o' the
boat, and very nigh droppin' me in the sea, six
strong fellows seized me by my head, my arms, my
clothes, anythin' as come 'andy, an' then they
hauled me over the rail an' aboard the cutter, just
as the boat shot down agin' in the trough o' the sea.
That's all, sir—leastways that's the worst part o' the

story, for every mile o' the tossin', tearin' run
to Lunnon in the carrier, bad as it was, was
bringin' me nearer the 'orspital.   Now, what I've
got to say is jist this—if folks ashore 'll do summat
in the way o' doctorin' for us *out in the fleet*, they'll
save many a life, an' many a limb, an' any quantity
o' sufferin'."

So spake old G——, and as he finished I silently
prayed, " O God, if it be true that Thou pitiest them
that fear Thee, ' like as a father pitieth his children,'
then of Thine infinite mercy and compassion, send
help and succour to these poor outcast toilers."

Skipper R——, a massive, stalwart fisherman,
with a voice like distant thunder, told of an occurrence twenty years ago, of which he was eye-
witness.

" The weather was," said he, " well, it was North-
Sea weather, sir—regular Dawger gales, and that's
saying about enough to make you understand it was
pretty bad.   I was aboard a small 45-ton smack, the
E—— C——, one of the old Barking fleet, and
though she was a tight, well-built little craft, still she
was little, and that meant that we took a good deal
more than spray aboard !   Well, one big thumping
sea pretty well smothered us, and when the decks
were a bit clear, there was poor A—— V——
lying writhing and groaning against the mast.
We soon found out what was the matter.   The

tremendous weight o' water had driven him violently against the winch, and there the poor chap lay with a bad compound fracture of the thigh. The weather was so baffling, dead head-winds and furious seas, that although we started for home at once, it wasn't till the ninth day after the accident that we were able to carry our shipmate ashore to the surgery at Barking. Now what a blessing it would have been to have the surgery out at sea!"

"Once," continued R——, "when I was working as a hand aboard the steamboat, it was an awfully rough morning, and one of the boats delivering fish was lifted on a big wave and capsized clean topsy-turvy on the steamer's deck. One of the boat's crew was already aboard the carrier, another fell on deck, while the third was shot overboard into the sea. Happily we saved him, but his head was terribly gashed and one of his ears cut right off. We had some Friar's balsam aboard, and dressed it for him as well as we could in our rough way, and then the boat being re-launched, he was sent back to his own vessel, and they bore away for Yarmouth the same day.

"Another case I remember, while I was aboard the steamer *Hallett*. It was in the month of November about sixteen years ago, and the fleet was working at the east end of the Silver Pits. I forget the name of the smack, but it was the skipper

I'm more concerned about. Skipper Greenwood was his name. The fleet had all got their gears down one Tuesday night, when towards morning it came on to blow very hard, and all the vessels were hauling their trawls in a desperate hurry. Aboard Greenwood's smack they had got the gear well on the rail, but hadn't lashed the beam, when a heavy sea struck the starboard side, and caused such a lurch as to send the beam and all the gear pitching back into the sea. The skipper happened to be standing just inside the coil of the bridles, and instantly, before he had time to move, he was dragged against the side of the vessel, the whole of the heavy gear, beam, net, fish, and all, held fast by the skipper's leg! I needn't say the crew rushed to the capstan and quickly hauled in enough of the weight to enable them to release the skipper; but the mischief was done, for the flesh of his leg was cut through to the bone, and the bone itself badly broken. The breeze increased to a gale, and for three whole days that poor skipper lay in his agony down in the cabin. On the Saturday morning, the weather being a little better, his crew lashed the smashed limb to the side of a fish-trunk, which they broke up on purpose, and then they ferried the poor chap aboard the *Hallett*, where we lowered him as gently as we could, feet foremost, into the cabin. We left the fleet at noon on Saturday, and brought up off Billingsgate on Sunday night. Then four of us got a shutter, lashed him to it, ferried him across the river, and carried him up to Guy's Hospital. Poor chap! I shall never forget him. When we took him up out of the *Hallett's* cabin, the slightest move seemed to hurt him terribly, and he just screamed with the pain. The doctors said the case had been made a lot worse by the delay and exposure, and they had to keep him in the hospital nearly four months before he was cured, and even then he walked with a bad limp ever afterwards till his death."

Reader, do you protest against the recapitulation of such horrors?

It has been said to me, " Don't harrow our feelings by relating these details; to dwell upon scenes such as you have described would make us morbid and miserable."

Indeed, I don't tell these stories to make you unhappy, but are you and I to have a monopoly of joy? For my own part, if I read my Bible aright, and judging from oft-repeated experience, I am unaware of any truer, purer joy than the joy of being allowed to brighten other lives. There is grand truth and force in the lines—

"For the heart grows rich in giving; all its wealth is living grain;
Seeds which mildew in the garner, scattered, fill with gold the plain."

And with regard to the stories of suffering and peril —although I have not told a thousandth part—they are mentioned for the one purpose of drawing forth sympathy and help.

From that species of happiness which centres in self, which takes no pleasure in ministering to another's needs, let us exclaim from our hearts, " Good Lord, deliver us ! " It is piteous, indeed, to hear of a man who can pay two hundred guineas at Covent Garden for flowers to decorate his dinner-table, and yet refuse to help a work of philanthropy on the plea of " hard times." Is *this* Christianity ? And yet that person would be vastly surprised if one dared to doubt the reality of his Christian pro-fession.

May the living God awaken our conscience and teach us earth's highest privilege—to walk con-sistently in the footsteps of Him Who said, " If any man will come after Me, *let him deny himself*, and take up his cross daily, and follow Me."

But, thank God, there are many thousands who do seek to

"Scatter seeds of kindness for the reaping by-and-bye ; "

and upon them this chapter will have but one effect, awakening sympathy with the smacksmen, deepening that sympathy where it already exists, and strengthening the determination to aid this work of mercy to the utmost of their ability.

CHAPTER VII.

THE FIRST VOYAGE.

" So sometimes comes to soul and sense
The feeling which is evidence
That all our sorrow, pain, and doubt,
A great compassion clasps about,
And law and goodness, love and force,
Are wedded fast beyond divorce.
  .   .   .   .   .   .
So, to the calmly gathered thought,
The innermost of truth is taught,
The mystery dimly understood,
That love of God is love of good."

I HAVE said that the new mission-ship was an object of derision to certain people before she left port. This perhaps was to be expected; but it may surprise the reader to learn that she was laughed at on joining the fleet, greeted with scorn by the very men for whose benefit she had been equipped! How could it be otherwise? They had yet to learn that Christianity does not, as they supposed, consist alone in singing psalms, but that the blessed Lord Jesus was Himself the most practical philanthropist the world has ever seen; and this new ship

came amongst them in His Name, and the workers
on board meant to follow His methods, confident
that by His grace they would succeed in the long
run, although they, like their Master, might at
first be misunderstood. True there were many who
were looking for the "Bethel-ship," and boisterous
cheers rang across the sea as she passed, here and
there, the smacks commanded by godly skippers.
The vast majority, however, were disposed to regard
the scheme as a new-fangled notion of some quixotic
landsman, and they agreed with the owner who had
foretold " one voyage, and then we shall hear no
more of *that* whim ! "

Had this been merely a commercial speculation,
there was more than sufficient discouragement to
damp the ardour of the most enthusiastic promoter.
But it was not only started with the absolute conviction that the work was of God, and could not be
overthrown, but also in the full expectation of con-
temptuous indifference, if not positive opposition.

Forewarned is forearmed ; so, with all these
probabilities in view, much prayer was offered
beforehand that our Master would " give testimony
to the word of His grace," and silence opposition
from the outset by proving to the whole fleet that
the Mission was one not of mere tract-distribution,
but bent on an errand of mercy, of physical as well
as moral and spiritual good, to every man and boy

in the service. How wonderful, how complete, how like Himself was the answer to this prayer!

On the day the *Ensign* joined the fleet, a skipper, leaning over the rail of his smack, scanned the new ship as she sailed by, noticed the great twenty-foot flag, and turning to his mate exclaimed, " What's the good of her? What do they think they're goin' to do with her?"

In God's good providence that man was one of the very first in the fleet to prove the good of the mission-ship.

I was myself present at the second Sunday service held in the fleet after the arrival of the *Ensign*, and this skipper, prompted by curiosity, attended, accompanied by his son, a boy about ten years old. The great 20-feet flag was for that occasion transferred to the steamer *Frost*, where, by the captain's kindness, both morning and afternoon services were held. The weather being very unsettled, with a threatening of more wind, many were prevented coming in the morning; but, spite of all difficulties, a large company responded at three o'clock to the call of the steamer's whistle, and, assembling in the hold, which had been carefully syringed and mopped for the occasion, listened attentively to an address by a Christian brother who had accompanied me. Very touching were the petitions afterwards offered by several smacksmen, very fervent their thanks-

giving, and all their visitors were deeply moved by
the triumphant closing hymn, so appropriate to the
circumstances of these brave fellows. The "bright,
beautiful home" was the burden of their song :—

> " Soon shall I join that anthem,
>   Far beyond the sky ;
> Christ is my salvation,
>   Why should I fear to die ?
> Soon my eyes shall behold Him,
>   Seated upon the bright throne ;
> Then, O then shall I see thee,
>   Beautiful, beautiful home ! "

It was a glad avowal of simple faith in Christ
from the lips of men accustomed to facing death,
and it was sung too in the presence of others who
had not yet decided, and who keenly criticised the
profession of their mates. Often had the Christian
smacksmen sung the same words together on the
eve of a gale which conveyed one or more of their
company to the *home* and the *Christ*.

On the third Sunday, Skipper H—— and his
son were at both services, and the father appeared
to be greatly impressed. After the service had ended,
Skipper Budd urged the father to sign the pledge,
and noticing the little lad looking very earnestly at
him, he asked if he would like to sign.

"Yes," said the boy, and with the father's permission he signed.

"Now," said Budd, " you cannot refuse, as your

lad has set the example, and will be helped by your signing too."

The conflict was severe but brief, and yielding to Budd's prayerful persuasion, in the result the father also signed the pledge, and both have kept it ever since.

A few days afterwards Skipper H———'s vessel received some damage during a gale of wind from the north-east. A block fell from aloft to the deck, and in falling struck the skipper's head, severely gashing it. Under the old régime he must have been conveyed to the steam-carrier and sent to London for hospital treatment, with the chances vastly in favour of erysipelas supervening by reason of exposure and neglect. But now—what? The mate ran the smack down towards the *Ensign*, the crew promptly helped their wounded skipper into the boat, and, accompanied by his little son, rowed him with all speed alongside the new craft, as to whose vocation he had expressed such cynical doubt.

A hearty welcome awaited the sufferer, kind hands assisted him into the cabin, the medicine-chest was opened, and Skipper Budd skilfully cut away the hair, cleansed, plaistered, and bandaged the wound, and the poor man rose from his seat feeling already half way towards recovery.

" What's to pay ? " he inquired.

" Pay ! " laughed Budd. " Pay ! Why, old

friend, there's *nothing* to pay. The blessed Gospel is *free*, and aboard this vessel the medicine-chest is all a part of the Gospel. But the good old book says, 'What shall I render unto the Lord for all His benefits towards me?' Just come along into my cabin, and we'll ask God to heal your soul as well as your body."

And so it came about that one of the first instances of physical relief being afforded proved also the first case of true conversion to God, for in Budd's cabin that day Skipper H—— surrendered himself to the Saviour, and for the past five years has been living " soberly, righteously, and godly."

This was one case, but others followed in quick succession. It soon became known in the fleet that simple medical and surgical assistance were to be had gratis aboard the new ship, and no man came for medicine or to have his wounds attended to without hearing of the Great Physician, our blessed Lord Jesus Christ. The mission-ship grew daily in favour, not only with the Christian men, who now for the first time had an opportunity of gathering for worship without fear of molestation or discharge from their employment, but with all who had occasion to prove on board of her how real and practical is true religion.

Amongst other cases treated were the following. One of the crew of the *Bessie* (commanded by Skipper Smith, who subsequently entered the mission-service, and lost his life in the *Breeze* disaster) placed his hand over the side of the boat during the delivery of fish, and the boat surging against the steamer, the hand was instantly smashed, being laid bare to the bone on both sides. After dressing the hand, Budd spoke to the sufferer as to his soul's welfare, pointing out that his life might have been taken, instead of there being merely the injury to his hand. This man was sent immediately to the London Hospital, and did not return to the fleet, but many prayers followed him.

The skipper of the *Agnes and Ida* nearly severed his left hand by a blow from a large hatchet, and must inevitably have gone home but for the presence of the Mission-ship. The injured limb was carried in a sling for some time, but the skipper managed to remain at his post.

One morning Budd placed the *Ensign* astern of the steam-carrier, in a convenient position to intercept the boats returning to their vessels after delivering fish. Within a few minutes ten boats boarded her for medical and surgical aid. One fisherman was suffering from a very bad poisoned hand, and no sooner were his own rough bandages removed, in order to the application of proper treatment, than the poor man fell fainting on the cabin floor.

There was no time for administering restoratives; the other nine patients were waiting, a smart breeze was blowing, with every prospect of a gale, and each man was anxious to get back to his own vessel before the weather grew worse; so Budd dealt with the cases as rapidly as possible, speaking a word here and there for his Master as each passed out of the cabin.

Meanwhile the first man had recovered consciousness, and the hand having been carefully cleansed, dressed with healing ointment, and skilfully enveloped in suitable bandages and placed in a sling, the sufferer was assisted over the side into his boat, fervently invoking blessings on "this 'ere wessel."

"Ay, ay!" shouted Skipper Budd as the boat pulled away, " but remember I'm only the *assistant ;* it's the blessed Lord Jesus Christ that's the Great Physician."

I cannot do better than quote Budd's own views of the work at that time, as expressed in a letter he addressed to me :—" Many of the men come aboard asking, 'Is it true as you've got medicines here for all the fleet, and nothin' to pay for 'em ?' 'Yes,' I tell them, 'free as the Gospel, without money and without price.' It all seems so wonderful, it's hard to believe at first, after living so many years with no one to care for us but our own relatives ashore, and I feel assured that this part of our work has secured the lasting gratitude and esteem of the men of the fleet."

That letter had reference to the earliest infancy of the Mission, when the experiment had not been tried four months; but what is the verdict now, after a lapse of five years? Let my readers inquire in any of the fleets where mission-vessels are stationed, and they will hear but one remark—the hearty ejaculation, " *God bless 'em !* "

Thus the work of healing for body and soul progressed side by side. When a man had been relieved of severe bodily pain, he could not, for very shame, refuse the invitation to " come again," and in a great number of instances this coming again resulted in coming to the Saviour. From this time victory became assured. Men who had gone to sea wild, profligate, godless, returned at the close of the voyage completely changed. Wives and little ones were made to rejoice, the police found their labours considerably lightened, and employers quickly discovered that a sober, godly servant was worth more than a drunken, godless one.

This prompt treatment of disease and injuries on the fishing-grounds had another most important result. Numbers of men who, without the aid of the mission-ship, must have gone home for cure in the hospital, were able after a few days to resume their duties aboard the smacks, and this it will be seen was in the aggregate an enormous gain both to the men and their families, and also to the employers. Take, for example, the case of injury to Skipper H——'s head. In the absence of help, he must have made the journey to the Thames by steamer, while the mate took the smack into Yarmouth for a fresh skipper. That would have involved at least a week's loss of fishing to the owner. To their honour be it recorded, that no sooner was this fact well ascertained, than the large owners spontaneously offered their congratulations, and proved their sympathy with the effort and their appreciation of its results in a highly gratifying manner. Having been ridiculed at the outset by some, I had very naturally determined not to apply to any of the owners for pecuniary assistance. What then was my delight on receiving, within nine months of the *Ensign's* first cruise, a letter from Messrs. Hewett & Co. saying, " Our men have been completely revolutionised; we believe great good has been done, and we gladly become annual subscribers of £10, 10s. to the funds of the Mission." The same firm also gave a donation of £50. Here then was cause for sincere satisfaction and thankfulness. Not a penny had been solicited; the spontaneity of the gift and its accompanying letter rendered the testimony all the more eloquent and valuable.

Moreover, it was given, not by private philanthropists, but by a Board of Directors calmly sitting round their table and voting away the monies of the company in aid of a *Mission*. Clearly the operations of the said Mission must have been of a very practical character, and have accomplished results favourably affecting the company's dividend, or most certainly shrewd business men would not thus be found contributing to its support.

But this was not all. Very shortly after the receipt of this agreeable communication a smack-owner placed a cheque for two guineas in my hand, saying, "That is my first annual subscription." I happened to know that he was one of those who had laughed when the work began; so, before appropriating the cheque I asked, "What provoked you to give that money?"

"Oh," he said, "you are converting the North-Sea smacksmen, I believe."

"Certainly not," I replied. "I trust, however, that God is converting a great many of them."

"Oh, I see. Well, I don't profess to understand much about it, but if converting the smacksmen means that they won't sell my nets to the *coper*, it will pay me very well to give you two guineas a year towards the cost of converting them."

Here was conversion viewed from a business standpoint; but I took the cheque and rejoiced

G

that the employers of labour were thus proving that
" godliness is profitable unto all things, having promise of the life that now is, and of that which is
to come."

Such was the cheering testimony from those who,
next to the wives and families, were best able to
judge of the character of the work accomplished by
the mission-agents. As to the people who, more
than any others, could testify to the reality of the
change—the relatives of the professed converts—they
were simply overflowing with gratitude for what
had been brought to pass,—so unlooked for, yet so
unspeakably welcome.

The captain of one of the steam-carriers wrote
to me at this period :—" The last time I was out
with the fleet, while standing on the bridge with
a crowd of smacksmen below me, I heard shouts
of, ' Here she comes !' ' Isn't she a beauty !' ' God
bless her !' and looking round saw the *Ensign*
coming up with her big flag flying ; and her captain was soon aboard with books, tracts, and bundles
of woollens, and many a man, for the sake of the
woollens, took—and read too—the tract or text that
was slipped inside them. But if you want a testimony as to the vessel's value, go to the smacksmen's
houses and hear what the wives have to say."

A woman, whose life for several years had been
one prolonged misery, and who looked forward with

terror to the eight days which her drunken and tyrannical husband would spend ashore, exclaimed, with tears of joy streaming down her face, " Oh, sir, my husband isn't the same man now. In the old days, if I wanted to find him while he was ashore, I knew quite well he was sure to be in the public-house ; and the children, poor things, were frightened to go a-nigh him. But now, he's that quiet and nice and kind, and he doesn't go a-nigh the public-house, but takes the children for walks, and such like, and on Sundays we all go to service together."

This poor woman but gave utterance to the feelings and experiences which she shared with many others, and there were those amongst the wives and mothers who for years had been Christians, and had, without ceasing, prayed for their unconverted relatives at sea. Besides, in many cases, the men, who had themselves "tasted that the Lord is gracious," came home to play the part of evangelists to unsaved wives and families, and thus the good resulting from the mission-vessel's work away at sea was not confined to the fleets, but extended in an ever-widening circle amongst the fisher-folk in the towns and villages on shore.

One immediate consequence of all this was that the men in other fleets cried out for a mission-vessel. " Why don't you send *us* a Bethel-ship ?

What have *we* done that we shouldn't have a vessel
with *our* fleet ? " It was difficult to persuade these
clamouring applicants that mission-vessels were not
carried in one's pocket, or brought forth fully
equipped by the wave of a magic wand; but, all
the same, there was immense satisfaction and joy
in the assurance that this eagerness to have a mission-vessel was in itself sufficient proof of the enthusiastic appreciation in which the pioneer-vessel
was on all sides held.

CHAPTER VIII.

GLIMPSES OF THE SPIRITUAL WORK.

" Far, far away, like bells at evening pealing,
   The voice of Jesus sounds o'er land and sea ;
And laden souls, by thousands meekly stealing,
   Kind Shepherd, turn their weary steps to Thee."

" WHAT has come over these fishermen ? " said a
gentleman who had not visited Gorleston for several
years. "The place hardly seems the same as when
I was last here."

" No," said the person addressed, " thank God it
is not the same. We may safely say ' old things
are passed away, all things are become new.' And
the change has certainly been brought about by
means of the mission-ships ; for many smacksmen
who have left the harbour careless and godless have
come back at the close of their voyage quite different
beings, shunning the public-houses, going about
respectably dressed, and taking their families with
them to the house of God."

A friend who was passing through the streets of
Gorleston one Sunday afternoon observed a large

crowd collected near the pier and watching intently
some vessel outside the harbour.   On closer examination, this proved to be a smack which had just
arrived from the fishing-ground, and was standing
off and on waiting to get into the port.   This in
itself was nothing unusual, but at her masthead was
flying a flag which some of the crowd thought to be
a mission-flag; yet as it was well known that her
skipper was a godless man, it seemed hardly possible
that he would come into port flying such a flag.
Just then a fisherman who had lately come home
from the fleet informed the watchers that the skipper had been converted to God at one of the services held at sea, and that he was really flying a
mission-flag, which he had obtained from the *Cholmondeley*.

The next day an opportunity occurred for speaking to the new convert, and with a joyous smile he
said, referring to the incident of the previous day,
" I thought I'd better hoist my new colours before
coming into harbour, as I didn't want to be ashamed
to let my old companions see that I had come over
on the Lord's side."

" Praise the Lord," exclaimed several Christian
men who were standing by.

Such results as this were calculated to call forth
fervent thanksgiving for the genuine character of the
work hitherto accomplished, and to fill our hearts

with encouragement and hope. One striking feature of the effort was (and has since continued to
be), the constant habit of waiting in prayer at the
throne of heavenly grace, and, as is ever the case,
this practice received its own reward in very remarkable answers, or, as an aged Christian expressed it,
" remarkably like God."

For example, two vessels in the " Short Blue "
fleet, known as the _D_—— and the _C_——, were so
exactly alike that their own skippers scarcely knew
them apart. The main difference lay in the skippers themselves. R—— of the _D_—— might well
have borne the same name as his vessel—a bright,
happy, open-hearted Christian, while the master
of the _C_——, though what was called a jolly good
fellow, was a great friend of the _coper_. One sultry
summer's afternoon the smacks had their gear down
for a day-haul, but as the wind completely died
away, it was quite practicable to hold a prayer-
meeting on board the mission-smack _Cholmondeley_,
then stationed with the " Short Blues," and having
a special missioner on board from London. The flag
was accordingly struck as a signal to the fleet that
service was about to be held. Upon the deck of
the _Cholmondeley_ stood, amongst others, the admiral
of the fleet, himself but recently converted to God,
during a serious illness which had confined him for
weeks to the hospital. While the hum of conversa-

tion was at its height, the mission-skipper was observed to shade his eyes from the intense glare, and after regarding for a moment or two a vessel some 200 yards on the port quarter, he exclaimed, "Why, there's R—— signalling. He wants to join us, and his own boat is on deck. Fred, do you think you can scull and fetch alongside of him? Skipper R—— will help you to pull back."

Fred thought he could, and while he is doing so, we may note that there was one vessel there that afternoon which, having no fishing gear on board, was free to cruise about the fleet, threading her way here and there, wherever there seemed to be the chance of sale or barter. That craft of ill omen, the devil's mission-ship, was on the look-out for prey, and while Fred, with his eye on the signal (a bread-bag or an oil-skin frock suspended on an oar, termed by the smacksmen a " creagan "), was making for the supposed *D*——, the *coper* might have been seen bearing down in the same direction, although she had not as yet sighted the signal. Arrived within hailing distance, Fred shouted, as only a North-Sea fisherman can shout, "*D*—— ahoy!" Instantly a head appeared above the rail, and with a broad grin the skipper responded, "This vessel ain't the *D*——. We're the *C*——. What do you want with me? I had the signal out for the *coper*, not for you."

Poor Fred was utterly chagrined, and having made his boat fast alongside the *C*—— with the rope the skipper had thrown, he exclaimed, "Well, skipper, here's a go.   I was told you were the *D*——, and was sent to bring you off to the prayer-meeting."

At this the grin developed into a loud laugh, for the skipper of the *C*—— was about the last man in the fleet to be guilty of attending a prayer-meeting.   Still time was pressing, and although Bill had found it an easy matter to *reach* the vessel, it was absolutely impossible for him to return without assistance.

"Skipper, would you let me have one of your crew," he inquired, "to help me back to the *Cholmondeley?*   We'll take care to send him home again."

"No, I can't well do that," said the skipper, "but I don't mind lending you a hand myself, if you'll send me back at once with a couple of men to pull me."

The bargain was struck, and a few minutes later, great was the astonishment of the smacksmen assembled on the *Cholmondeley's* deck at seeing the skipper of the *C*—— coming, as they supposed, to the prayer-meeting.   The moment the boat sheered alongside, a perfect forest of hands was held over to greet the new-comer, while hearty cries of

" What cheer ? " " What cheer, old fellow ? " " Glad
to see you," showered down upon him the warmest
of welcomes. But the admiral put a stop to this
with " Come on board, old man; you will have
your shoulder put out of joint." And indeed there
was danger of some such accident in endeavouring
to shake hands from a boat while constantly rising
and falling with the swell.

This coming on board was more than the skipper
had bargained for, but he was not the man to turn
his back on old friends, and many of these, the
admiral included, had been his " pals " in other
days on board the *coper*. So it came to pass that
he, who had vowed again and again that he would
give the " Bethel-ship " a wide berth, found himself the next moment standing on the deck of the
Cholmondeley, amid the hearty greetings of the
congregation, compelling the mental admission
that it was not such a bad place after all! Yet
even now he had no intention of remaining; but
before he had time to explain that he had merely
come with the object of doing a kind turn to Fred,
the missionary passed the word round, " Now, my
lads, let's go below," and the skipper of the *C——*
found himself going down with the rest, where he
never had been before. After the first burst of
happy song, he heard one after another speaking
reverently and earnestly to their Father in heaven.

It was all new and strange, and he began to feel
very uneasy, for it appeared to him that if all these
prayers were real, God must be very near to them.
And presently, when one man fervently exclaimed,
" O Lord, bless the skipper of the *C*———," there
was instantly a chorus of " *Amen !* " from the whole
assembly.   This was quite too much for the poor
fellow.   He had never in his life drawn near to
God, and now to find himself the subject of inter-
cession, to hear the earnest pleadings of others for
his soul's salvation, brought him consciously into
the very presence of the living God, and made him
cry out, " Lord, have mercy upon me."   The good
missionary who was at that time quartered on board
the *Cholmondeley* thereupon pointed this penitent
to the Lamb of God, and had the joy of hearing
him, before the day closed, express trust in Christ
as his Saviour.   At the end of the service, when the
members of the congregation were chatting in groups
on the deck, waiting the return of their boats, the
strange event of the day was naturally the chief
topic of conversation, and one skipper remarked—

" Well, that *was* a funny mistake."

" Mistake ! " exclaimed the admiral, turning
sharply round.   " Mistake do you call it ?   At all
events, *God* made no mistake.   He wanted the
skipper of the *C*———, and He let you make a mistake in order to get him here."

Here was another victory for Christ and another blow to the *coper* traffic; for never more would a "creagan" be hoisted on board the *C——* as a signal to the grog-shop, and thus the foreigner lost the patronage of a whole ship's company.

The habit of seizing every opportunity for conducting Divine service was not, however, peculiar to the "Short Blues," but other fleets observed the same wholesome custom, and were also equally fond of long-continued religious exercises, which are unknown to congregations on land, but a common practice at sea.

Skipper Cullington relates an interesting story illustrative of this, and at the same time proving how the Holy Spirit was working amongst the fishermen, and leading some of the worst and wildest to the Saviour's feet.

It was a lovely summer's day in the Great Northern fleet; not only very warm, but so calm that the sea had the appearance of molten glass, with not even a ripple on its surface. About two o'clock Cullington was struck with the bright idea of lashing several vessels together, so that not merely those who were able to come away in the boats, but every man and boy on board might gather to the service. The reader must not conclude that this was Sunday. Every day in the week the mission-vessel is open for Divine service, subject, of course, to the

exigencies of the weather and the fishing.   On this
particular Tuesday Cullington remarked to a skipper sitting beside him, sipping the orthodox mug
of tea, " What a grand chance to lash the wessels
alongside o' one another an' hold a service."

" You're right, old friend," responded the man
addressed.   Then, jumping to his feet, and taking
a hasty survey, he exclaimed, " Let's be at it at
once."

" At it " they all went in tremendous earnest,
and within three-quarters of an hour no fewer than
ten vessels were lashed side by side, the mission-
ship being in the centre.   This was not accomplished without much labour, but boats were thrown
out, and willing hands made light work, the result
being that by three o'clock no fewer than fifty-two
men and boys were assembled in one group on the
deck of the mission-ship, and with the exception of
a brief half-hour for the evening meal, there was a
continuous service for eight hours.   Singing, prayer,
addresses by several Christian fishermen, and by a
lay missionary who was spending a month in the
fleet, occupied the time until the clock in the cabin
struck eleven.

" You'd better give out, old skipper," said one of
the men, addressing Cullington ; " you're as hoarse
as a crow."

" Well," responded the enthusiastic little man,

"I'll grant ye we can't see to sing any more out here on deck, but we'll go below and pray, for I'm anxious about several o' these fellows."

So the word was passed round, and the visitors dropped one by one through the open hatchway into the hold, where lamps were provided and several earnest addresses were given, beseeching the careless and the unsaved to "be reconciled to God."

Cullington was right. There were some in that strange company who were known as the best customers of the foreign *coper*—men who, when ashore, were always in trouble themselves and causing trouble to their wives and families, and after these especially was the heart of this good man yearning.

As time passed, it became evident that the word spoken was reaching some consciences, for sighs were heard from corners of the dimly-lighted hold, and presently one big rough smacksman groaned forth, "O God, I can't hold out no longer. Lord have mercy on me."

Finally, the gathering dispersed at 1.30 A.M., after remaining together ten hours and a half.

The lashings were cast adrift, the ten vessels hauled clear of one another, and when at last the sounds of public worship ceased, there were still silent thanksgivings in many hearts; for three skippers and a cabin-boy had not only become pledged abstainers, but had openly confessed the Saviour.

By that day's event the *coper* lost three of his customers—nay, more than three; for when the skipper of a smack refuses drink, he refuses it for himself and his crew.

But here, as in other cases, we were confronted with the perplexing problem, "How are these men to get their tobacco?" 'Twere hard indeed to say to a man, "Now, in addition to the many privileges which have become yours as a believer, there is this further boon—you are to be allowed in future to pay 4s. per pound for your tobacco, *i.e.*, 2s. 6d. per pound more than you paid in your evil, drinking days."

Of course this was most ridiculous, and it became a question of purchasing tobacco from the *coper* or giving up the pipe altogether. Some adopted the latter course, but only very, very few, for tobacco is to many of the fishermen almost a necessity.

The others, who remained smokers, were of course obliged to purchase from the grog-shop, where, in addition to the oily persuasiveness of the foreign skipper, they were exposed either to the pleadings or the taunts and jeers (ay, and sometimes the curses and blows) of their old companions.

This was a most serious and alarming state of

things, and I felt that sooner or later this question of the tobacco supply would have to be faced and settled in favour of the men, who were now practically at the mercy of the foe.

Yet, in spite of all hindrances and opposition, the good work went bravely on, and one unfailing test and proof was to be found in the fact that the *copers* felt the pinch of hard times. The tobacco was merely a lure, a decoy-duck; and when so many customers who used to make large purchases of aniseed brandy began to confine themselves to " Rising. Hope," the hopes of the foreign mischief-makers were far from rising, and it will easily be credited they were far from regarding the mission-ships with a friendly eye. These new craft had indeed proved to be anti-*copers*.

By the autumn of 1884 matters were rapidly reaching a crisis. The foreigners were growing desperate, and one of them, an Ostend skipper, openly declared, " Those cursed mission-ships are ruining our trade, and if many more of them come, there'll soon be no *copers*."

This was cheering news indeed; and while such tidings reached me from sea, the testimony on shore was equally gratifying. The Mayor of Grimsby remarked at a public meeting, " I regard the mission-vessel in the Grimsby fleet as a blessing to the trade of the port." Similar pleasing statements were made in other towns by magistrates, clergy, and police; and many private residents of the fishing-towns added their voluntary endorsement of the official verdict.

With all these results present to my mind, I could but say to a dear friend, who, at the close of 1884, was offering his congratulations, "Yes, the retrospect is wonderful indeed, considering that the Mission has only been in active operation two years and a half. The results are infinitely beyond my expectations, though certainly not beyond my hopes. I have loved those words of Samuel Rutherford—

> 'If but *one* soul from Anwoth
>   Meet me at God's right hand,
> My heaven shall be *two* heavens
>   In Immanuel's land.'

But, thank God, it is not *one* only, but many, probably hundreds, who have been brought to trust the Saviour since the first Mission-ship sailed in 1882."

H

CHAPTER IX.

TWENTY-FOUR HOURS OF A SMACKSMAN'S LIFE.

" No coward soul is mine,
No trembler in the world's storm-troubled sphere :
I see heaven's glories shine,
And faith shines equal, arming me from fear."

THE first time I stayed aboard a trawling-smack in one of the Yarmouth fleets, the cry of the watch on deck, " Haul here! Haul the trawl! All haul, all haul!" effectually roused me at 5 A.M., and being anxious to go through the mill, and, as far as possible, share the smacksman's labours, I quickly turned out and joined the crew at the capstan. The modern plan of fitting the trawlers with steam-capstans had not come extensively into vogue, and our vessel's gear was worked by one of the " patent manuals." At first the handles flew round merrily enough, but by-and-bye, when the warp was " up and down," the strain became fearful. Tugging, pushing, panting, the labour continued without cessation until

nearly eight o'clock, and oh! the sense of relief
when at last the trawl came alongside, and the
skipper shouted, " Belay all ! "

Now, I thought, I shall thoroughly enjoy some
breakfast, for three hours of North-Sea morning
air and incessant labour had combined to make me
exceedingly hungry. Misguided land-lubber that
I was! The work was merely changed ; it was very
far from being over. Seeing no sign of a meal, I
ventured to say—

" Skipper, what time do you breakfast ? "

" When our work's done, sir."

" May I ask when that will be ? "

" Maybe twelve o'clock, maybe one — depends
upon the catch."

" But," I remonstrated, "you don't mean to
say you can work for seven long hours without
food ? "

" We breakfast when our work's done, sir," and
with that reply I was fain to be content, until it
happily occurred to the worthy skipper that perhaps
I was unaccustomed to such long fasts, and turning
to the cook, he bade him " go below and fetch the
gentleman some coffee."

Now, if I have one special weakness, it is for
coffee. Whether it be such excellent *café-au-lait* as
they give you at Amsterdam, or the delicious *café-noir*
with which the amiable monks of La Grande Char-

treuse regale their guests after a vegetarian dinner—
there is no fragrance more pleasing than that of really
good coffee. But when the cook appeared with the
cup of dirty-looking liquid, I wished I had asked for
a glass of water. It had neither the colour nor the
flavour of coffee, but I managed one sip, and then
set the cup down in disgust, and pleaded for something to eat. The mate, a facetious fellow, noticed
my repugnance, and remarked, with a view to com-
forting me, " Anyhow, sir, it's wet and warm."

Meanwhile, the cook had been despatched for
some bread, and in my simplicity I had visions of
an appetising slice of bread and butter. Another
disappointment! Their "bread" was the hardest
of sea-biscuits.

However, I managed to take the keen edge off
my hunger, and set to work again with the men,
though when it came to cleaning the fish prepara-
tory to packing them in the trunks for conveyance to
the steamer, my help was valueless, and so I contented myself with looking on and chatting with
the mate. He could not get over his amusement
at my chagrin in the matter of breakfast, and when
opportunity occurred he would, with a sly chuckle,
return to the charge.

" Didn't much like our coffee nor our bread
neither, did yer, sir ? "

" No, mate, I can't say I did ; but I didn't come

to sea for pleasure, but to find out something of
the life you fellows lead. Now tell me, how is it
you can work so hard for seven hours at a stretch
without food ? "

" Well, sir, for one thing, we're used to it, and use,
they say, is second natur' ; then when we begins our
breakfast, we goes it ; and again, yer see, we keeps
ourselves from gettin' bad by usin' a bit o' baccy."

And so they did, taking tobacco in two forms—
not only in the pipe, but cutting off a plug from
their " pocket-piece," and chewing it persistently, as
I discovered by observing now and then a slight
protuberance of the cheek.

By half-past ten o'clock all the fish were sorted,
cleaned, and packed in trunks for conveyance to the
steam-carrier.

" Now, my lads," cried the skipper, " be sharp.
There's a nasty look to windward, and we must look
alive if we mean to get the fish away to-day."

" Why, skipper, I thought you were so forward
with your work that there would be no risk of
losing the steamer."

" That's quite true, sir, but it's the weather I'm
thinking about, not the steamboat. If I'm not greatly
mistaken, there's a gale o' wind brewing. Just look at
that sky and listen to those Mother Carey's chickens ;
they're quite signs enough for a smacksman ; and
if you ain't convinced, you may satisfy yourself by

just taking a look at the barometer, which has been falling these two hours. It mayn't last any time, but I reckon we're bound to have it before long."

While the conversation was going on the skipper's hands were not idle.

The skipper who succeeds in the North Sea is the "*come-boys*" man (the "*go-boys*" man might as well stop ashore); and our friend was not content with directing, but with a cheery cry of "Lend a hand here," he would lead the way wherever the work was hardest and most pressing.

"Why don't all the fishing-smacks carry barometers?" asked a lady who was one day greatly interested in my story of the Mission, and appalled at the sacrifice of life in the North Sea.

"They do carry barometers."

"Then how is it we hear so frequently of vessels being lost? I should have thought the chief use of a barometer would be to indicate an approaching storm, and enable the master of the smack to run home in time to escape it."

"Well," I explained, "there would be two serious difficulties in the way of running home. In the first place, the smack would probably be from 100 to 300 miles away from home, and the gale would have time to blow itself out before port was reached. Then, again, the smacks are equipped and sent to sea for the purpose of trawling, not to spend their time in running home. If his vessel were actually caught in a gale and disabled, then of course she must be taken home for repairs ; but, on the other hand, the skipper who would not even stay to face the gale, but arrived in harbour for no better reason than because the barometer was falling, would, I suspect, be promptly discharged by his employer, and his berth be filled by a man who understood, and was prepared to carry out, at all risks, the duties of his calling."

I had now an opportunity of seeing, from a different standpoint, the dangerous service which had on former occasions so impressed me when witnessed from the bridge of the carrier. The stern of the massive boat was hoisted on the vessel's rail by the combined efforts of the whole crew (the skipper being for the moment at the tiller), and then with one mighty effort, in response to the mate's cheery cry of " Shove together, my lads ! " the boat was bodily pushed over into the sea, and lay alongside, tugging at the painter with convulsive snatches, like a restless hound eager to be freed from the leash.

The third and fourth hands, in full regalia, leaped into the boat, and commenced stowing the boxes of fish under the thwarts ; this done, the fifth hand joined them, and the skipper passed down the " fish

note," which the third hand carefully hid away in his
sou'-wester, and the smack having now arrived within
four hundred yards of the carrier, the boat was cast
off, and made its way over the intervening space of
what was rapidly assuming the appearance of a boiling cauldron.   To me the spectacle was appalling
enough, but the others seemed to make light of it,
although I fancied there was just a shade of uneasiness on the skipper's face.

"How do you like the prospect for your boat's
crew, skipper?"

"Not at all, sir.   There's a nasty swell this
morning, and this rising breeze makes the sea very
choppy.   I almost wish I'd kept the boat aboard."

"Then why didn't you?   You're your own master."

"True, sir, and I shall only have myself to blame
if anything goes wrong; but you see other boats
were putting off, and I didn't like to be behind the
rest of 'em; but I shall be uncommonly glad when
that boat comes alongside again."

Meanwhile the perilous task proceeded, and more
than once, as two seas, careering at right angles,
suddenly converged, it seemed for a moment that
no power could prevent a catastrophe.   Yet the
staunch boat, now little more than a red speck in the
distance, rose amid the wild smother of the breaking
surge, and held on her course for the carrier, whose
unwieldy bulk rolled and plunged madly among

the cross seas. Away beyond were smacks, some
of which, like ourselves, had sent away their boats,
and were now waiting their return, although others
had evidently concluded that discretion is the better
part of valour, and were heading away after the
admiral, who had lost his gear through coming fast
to a sunken wreck during the night.

Presently our boat was observed to reach the
steamer, and the skipper uttered a sigh of relief
as he saw one half of the dangerous errand safely
accomplished. Then came the return journey.
True, the boat was not so heavily weighted, for
twelve trunks of fish, representing a total of eleven
hundredweight, had been transferred to the carrier;
but to be without ballast was not altogether in
favour of a safe passage, especially as the force of
the wind was momentarily augmenting, and shaved
off the crests of the travelling seas as with a knife,
driving volumes of salt spray high around our
vessel as the blast came tearing through the rigging
with ever-increasing velocity.

No more skylarking now! Each man seemed
profoundly impressed with the gravity of the situation, and by common consent there was dead silence,
while every eye was fixed on the red speck, at one
time carried high upon a huge wave, then for
several seconds entirely hidden from view. The
suspense was terrible, and we all knew well that

nothing could save our three shipmates if their frail
craft were capsized by the vicious seas. Still, on she
came, the distance quickly diminishing; for the
three men who strained and pushed at their oars
were evidently keenly alive to the necessity for haste,
and they urged the boat up and down the liquid
hills and forced her through the broken water
with the determination of brave men wrestling with
death.

They were now within hailing distance, and our
skipper, who, with knitted brows and compressed lips,
had been anxiously watching their progress, for the
first time broke the spell by crying in stentorian tones,
"Keep it up, my lads; another dozen strokes and
you'll fetch alongside of us." . . . The last word was
cut short and terminated in a groan, which was re-
echoed from every lip, for the bow-oar was seen to
snap just as a rushing eddying roller caught the boat's
quarter, and for one instant all appeared lost. But
no; although the volume of angry water roared and
hissed around, the danger was averted by the skill
and presence of mind of the third hand, who, shouting to the bow-oar to pull away with the broken
piece, managed, by skilful manipulation of his own
oar, to keep the little craft from canting. Within
ten seconds the swirl of a breaking sea swept the
boat with a crash alongside the smack, and before
she could recoil from the blow the painter had been

thrown and caught, and in another moment the
three dripping and exhausted smacksmen were safe
upon our deck.

"Praise the Lord for His great mercy," fervently
ejaculated the skipper, immediately adding, "You'll
never catch me sending a boat away in such weather
again;" and to both the praise and the promise we
all responded "Amen!"

Now came the question of getting the boat on
board. It was already half full of water, and would
undoubtedly swamp if left afloat much longer, or
else be staved in against the side of the vessel.
The stern-rope was made fast, the burton hooked to a
strap in the boat's head, the tackle hooked to a ring
in the stern, the painter pulled tight aft and attached
to the capstan, and the other part of the stern-
rope made fast to the mizen-rigging. The whole
crew then hoisted away on the burton, gathering in
the slack of the stern-tackle to prevent the boat
swamping, until the forepart of the keel rested on
the vessel's rail, then one haul on the stern-tackle,
and the boat was on board. During this somewhat
ticklish operation the smack had been lying-to with
the foresail a'weather; but now the skipper cries
"Let go!" The taut and trim little dandy immediately pays off, and rapidly gathering way, heels
over to the breeze and races after the admiral, whose
vessel is already hull down on the western horizon.

The cabin-clock is heard striking twelve, and as the sky is evidently clearing and the wind and sea perceptibly falling, we all, with the exception of the fifth and sixth hands, go below, whence the odour of fried-fish has been for some minutes warning us that breakfast is ready. Now indeed these men verified the mate's assertion. Seven hours of continuous labour had given them prodigious appetites, and the fish and sea-biscuits vanished with amazing rapidity, being washed down by heavy draughts of tea.

During breakfast the fifth and sixth hands remained on deck, but the moment the others had finished their meal, the men above were relieved by the fourth hand, whose business it was to keep the watch until 5 P.M. The ever-active skipper kept an eye on the man at the tiller, but the mate and remaining hands, with the exception of the cook, kicked off their sea-boots, divested themselves of their " oily frocks," turned into the bunks, lighted their pipes, closed the sliding door until not a breath of air could penetrate, and then speedily relapsed into a sound slumber, the result of the combined effects of seven hours' herculean labour and a heavy meal.

Having watched this operation, and wondered whether they would all be asphyxiated, and how soon death would ensue, I came to the conclusion that even the atmosphere of the cabin itself was too heavy and polluted for my lungs. So taking a book, I went on deck, and finding the weather had moderated, wrapped my rug around me and ensconced myself under the weather quarter, as near as possible to the fourth hand, who was in charge of the tiller. Not many minutes had elapsed before the cook (the smallest hand in the ship), emerged from the companion and approached me, holding, with a very mysterious air, a small net to which a stout line was made fast.

"What have you in that net?" I inquired.

"It's the salt beef for to-morrow's dinner, sir, and I'm going to lash it to this cleat, so as it may tow under the wessel's stern to take the salt out."

"But if that is for to-morrow's dinner, where is the beef for this evening?"

"Why, here it is," said he, hauling on board another small net similar to the one he had just cast over the stern—"it has been astern of her since this time yesterday."

"You see, sir," chimed in the fourth hand, "that 'ere beef gets uncommon salt when it's bin in the harness cask for six weeks, and we're obliged to get some of the brine out of it, or we couldn't tackle it nohow."

"And so you find that the best way to extract the salt from the beef is by towing it in the salt sea?"

"You're right, sir; that's how we're forced to do it."

This was all new to me, and my curiosity being excited, I followed into the cabin to see the end of this novel style of cooking.

A huge pot was boiling furiously on the fire, and what with the smell of fried fish still remaining from breakfast, the stale fumes of tobacco, and the heat from the nearly red-hot stove, the atmosphere of the cabin was quite unbearable. The cook promptly removed the lid from the great saucepan, and popped in his net of salt beef. It struck me that the water looked very peculiar, so I asked —"Is that *fresh* water, cook?"

"No sir, it's *sea* water. We can't afford to use fresh water; we only carry enough for drinking."

"And what have you got there?" I inquired, seeing him produce a large tin dish and a bundle from a dark recess.

"This is the taturs, sir, and that's the pudden;" and without more ado he bundled the potatoes and pudding into the same saucepan of sea-water in which the beef was already cooking.

When, at five o'clock, dinner was announced, the potatoes proved to be very good indeed, the pudding rather heavy (though many times since I have found the North-Sea puddings of most excellent quality), and the meat terribly tough and very salt, in spite

of its twenty-four hours' soaking, while externally
it had the appearance of a wedding-cake, being
incrusted with dry white salt within a few moments
of its removal from the boiling sea-water.   All
hands turned out from the " bed places," and apparently the long sleep had induced a return of the
morning's appetite, for the meat and potatoes soon
disappeared before the vigorous onslaught; then
followed the suet pudding, with just a suspicion of
treacle, and finally the inevitable " drop o' tea."

During dinner the fifth and sixth hands were
again in charge of the deck, and the meal was
barely finished when the cry " Admiral's signallin',
Skipper," brought us to our feet, and a moment
later every one was on deck.

The admiral's flag had been hauled down as a
signal to " put to " on the port tack, and for the
next half hour all hands throughout the great fleet
were busy preparing to shoot the gear.   The fore
trawl-head was partially hoisted out by the aid of
the boat-tackle, when a sharp cry of pain startled
us, followed by the exclamation, " O Skipper, heave
the beam off, my fingers is jammed."   Poor man!
It was the third hand, who, not being quite smart
enough in his movements, had allowed his fingers
to be entrapped and crushed by the great oak beam,
as the smack took a heavy roll to port, causing the
beam to lurch back against the rail.   It was the

work of a moment to lift the trawl sufficiently to enable the sufferer to withdraw the injured hand, but what was to be done with him? The fingers were horribly crushed and bleeding, but the nearest surgery was about 305 miles from the spot where we were cruising, so, as in hundreds of previous instances, the injured man was the next morning ferried away to the steamboat, for conveyance to Hospital, while by the same steamer the skipper wrote a note to his owner asking for a fresh man to be sent out to him immediately, to fill the vacancy thus occasioned.

When all was ready I was surprised and delighted to see the skipper reverently raise his cap and briefly invoke " the blessing of the Lord " upon the night's labour.

Then, at the command " Let go!" the ponderous trawl splashed into the sea and quickly disappeared, the warp rushing rapidly through the gangway until fully sixty fathoms had been paid out, when the sudden slackening announced that the gear was on the bottom.

The trawl rope-stopper was then made fast, the foresail let go, the tiller lashed amidships, and under ordinary circumstances the third and sixth hands would have taken the first watch.

Of course after the accident just related this was quite out of the question, and as I was not particularly tired, and the skipper seemed good for a yarn or two, we decided that he and I would remain on deck until midnight. Before the rest of the crew went below we read a chapter by the light of the binnacle-lamp, sang the hymn commencing

"Abide with me, fast falls the eventide,"

and after brief prayer all dispersed to snatch a few hours of slumber before the admiral's signal woke us to the cares of the morrow.

"You see, sir," began the skipper when we were left together, "if you had come out in the winter instead of the autumn, you'd have found us making two hauls, one at about eleven o'clock at night, and the other at daylight."

"That midnight haul must be very trying for you."

"Well, you see, sir, the most part of our life is what you may call 'trying,' whether it's day ferrying or night hauling, and a little more or less 'trial' don't make overmuch difference; but there's no mistakin' it's hard enough to turn out on a winter's night, when there's not only a rough sea, but a bitterly keen piercing north-east breeze, with a spice of snow. Do you suppose, sir, that the folks ashore thinks much about us when we're in that plight?"

"I'm afraid not very many 'folks ashore' know

I

anything of the trials and privations of a smacksman's life at present; but I hope, before long, the condition of things out here may be as fully known throughout England as it is to yourselves, and when that day comes, we may expect to find thousands of Christian people, not content with knowing about your troubles and dangers, but striving their utmost to alleviate your sufferings, and to throw a few rays of sunshine into the dull monotony of your existence."

"Ay, it'll be a blessed day when that comes about, for sure," quoth the skipper.

And then he explained to me about the midnight haul in winter time, when the running gear was often stiff as bars of iron, and the fish themselves frozen hard like so many blocks of wood within a few moments of coming out of the net.

"If the admiral hauls at eleven o'clock, we reckon to get supper (tea, biscuit and butter) by twelve. But, bless you, if it's a bit extra rough, it's as often as not four o'clock in the mornin' afore we've time to go below."

"Don't we feel tired, did you say, sir? I should just think we do. Why, I've been out on a winter voyage, and not had a settled bit o' sleep for the whole eight weeks, on account of the toilsome baffling weather; but then it's no use complainin', the work's got to be done, and if we don't look well after the vessel, we may all lose our lives, so we just go on day and night, and uncommon thankful we are if we manage to get home to port again safe and sound."

" Do you often come fast to sunken wrecks ? "

" Yes, sir, more especially in the winter.   I remember one time when we found ourselves fast about three o'clock in the mornin'.   It was coming on to blow hard, and there were we hard and fast to that wreck till five o'clock the next evening, and no time to go below for a meal for the whole fourteen hours.   If ever I felt right done up it was that day.

" I recollect another time the cod-end had just come aboard when first one of the men and then another gave a yell and bolted down below.   It was an uncommonly dark night, and I couldn't see what there was to frighten the crew, but it was no good a-stoppin' on deck all alone, so I followed 'em into the cabin and asked what all the row was about. ' O Skipper,' sings out one of 'em, ' there's the devil in the trawl.'   ' Nonsense,' says I.   But what could I do by myself ? so I just stopped below with 'em.   Never a wink of sleep did any of us get, and at the first streak o' dawn I crept up the companion, and there, instead of the devil, there was a great bullock in the net, with his tremendous horns pokin' out about a yard on each side !

"But, sir, we've had lots worse than a bullock in the net; an' when we brings up the bodies of our brother fishermen who've fell overboard from other smacks, why it's enough to turn us all agin the trawling. But—there, there, I'd better not go on upon this tack or you'll be dreaming about it."

At midnight the mate and the fifth hand came on deck for the remainder of the night, and we had just settled fairly off to sleep, when the cry of *"Where are you coming to?"* uttered just above our heads, rang out in the stillness, and caused all to rush on deck. I was nearest the companion, and therefore the first to reach the deck, when, to my horror, I saw a large screw steamer just tearing by within a few yards of us. In another moment she had disappeared in the inky blackness of the night, and we were left—safe, but with nerves somewhat shaken by the close proximity of a disaster which, in all probability, would have cost the lives of all on board.

One crash, one wild cry of horror, and the great steamer would have passed on her course, crushing beneath her keel the fragments of the little smack, while the insatiable sea would have swallowed eight more victims.

But no, we were spared, and with one consent all joined in singing, as we stood bareheaded on the deck—

" Praise God, from whom all blessings flow ;
Praise Him, all creatures here below ;
Praise Him above, ye heavenly host ;
Praise Father, Son, and Holy Ghost."

And then, commending ourselves afresh to our
heavenly Father's care, we finally went to rest, and
slept undisturbed until roused to commence the
duties of another day of toil.

CHAPTER X.

SELF-HELP.

" This genial intercourse and mutual aid
　Cheers what were else an universal shade,
　Calls Nature from her ivy-mantled den,
　And softens human rock-work into men."

ON several occasions I have found it necessary to
protest against the thoughtlessness of well-meaning
people, who, partially informed upon the question,
have indulged in wholesale condemnation of smacksmen as a class, simply because of the sins and im-
proprieties of individuals.

For example, in 188–, a Hull skipper named
. . . But no; it can serve no useful purpose to
repeat his name ; he is gone, poor man, and we, who
are sinners ourselves, cannot do better than quote
with regard to him Hood's touching lines, and content ourselves with—

" Owning his weakness,
　His evil behaviour,
　And leaving with meekness
　His sins to his Saviour."

This skipper was convicted of the murder of his cook, a lad fourteen years of age. The poor child had been subjected to a course of gross and utterly unpardonable ill-usage by both master and mate, and the wretched skipper met his fate on the gallows, while the mate—whom many smacksmen to this day consider to have been the real murderer—suffered some months' imprisonment, and on the expiration of the term was obliged to fly the country.

How people have plagued me about that case, both in conversation and correspondence. Over and over again it has been cited against me, at the close of a lecture or drawing-room meeting, in order to prove the incorrigible depravity and iniquity of the whole race of deep-sea fishermen. People seemed to regard that unhappy murderer as a fair sample of the population inhabiting the trawling fleets.

One answer readily suggests itself, and this I have invariably given. " Assuming that your estimate of these men were true, surely, on your own showing, there is still greater need than I had represented to you for liberal support of this institution, whose mission on the high seas is to reform, to elevate, in the truest sense to *convert*, the smacksmen."

I was not merely amused, but struck by the point and force of the *double entendre*, when a friend one day drew my attention to the following paragraph in *Punch* :—

" *Mission to Deep-Sea Fishermen.* — This sounds practical. Of course, the *deeper* the sea-fishermen, the greater the need of the mission ! "

To assert, however, that fishermen as a class are bad, is simply a monstrous calumny. It is quite as ridiculous to saddle the responsibility of the wicked act just referred to upon all the men of the Hull fleets, as it would be palpably insane to blame the inhabitants of the village of Rugeley for the evil deeds of the poisoner Palmer, or the whole Irish people for the assassination of Lord Frederick Cavendish.

The Hull fishermen can afford not only to repudiate with indignation the charges thus recklessly levelled against them, but are able, on the other hand, to point with justifiable pride to works of mercy and charity, the result of local effort, and if not actually created, at all events fostered by the smacksmen themselves.

The fishing industry has for several years been in a deplorable condition, affording no chance whatever for even the most diligent to prosper. But six years ago, before the period of depression set in, I knew several well-to-do owners, who, having begun life as smack-apprentices, had, by steadiness and sobriety, addēd in some cases to high Christian

principle, successfully worked their way upward,
until they occupied positions of influence in the
towns of Hull, Grimsby, Great Yarmouth, and
Lowestoft, and had earned the universal respect
and regard of their fellow-townsmen.

Here then was an additional reason for a Mission
to the Deep-Sea Fishermen. Apart entirely from
the spiritual question, it appeared to me that if
some here and there had risen from the ranks by
sheer perseverance and pluck, without adventitious
help, surely there must be many more who, by
assistance from without, wisely and kindly directed,
might presently come to the front, and distinguish
themselves in their own walk of life, if indeed they
did not—

> " . . . Rise on stepping-stones
> Of their dead selves to higher things."

The witty reference to the Mission already quoted
is suggestive of several standpoints from which to
view the smacksmen; but look as closely as one
may, and from whatever side, the fact remains that,
on every ground, spiritual or philanthropic, human
or divine, they are a class who deserve, and who
should receive, our ungrudging and most liberal aid.

Too long have we held aloof—through ignorance,
I admit—from our brethren who are thus risking
their lives at sea; and now that we are ignorant
no longer, but fully informed both as to their needs

and the proper means of supplying them, it behoves
us to—

> " Chase back the shadows, grey and old,
>   Of the dead ages from their way,
> And let their hopeful eyes behold
>   The dawn of a millennial day."

How often have I felt shamed when observing
the unstinting generosity evinced by smacksmen
towards a brother-fisherman in distress ! If John
or Bill or Charlie be out of work, or " on a lee
shore," there is no hesitation—unless the man in
question be an incorrigible loafer—in extending
help to him in his poverty ; but the occasion of
all others for the display of genuine charity—I
use the word in its highest sense—is when death
has brought sadness and bereavement to the fisher's
home. It has been my privilege to gain many a
glimpse behind the scenes in times of sorrow, and I
have personally witnessed acts of self-denial which
would put to the blush the benevolence of higher
social grades. In the one case, it is giving, out of
their abundance, some portion which can be spared
and will not be missed ; in the other, it is the
practical exemplification of the lines—

> " Is thy cruse of comfort wasting ? Rise and share it with
>   another,
> And through all the years of famine it shall serve thee and
>   thy brother ;
> Love Divine will fill thy storehouse or thy handful still renew ;
> Scanty fare for one will often make a royal feast for two."

Yes, I trust I have learned some lessons of highest value from my fisher-friends.

We find in Psalm cxxx. the expression, " Out of the depths have I cried unto Thee, O Lord." What first struck me in the trawling fleets was the absence of spiritual help or sustenance for the few who professed the Name of Christ. Of them it could truly be said that *" out of the depths"* of sorrow and despair they had cried to the Lord for succour. The Mission brought it to them in the shape of a floating House of God, where they might gather for worship without fear of molestation, and where they might pour out their supplications at the Throne of heavenly grace on behalf of their unsaved brother-fishermen. There were many, alas! who were in the depths of degradation and sin, their necks under the heel of the enemy, and to them the Mission brought a gospel of emancipation from guilt and from judgment, so that they might be raised *" out of the depths,"* and brought into the conscious enjoyment of Divine favour and blessing.

The third verse of the psalm says, " If Thou, Lord, shouldst mark iniquities, O Lord, who shall stand ?" And truly it has been hard for me at times to listen to the severe strictures passed upon the smacksmen by folks on shore, who, while professing to be Christians, appeared to forget the cardinal lesson their Master taught when He said, " Let

him that is without sin among you cast the first
stone." Granted that smacksmen, many, even the
majority of them, were openly profane, and absolutely careless as to the claims of their Redeemer,
who are we that we should lift so much as a little
finger against them ?

> " A Briton knows, or, if he knows it not—
> The Scripture placed within his reach—he *ought*,
> That souls have no discriminating hue,
> Alike important in their Maker's view ;
> That none are free from blemish since the Fall,
> And Love Divine has paid one price for all."

We have been cradled and educated in Christian
truth and principle. They were hurried away to
the wild sea-life at an early age, when we were
but a little in advance of the nursery. We have
enjoyed *ad libitum* the privileges of mental, moral,
physical, and spiritual culture. They, poor fellows,
with absolutely none of our advantages, have, on
the other hand, been exposed to peril, privation,
and suffering, of which landsmen can form but the
dimmest idea.

Thus, away there on the ocean, these sons of toil
have developed certain valuable traits of character
which many a professing Christian appears to lack
entirely; and the more I have mixed with the
smacksmen, the more have I been struck with the
unselfishness, the manly bearing, the outspoken

frankness, the resolute bull-dog tenacity of purpose, the unflinching courage and coolness in the face of danger, which mark them as immeasurably superior to . . . well, to be plain, to many of their traducers.

Lord Northbrook, some years ago, when First Lord of the Admiralty, assured me that the North-Sea trawling fleets are regarded as the chief recruiting ground of the Royal Navy; and at the present moment 4000 smacksmen are enrolled in the Naval Reserve, and are called out for four weeks' annual training.

Can we be surprised that these men, sundered from all home care or affection, have displayed "the vices of their virtues," and become, hundreds of them, enslaved by the tempter in the person of the foreign *coper?* Their very susceptibility to kindly influences, and their disposition to manifest kindness to others —to accept the advances of so-called good fellowship, and to prove themselves good fellows in return —have contributed to make them an easy prey to the destroyer.

What a grand opportunity for the servants of Christ! Let but the Saviour be presented in His own true attractiveness to the hearts of these fishermen, and at once, like their Galilean prototypes, they will "follow Him," and become themselves the most energetic, the most earnest, and the most successful of missionaries.

I love to note the points of resemblance between
the brave fellows who man the trawling fleets and
that fisher of long ago, who by the Lake of Genne-
saret heard the voice of the Son of God, saw His
miracle, and then cried, " Depart from me, for I am
a sinful man, O Lord."

I love to remember that, in the same reassuring
tones of infinite grace and divine tenderness, the
Saviour says to-day, as to Peter of old, " Fear not !
from henceforth thou shalt catch men."

I love, too, to watch the effect upon my friends
of the Dogger Bank of this summons from the
Master.   The title of this chapter is " Self-Help,"
and most certainly in spiritual matters the smacksmen resolutely and diligently set to work to help
themselves.   What specially charmed me in 1881
was the intense reality and fervour of those who
knew and loved the Lord Jesus.   They were but a
handful amongst the mass, but they were on the
winning side, and they knew it, and spoke and
acted accordingly as men deeply imbued with a
sense of responsibility to bring every one of their
brother-fishermen to the same Saviour whom they
had learned to love, and whose love to them, shed
abroad in their hearts, was the animating, energising
power of their lives.   None could come in contact
with such men without feeling impressed by their
consistent piety.   The point and full meaning of

that passage of Holy Scripture—" The love of Christ constraineth us"—was more clearly understood after watching the evangelistic efforts of these simple souls, irresistibly reminding one of the fact that two fishermen were the first persons whom our Saviour called to follow Him (St. John i. 39). One of them, Andrew, immediately set forth upon a mission, and finding his own brother Simon, also a fisherman, he " brought him to Jesus."

I can never forget the effect produced upon a group of these Christian smacksmen by a short address upon the fifth and sixth verses of the psalm already quoted, the exposition of course having particular application to their own circumstances of trial, and isolation from the " means of grace." The verse, " *My soul waiteth for the Lord more than they that watch for the morning*," had special force and meaning for men accustomed to spend long hours upon deck in the biting cold and inky darkness, or sometimes the blinding snow, of a winter's night in the North Sea. And now they were reminded from God's Holy Word that for those who waited thus there should surely be " redemption " and " mercy ; " that for the upright " ariseth light in the darkness."

Thank God, since then the promise has been fulfilled, " Unto you that fear my name shall the Sun of righteousness arise with healing in his wings."

Whatever developments of the Mission to Deep-Sea Fishermen the future may have in store, I, at all events, shall always take pleasure in reverting to the time when there were but few in each fleet —in some fleets not more than two or three—who " feared the Lord, and that thought upon his name." And although the helpers on shore may now be reckoned by thousands, and in scores of households the smacksmen are remembered daily at family prayers, my mind dwells with delight upon the memory of those good and true and stalwart Christians, standing firm in their own profession and offering prayer without ceasing for an outpouring of Divine blessing upon the men around them.

Of necessity it has followed that " the Lord hearkened and heard, and a book of remembrance was written before him." And for them He has indeed redeemed His pledge :—" Prove me now herewith, saith the Lord of hosts, if I will not open you the windows of heaven, and pour you out a blessing, that there shall not be room enough to receive it."

CHAPTER XI.

NORTH-SEA HEROES.

" Prayers of love like raindrops fall,
Tears of pity are cooling dew,
And dear to the heart of our Lord are all
Who suffer, like Him, in the good they do ! "

THE spring of 1883 was marked by a fearful storm,
resulting in great damage to property and the loss
of over 360 smacksmen and boys. This is still
mentioned, and for years to come will probably continue to be known, as "the great March gale."
Never can I forget the visits I paid to Hull, Grimsby,
and Great Yarmouth at that time. In the streets,
the churches, in public halls—everywhere the pre-
vailing colour was black. Widow's weeds, children's
mourning—black, black, wherever one turned. The
chief, or rather the *one* topic of conversation, was the
awful visitation to which the community had been
subjected. In private houses, in trams and omni-
buses—always the gale, the gale.

It was distressing beyond description to converse
with the women, who in some cases had lost a

K

husband and several sons. One poor widow told me her husband was taken from her in a similar gale several years before, and now her only son had followed his father, and she was left absolutely penniless. "And oh, sir," she cried, "he might have been saved if he had only listened to his mother."

" How so ? " I inquired.

" Why, sir, when my boy was at home last, I told him of the storm-warnings they had sent over from America, and begged him to stay ashore for a week or so. He promised he would, but I suppose his love of the sea, and his fear of being laughed at, overcame his resolution. At any rate, he went to sea, and the vessel was lost with all hands."

This is a fair sample of scores of sad, heart-breaking stories which were brought before me, and the memory of that great sorrow can never be effaced from my mind. May God defend the families of the smacksmen from the recurrence of such an overwhelming disaster !

That March gale furnished, however, as indeed nearly every North-Sea storm does, occasion for the display of those qualities of cool daring and generous disregard of personal safety which have ever characterised the smacksmen when an opportunity has occurred for rescuing others from imminent danger.

It has been my wish in these pages not merely

to narrate the history of the M.D.S.F. *per se*, but to present to the reader a fair, and I trust impartial, portrait of the class on whose behalf the Mission was founded—a class which has been sorely maligned and misunderstood.

It is, therefore, in partial fulfilment of this purpose that I furnish the following facts, illustrative of the undaunted courage of the North-Sea smacksmen. It must be understood that the cases cited are merely culled here and there from a vast number within my ken, the mere enumeration of which would fill this volume.

To begin. The smack *Cavalier*, a thoroughly first-class vessel, left Hull in February 1883 for an eight weeks' voyage. All went well until the 2nd March, when the wind freshened and rapidly increased to a heavy gale. At 7.30 A.M. on the 3rd, when the *Cavalier* was riding to the gale with every possible stitch of canvas stowed, a heavy sea struck her, tearing out both the main and mizen masts, and leaving merely a bare and shattered hull. For upwards of thirty hours the vessel lay on her side amongst the seething seas, and during the whole of that time the mate stood in the cabin up to his elbows in water, which constantly washed over his head. The cook, meanwhile, was on the ladder, taking from the mate the full buckets and emptying them through the open companion. ·The skipper and the third and fourth hands were hard at work on deck, endeavouring to get the anchor overboard. This was safely accomplished by 3 P.M., and during all that time the seas had been breaking on board with such force that three of the deck-beams were smashed, and but for the fact that empty fish-boxes were tightly stowed from floor to ceiling in the hold, it would have been quite impossible to keep the hull afloat. After the anchor was let go, the vessel rode more steadily, and all five of the crew devoted themselves to the work of baling out the cabin. By 7 P.M. the weather-side of the floor was visible, and after much difficulty (for there were only two dry matches on board, and one missed fire), they managed to light the stove. They then endeavoured to heat an iron bolt, in order to pass it through a handspike to serve as a pump brake, for it was most important to pump out the vessel; but another huge sea broke on board, filling the cabin and extinguishing the fire, and with it the hopes of the crew. All through that terrible night the gale raged, and the five poor fellows in the water-logged smack, while constantly baling out the sea, prayed for daylight and for succour, though not knowing whence help could come.

At 9 A.M. on the 4th a steamer was sighted, and during the morning several more passed close to them, but did not dare to offer assistance. About noon the Grimsby smack *Blanche* was seen bearing down upon them, and then indeed they were filled with hope, for their brother-fishermen would not dream of deserting them. Spite of the tremendous sea still running, the skipper of the *Blanche* threw out his boat, and in a few moments the rescued men, who during all that fearful time had tasted neither food nor drink, were safely ensconced on the lockers around the cabin-fire, and eventually were landed at Grimsby.

. . . . . .

At daybreak on a winter's morning about ten years ago, when a tremendous gale was blowing on the Dogger Bank, a heavy sea struck the smack *Bessie* and bore her down on her beam-ends. Six of the crew were on deck at the time, but the seventh, who was in the hold, was killed beneath the tons of ballast which burst up the ballast-deck and fell to leeward, burying the poor fellow alive, his feet only being visible.

Skipper Steele, master of the *Fawn*, seeing what had occurred, instantly bore down towards the wreck, and descried the six survivors clinging to the weather-bulwarks, the smack meanwhile rapidly settling down. The gale was far too heavy to allow of a boat being launched, unless for life-saving purposes; but as the mate and third hand volunteered to run the risk, the boat was thrown out, and these brave men made their way to the *Bessie*, and succeeded in rescuing the six unfortunates, now so completely exhausted as to be quite unable to lend a hand in pulling back to the *Fawn*. After several hair-breadth escapes of being capsized or swamped by the mountainous seas, rescuers and rescued returned to the vessel in safety. This was an exceptionally dangerous service, and through the influence of Mr. Hallett (chairman of Hewett & Co., Limited), the two men, whose names were Mann and Love, were each awarded the Royal Humane Society's medal, the presentation being made by the Mayor of Great Yarmouth.

Towards evening on the 3rd December 1863, during a heavy gale, the smack *Fox* of Great Yarmouth fell in with the Swedish brig *Speculant*, dismasted, her boat stove in, and in a very critical position. The *Fox* was close-reefed at the time, and naturally anxious to get more sea-room, as the wind from W.N.W. was blowing them on a dead lee shore. Notwithstanding this, the skipper without hesitation got a line on board the brig and made fast a tow-rope.

After towing for two hours the warp parted. It was now pitch dark, the weather still very boisterous, and the Texel light in sight. The *Fox* sailed round the brig and endeavoured to heave another line

HOISTING THE BOAT.

aboard, but the Swedes failed to secure it, and hailed " for God's sake come and take us off."

Spite of the heavy sea running, the smack threw out her boat, and the third, fourth, and fifth hands pulled to the stranger. The crew of six immediately jumped into the boat, and as the Swedish captain refused to leave the brig, the *Fox's* third hand bundled him in after his men. It was with the utmost difficulty, and not a moment too soon, that the deeply laden boat returned to the *Fox*, whose skipper had all his work cut out for him in thrashing out to sea in the teeth of the gale, and it was not until the 7th December that he was able to land the shipwrecked crew at Yarmouth. No notice was taken of this brave action by the English authorities; but six months later the Swedish Government sent £40 to the owner and crew of the *Fox*.

I have invariably noticed that the smacksmen appear to attach little or no importance to these acts of conspicuous courage. A man sees others in distress, he knows there is a chance of his saving them, and without a moment's hesitation he plunges into the work of rescue, apparently oblivious to all sense of personal danger, and when, ultimately, he returns victorious, he quietly goes about the routine work of the vessel as though nothing unusual had occurred. For example, when, a few years ago, Messrs. Hewett & Co's. smack *Retriever*, and the smack *Confidence*, belonging to Mr. Roberts, of Grimsby, saved a ship's crew of seventeen hands during a heavy gale, the shipwrecked men being conveyed to Grimsby on board the *Confidence*, Skipper Norgate and the crew of the *Retriever* only casually mentioned the circumstance when they came ashore, and did not appear to think they had done anything extraordinary, although the deed was a very brave one, and attended with unusual peril.

Quite recently a boat from the *Vulcan* (Skipper Polequeska) saved the crew of the ship *Gylding* of Fano during a gale, the *Gylding* foundering shortly afterwards. The crew of the *Vulcan* were merely thanked for this service.

While engaged in writing this chapter, news reaches me from Mr. Harvey-George of Gorleston of the rescue by the steam-trawler *Lord Alfred Paget* of the crew of a Norwegian ship numbering eleven hands, this ship also foundering immediately after the removal of the crew. Again only thanks !

Much as we may rejoice in these evidences of true courage, unprompted by the prospect of fee or reward beyond the gratitude of the saved and the consciousness of duty bravely done, there can scarcely be two opinions as to the great utility and advisability of securing to these brave men some distinct and practical expression of public approval of the services so nobly rendered. With regard to this I quote, and most heartily endorse, Mr. Harvey-George's remark: " I think that in cases such as the *Lord Alfred Paget* and the *Vulcan*, the men ought to have some tangible acknowledgment, as it would be satisfactory to them and would encourage others to act in the same way." It is pleasant to hear from the same source, " Our men in the fleet are continually doing grand acts of bravery in rescuing comrades, but they seldom report the cases to me. They look upon it as a part of their ordinary duty ; they are, as a rule, most brave and fearless, and ever ready to risk their lives in saving others."

What Mr. Harvey-George states with regard to the "Short Blue" fleet is equally true of all the rest, and fully accords with the testimony of other owners, and with the inferences I have myself drawn from personal observation.

The following is extracted from a communication I have received from Mr. W. H. Ashford, the able manager of the Port of Hull Trawl Fishermen's Protective Society :—

" Men of Grimsby and Hull being in close proximity, we are able to gather from time to time accounts of the splendid services that have been rendered, and only this winter out of the port of Hull, and out of the port of Grimsby, there have been cases which have won the highest praise from those to whose knowledge the services have been brought. It was my privilege some time ago to bring before the general public at

Hull, through the press, a case which in my opinion has no equal in my time. The smack *Primrose* had left our port, and had worked a distance out to sea of between 200 and 300 miles, when they fell in with a Danish steamer in a disabled condition, and the captain and crew were calling to be taken off. Now, it generally happens—although I mention this, I am bound to say it—it generally happens that our men save the lives of foreign seamen when they have boats in a good condition of their own, but from some cause or another fail to make use of them. In this case in particular the crew of the smack *Primrose*, in a cross-running sea, in a small open boat, made three trips to the steamer, but in the third trip that she made to bring off the captain and engineers, the boat was lost sight of. That boat contained Harry Jones and the mate, and these two men were never seen any more. For forty-eight consecutive hours did that smack cruise about to try and find its boat (two long winter nights and days), but at last they had to give it up, and to return without two of its crew who had rendered such splendid service in that biting wind, cold enough to chill their blood, and now they leave wives and families to bear their loss. They, however, saved the lives of fourteen men, and only a fortnight ago, in the Danish Church at Hull, the pastor presented a cheque from the Danish Government for £100 to the captain, and to the widow a like amount, with a silver medal, which will be a lasting memorial of her husband's services. All these services as a rule are done without hope of fee or reward. There are many who can tell you that in all these cases owners are put to expense by the loss of the voyage, the provisions eaten up, and a new voyage has to be made ; and the British public know nothing of these services. I may take this opportunity of saying that in my opinion when such splendid services are rendered, there should be some international arrangement, in order that those men may not suffer pecuniary loss in rendering services in saving life at sea."

"I think it was nigh about the year 1860," said Skipper C——, "I was a hand aboard the

Alpha, one of the old Barking fleet. It was winter-time, an' a big gale sprung up an' blowed hard from the nor'ard and east'ard for several days. We was bound home to Barking when the gale started to blow, an' when our skipper seed as it were a comin' on worse, it didn't take him long to make up his mind as he'd run into Yarmouth Roads for shelter. Well, we shaped our course accordin', an' when we got pretty nigh abreast o' Cromer, about eleven o'clock in the morning, we caught sight of a foreign wessel alongside Haisborough Sands, an' bumpin' like a good 'un in the big seas. In corse we bore down, an' sure enough there was a big Spanish schooner with a flag o' distress a flyin'. Her rudder was knocked clean away, an' it was evident as she'd soon be a wreck if she stopped like that 'ere.

" ' Now my lads,' says our skipper, ' I'm thinkin' them furriners have throwed up the sponge afore they've any call to, an' I guess we'll save ship an' all, if so be we're smart about it.'

" ' Right you are, skipper,' says we ; an' with that he runs our smack right down as close as he could under the lee of the stranger.

" Then came the order 'Out boat!' and the skipper an' three of us chaps jumped into her, an' was a-standin' on the Spaniard's deck afore you could count twenty. We pretty soon diskivered how things was. There was the Spanish captain a-lyin' dead-drunk on the cabin floor; the mate was near as bad; an' as for the crew, why they was well nigh played out, what with the cold an' wet an' the hard work, not to say fear; for there they was down in the fo'c'sle with everything a-washin' about, and all of 'em in a mortal funk, an' was kissin' of crucifixes an' prayin' instid o' tryin' to get theirselves out o' the fix.

"The wessel had got a load o' toller from Roosha, an' was bound for London, with a crew of twelve hands all told.

"It seems, as we found out arterwards, as when the gale caught 'em the captain was already pretty well half-seas over with drink, an' too muddled to understand what he was about; so it weren't to be wondered at as he let the wessel run away with him, an' then when he found 'isself abumpin' on Haasboro' Sands, he jist lets go both anchors, an' that was how they was when we boarded 'em, a-ridin' close to the sands, with rudder clean gone, an' the mainmast sprung full five inches. Well, you may be sure, sir, as we hadn't gone aboard the wessel to stand alookin' at them fellers a-tellin' their beads, so our skipper picked up the sounder, as was lyin' alongside the pump, an' sounded the well. He found as the schooner had five foot o' water in her; so says he, 'Now, boys, these furrin chaps don't seem able to do nothin', so we'll just let 'em see as *we* ain't made o' the same sort o' stuff in these parts. Now, Bill (that was me, yer see, sir), you an' Isaac 'll have to stay aboard o' the schooner an' pump her. I'll take Dan in the boat, an' see if we can't get a warp made fast from the smack an' tow the old bunch o' boards off this 'ere sand, an' I make no doubt we'll manage it as the tide begins to turn.'

"All this while, yer see, sir, it was blowin' 'ard, an' the waves makin' clean breaches right over the schooner's decks; so me an' Isaac lashed ourselves to the pumps an' set to work. The pumps was in fust-rate trim, an' the water come out of her fine; but, would you believe it, we hadn't fetched more 'n half-a-dozen strokes when the whole garlicky set o' lubbers up an' tried to stop us. 'Well, that's a good 'un,' says I; 'here are we a-riskin' our own skins to save these fellers, an' they're all agin their own salvation!' However, Isaac an' me wasn't goin' to stand that sort o' nonsense—'twasn't likely; so we just beat 'em off with the pump-handles an' set to work agin. When our skipper seed their game, he jist went down in the cabin an' tries to 'spostulate with the Spanish captain. He wasn't so drunk but he could understand summat o' what was said to him, and he could speak a little English. At fust he was all for us leavin' 'em alone. 'Well,' says our skipper, 'if we leaves yer alone, what can yer do for yerselves, you're all dead-beat (dead-drunk he might 'a said!), an' yer rudder's gone, an' if yer stop where yer are, you'll be gone to Davy Jones afore mornin', sure as my name's Bailey.'

"Well, what with feelin' as he couldn't do no good for himself, and what with wantin' to be left alone with his bottle, he says, 'All right,' says he; 'you do what you've a mind.'

"With that the skipper comes on deck again, an' bids us go ahead with the pumpin'. But, d'ye know, it didn't seem as 'ow t'em Spaniards could take no for an answer; for by-and-bye back they comes a second time. O' course we couldn't speak their outlandish langwige, but there's a way o' makin' chaps o' that sort understand yer when ye're right down in earnest, which we was. So arter that they let us alone, an' we very soon began to make a powerful difference in the depth o' that water. Meanwhile our skipper 'ad bin away to the smack, an' run out some eight-inch trawl-warp over each bow, an' then away he comes again in the boat, an' makes the t'other ends fast on the starboard an' port quarters o' the Spaniard. Yer see, sir, his dodge was to clap some canvas on the foremast o' the schooner (the mainmast was too badly sprung to bear the strain), an' then up anchor an' make the schooner tow the smack. That way, you understand, the smack would act as a rudder to the big

vessel; but if we'd ha' put the schooner astern o'
the smack, she'd a run so wild, seein' as she had
no rudder shipped. So when all was made fast,
with jist about sixty yards o' space between the
two, the skipper, Dan, Isaac, an' me made sail on
the schooner, jist double-reefed topsail—for all this
time it was blowin' a gale—then the skipper and
Dan got away back aboard the *Alpha*, an' Isaac an'
me hove one anchor; but one pill o' that physic was
a dose, so we slipped the other cable, an' away we
goes, the smack hanging on astern.o' us under bare
poles, and steerin' us first rate.

"It was mighty slow work, but all the same she
did *move*, an' in an hour we were well clear o' the
sands, an' still able to keep the water under, though
it was uncommon hard labour; and when our skipper
sent the boat along at six o'clock to relieve us, it
was jist about as much as we could do to unlash
ourselves from the pumps, we were so dead-beat.
You mustn't go for to think as we was gettin' back
to the smack for rest—no, nor for food neither.
It was just swappin' the work, an' that was all.
We kep' that up from Tuesday mornin' at eleven
o'clock till Thursday evenin' at five, when a Lowestoft steam-tug come alongside an' towed us into
harbour. We'd bin all them fifty-four hours a-doin'
twenty miles, a strong gale blowin' the whole time,
an' takin turn an' turn about to steer the smack

an' pump the Spaniard. We hadn't one of us had a wink o' sleep, an' as for food, why we jist kep' goin' with munchin' a bit o' biscuit, with a plug o' baccy by way o' relish. We'd seen nothin' o' the Spanish captain nor yet the crew the whole three days, but jist before we got into Lowestoft our skipper goes down an' tells the captain as we were almost into harbour. Soon as we got alongside the quay, down comes the Custom's officers, an' says one of 'em—

" ' Where's the captain ? '

" ' In the cabin,' says we.

"With that they goes below, an' in another minute they comes on deck an' says—

" 'There ain't no captain down there; where is he ? '

" ' I seed him there myself five minutes 'gone,' says our skipper.

"Well, sir, we searched everywhere for that ere Spanish captain, but he was clean gone—bolted, an' none of us ever clapped eyes on him agin. An' no wonder, when you comes to think as he got that fine ship into trouble all through the drink, and but for our seein' his signal he might 'a bin there till now."

"Yours has been a most thrilling story, C——," I said; "but now tell me whether you got much in the way of salvage-money."

" Why, I believe as about £1400 was cleared over that job."

" Indeed! that was a good haul for you fellows, and you well deserved it."

" For us fellows, did you say, sir! Why, what do you suppose my share come to ? "

" I've no idea ; but possibly a hundred pounds."

" Fourteen pounds, sir, was every penny as ever came into my pocket."

The following story was related to me by H. G——, now a skipper, but, at the time of the occurrence referred to, mate of the *Forget-me-not*, a smack forty-three years old.

" It was in the year 1878," said G——, " when, on the 14th October, about two o'clock in the morning, we had our gear down in a dead calm with a heavy swell. Of course there had been a bit of a breeze the night before when we shot our trawl, but the wind had died away altogether and left this nasty swell. You know, sir, there's nothing so trying to a ship's rigging an' running gear as a calm with a heavy swell. I'd sooner, any day, have a strong wind, for then there's a perfectly regular strain on everything ; but when there's a swell and no wind, the booms go flying and banging from side to side, first starboard, then port, to and fro, to and fro, ripping and tearing everything. Well, at two o'clock that morning our main-sheet gave way, and

L

the boom began to play some pretty games. I soon
roused out all hands, and as soon as we'd fixed up
a new one, they went below again and turned in.

"No sooner was everything quiet than I noticed
something peculiar.   It was pitch dark, but I could
discern on the top of every swell, as it rolled along,
a great cloud of white spray rising—I may say without exaggeration, half as high as our masthead.
Not at all liking the look of the weather, I called
the skipper and told him about it.   He at once
roused all hands to heave the gear, but before we
had time to man the capstan, the wind suddenly
burst upon us with great fury.   We were instantly
hove with all our sails aback, and, the gear being
over the side, the trawl-warp began to tear out,
and when we attempted to check it, it snapped at
the gunwale, and there was all our valuable gear
clean gone.   By the wind having so rapidly shifted,
a heavy swell kept rolling up from to leeward, and
every roller came right up over the lee-rail, making
it dangerous for one of us to go to leeward.   However, in obedience to the skipper's orders to close-
reef the vessel, the fourth hand and myself were
getting the reef-earings adrift.   Just then a big
swell came rolling like a great mountain from to
leeward, and as it burst over our rail, it knocked the
fourth hand off his legs, carrying him clean over into
the sea.

"The thought struck me—'He'll be lost if I don't get him;' so grasping the end of the reef-earing with my left hand, I swung myself over into the sea, and made a clutch at him with my right. Happily I succeeded in seizing him, and then exerting my full strength, I drew myself and my charge back again aboard the vessel, where the skipper sent him below for a change and to keep quiet, as he was very much frightened.

"It was a remarkable thing that as the skipper and I were continuing the same work a few moments afterwards, another sea carried me overboard in a similar manner, when the skipper saved me exactly as I had saved the fourth hand. After that we got the vessel reefed snug, and the Blessed Lord took care of us during the remainder of the gale."

Quoth Skipper T——:—

"I've been to sea close upon forty years, and I can remember a' many cases of life-savin' in my time. Some of 'em has been just what yer might call *attempts*, as haven't been successful. Indeed I call to mind several very sad instances where not only the poor crews as were in danger, but them as went to save 'em have all been swallowed up in the cruel sea. But, on the other hand, I've seen, an' I'm glad to say I've had my part in, cases where we managed to do all we wanted to, an' it's been a real comfort to me many a time to know as I've been privileged to rescue a fellow-creature's life from a watery grave.

"The first case I remember was a great many years ago, when I was one of the hands aboard a tiny smack, not much more than half the size of the wessels they builds now-a-days. It was blowin' a reg'lar big thumping winter's gale, with the wind about N.N.E., an' we was close-reefed, as you may suppose. About noon, when we was not very far from the Barnard Sands, what should we see but a ship brought up close to the edge of the sands, in a most dangerous position, and with the sea makin' a clean breach over her. It was very clear as she couldn't bear up very long agin' that sort o' treatment. She appeared to be a fine strong wessel, but nothing as ever come out o' the shipyards could withstand the shock o' them big merciless seas.

"The worst part o' the business were as we couldn't get a' nigh 'em as the tide then was, so we lay-to an' waited our chance. Just afore dark the tide favoured us a bit, so we bore up for the wreck, an' when we'd crept within as near as we dared, we throwed out our boat, an' me an' two others pulled alongside of 'em. It was a perfect wonder as she'd held together so long; and what with the night settled down fast around us, an' the chance o' the wessel breakin' up or sinkin', we made up our minds as we'd take the whole crew o' twelve hands at one trip. It was a great risk, I'll allow, but we cal'c'lated all the chances, an' felt it was the best course; besides, it would a' been a heart o' flint as could a' resisted the cries an' pleadin's o' them poor fellows. For nigh eighteen hours they'd bin in the riggin', for no one could a' stayed on deck without bein' either washed overboard or drowned by the big waves as came tumblin' an' breakin' upon the wessel. Anyhow, right or wrong, wise or foolish, we did it, for, in moments like them, folks don't stop very long a' considerin'. Well, sir, there we was in a small boat fifteen of us, the sea ragin' fearful an' the wind shriekin' an' howlin' so you could scarce hear one another speak if you bawled ever so. It's true we hadn't far to go, an' a good thing too, or we'd never a' done it; for by the time we fetched alongside o' the smack we was just about sinkin'; but, thank God, every one was rescued, an' we'd no sooner got aboard our little wessel than we looks round an' couldn't see the ship. We thought at first as it was the darkness o' the night as prevented our distinguishin' her ;. but no. We cruised around and ran in a bit closer, an' sure enough she'd sunk clean out o' sight within five minits o' the crew leavin' her. I leave you to judge, sir, what feelin's o' thankfulness an' praise to God filled all hearts aboard the little smack that winter's night."

CHAPTER XII.

MORE HEROISM.

" Black clouds are scudding o'er a wintry sky,
  Deep shadows casting on the angry main ;
  And wildly shriek the shrill winds passing by,
  Like living creatures tortured in their pain.

  Helpless they are, yet courage does not fail,
  Calmly they front the elemental strife ;
  Dauntless and bold, they neither blench nor quail,
  And battle bravely with the storm for life."

To say there are heroes and heroes is to utter a
mere platitude ; but, all the same, I will let the
assertion stand without erasure, though leaving my
readers to supply the premises upon which the
conclusion is based.

I am anxious, however, to emphasise a remark
already made, that I have no intention of doing
more in these pages than furnish a cursory glimpse
at the subject which gives its title to both this
and the preceding chapter. Readers of the book
must draw their own deductions from the true
incidents herein related ; I content myself with

citing a few specimen cases out of the scores at my disposal.

To attempt more than this would be to convert the entire volume into a mere catalogue, so numerous are the recorded instances of the display of heroic courage and unselfish devotion by the men whom I count it a real privilege to number amongst my friends.

Skipper H——— G——— once told me the following story :—

"It was in the winter of 1866, just twenty-one years ago, and I was then making my second voyage as an apprentice aboard the smack *Welfare* of Ramsgate.

"We had left harbour on a single boating trip to bring home our own catch of fish, and it was the skipper's intention to run for Lowestoft and take in ice, as there was no depot for it at Ramsgate at that time.

"It was blowing hard, and as we got down as far as the neighbourhood of the Galloper Sands, which are very dangerous for vessels of great draught of water, I overheard the skipper and mate talking of the quantity of wreckage floating past, and by and by I heard, for I was below at the time, that there was a large ship ashore on the sands, and flying a distress signal. You may be sure I was up on deck in a minute after that, just in time to hear the skipper say, 'Well, it may be blowing great guns, but I ain't going to sail past 'em and offer no help, poor fellows, so here goes to find out what we can do for 'em.'

"There didn't seem the faintest chance for a small boat in such a high sea as was then running on the sands; however, it takes something more than a stormy sea to unnerve a British fisherman, so away we ran right down under the ship's stern, and hailed her. She proved to be the *Lucknow*, a first-class iron clipper, homeward bound to London from the East Indies with a cargo of silks and other goods of great value.

"Our skipper shouted to the captain, 'Do you want any assistance?' and the answer came back, 'No, we've a pilot on board.'

"'And a deal of use he's been to you, running you plump on the Galloper,' mutters our skipper.

"However, we couldn't force our help upon the captain if he was satisfied to stop where he was, with the chance of beating higher on the sands with the rising tide, so we hauled off again and lay-to for half an hour in smoother water, under the lea of the shoal. Noticing presently that the big ship was signalling for us we ran back as near her as we dared, and the captain of the Indiaman shouted through a speaking trumpet, 'Come on board!' Our skipper immediately laid the vessel to wind-

ward of the *Lucknow*, and having throwed out the
boat the mate jumped into her as she lay tossing
alongside, and shouting to us to let go the painter,
away he went plunging over the big waves, sometimes visible, at other moments completely hidden
from view between two great rolling seas. There
was no need for the use of oars to pull the boat,
for the high wind and heavy sea drove the little
cockle shell at a furious rate towards the ship, and
we noticed that the mate had the greatest difficulty,
and could only with the utmost caution manage to
steer his small craft by means of one oar over the
stern.

" However, he arrived safe alongside the big vessel,
and, what do you think ? The moment the boat
touched the side of the Indiaman the pilot wanted
to jump down into her, but our mate wouldn't let
him, so he was obliged to climb back on deck.

" When our mate stepped on board, the captain
gave up the entire charge of the ship to him, and
meanwhile we lay by in our little smack until
presently we noticed the sailors aboard the *Lucknow*
swarming up the rigging and loosing the sails, and
some of us wondered what they could be up to,
seeing as the ship was hard and fast on the sands ;
but our skipper says, ' Oh, they're all right ; Jim
knows very well what he's about, and I guess he's
found that the ship isn't much hurt, so there'll be

a chance of lifting her off as the tide rises, and
no fear of her sinking in deep water. You may
be sure he wouldn't risk it if she was a'leaking
badly.'

"While the skipper was speaking, the work
aboard the Indiaman had been going ahead, the
sails were hoisted up and sheeted home, and as
the big ship felt the press o' canvas she heeled
over, and we all thought the masts would be carried
away, and then they'd ha' been in a worse fix
than ever.

"But no, it was only just for one half minute,
and while we stood watching anxiously and wondering what would happen next, she began to lift, and
the next instant she slid off the sand into deep
water, and paying off in answer to her helm she
began to race through the billows like an express
train, and was very soon out of sight. As for us,
it came on to blow harder than ever after we'd
parted company with the ship, and we were three
whole days and nights reaching Lowestoft, with a
dead head wind, and very glad we were to get into
harbour after the buffeting of the gale.

"It turned out that when the *Lucknow* got off
the Galloper Sands she left part of her keel behind
her. It had been just a question whether the masts
or the keel would give way first, and luckily for the
vessel, and I may say luckily for our owner too, it

was the keel and not the masts. When we reached
Yarmouth Roads there was the *Lucknow* brought
up all comfortable, and riding with two anchors out
ahead. A couple of tugs towed her to London, and
we lay a whole month in Lowestoft waiting for the
salvage question to be settled, and I was told the
owner of the *Welfare* was awarded £2000, but
what share the skipper and mate got I never heard,
—the other three of us were all apprentices, so
of course we had no share. To my thinking the
mate deserved the biggest pull, though of course
he wouldn't get it."

Skipper J—— M—— said, "When I was
skipper of the smack *Brunette*, we towed out of
Yarmouth harbour late one afternoon, the weather
being a flat calm at the time, so as soon as we were
clear of the north buoy we let go the anchor.
Before daylight next morning the wind freshened,
and I was on the way early, and run down through
the Cockle Gat, with two reefs in the mainsail, and
six cloth jib set; and after passing the Cockle
lightship, I steered out of the Newarp Gat to sea.

"We hadn't proceeded far on our voyage, when
the mate called my attention to a ship under our
lee, saying, 'Skipper, that ship is ashore.'

"I said, 'impossible,' as I knew by the distance
we had run that we ought to be outside Haisborough Sands; but the mate said again, 'I'm

sure she is ashore,' and so it proved. We steered
for the ship, and found she was on Winterton
Ridge. As we passed her my mate said, 'O
skipper, the crew are all in the rigging.'

" ' Out boat ! ' I cried, and immediately put the
Brunette about, and by the time the smack was gone
about, the boat was in the water. I never saw a
boat launched as quick before. We then naturally
looked for the ship, and I said, ' Why, where is the
ship ? ' but she was nowhere to be seen.

"We bore up before the wind with boat astern,
ready manned, and were very shortly surrounded with
wreckage, and I spied one man on a piece of wreck
and steered straight for him. Poor fellow, he
shouted out, thinking we were going to run him
down ; but no, I was only steering close to him, so
the boat with a sheer could pick him up, and with
a good sheer the boat was cast off, and alongside
of the poor man, and had him in pretty quickly,
but alas ! all the others had perished. After the
poor fellow was recovered and rigged out with
dry clothing, he stated that they had passed the
Leman Light, and was steering southerly, luff a
luff (close hauled to the wind), and the captain
thought he was clear of all danger till he got up
to the Cross Sand, and as the wind was from
the south-east, all hands were expecting to be up
at Gravesend in a very short time, as the ship

was bound for London, and they were all writing letters to wives and parents, to post as soon as they arrived, when the ship struck, and the cry was heard through the ship, 'We're ashore.' The ship launched heavily over to port on to her broadside, then back right over on her broadside to starboard, and then right over again to port, then slipped off the Ridge into deep water and sank.

"You see," explained the narrator, "Winterton Ridge is very steep and most dangerous for big vessels, for the forepart of a ship may be in two fathoms water, and the stern in seventeen fathoms."

"We were fishin' over along Borkum Reef," said Skipper T——; "I can't rightly remember the date, but I was skipper o' the *Mizpah* at the time.

"It was very bad weather, blowin' hard, and havin' been up all night, and bein' full of anxiety about the safety of my wessel and crew, I felt just about done up and played out. So just as daylight was breakin', I said to the mate, 'I'll go below and try for a little sleep, if only on the locker.'

"'All right, skipper,' says he; 'I'll rouse you if there's any call for it.'

"Before I'd time to fall asleep, I heard a voice up on deck sayin', 'Hallo, mate! here's a smack's mainsail and boom close to us, and a boat bottom upwards.'

"I was up on deck in a trice, and there I saw at

a little distance from us, as well as the dim light would allow, a cutter-rigged smack, with all her sails gone, except a bit of a jib as they'd hoisted just to try and keep her to the wind.

"I at once tacked our wessel so as to run in closer and speak them, when I found she had been clean swept of everything, barring her mast and her bowsprit—sails, boat, everything gone.

"The moment I came within hail, the crew shouted, 'Come an' take us off board.'

"I replied that I wouldn't leave 'em; but I couldn't for the life o' me see how we were going to launch a boat in such a mountainous sea as was then runnin'. However, I brought the wessels as close as I felt was prudent, and then waited a bit for daylight, before decidin' what to do next.

"Presently the mate came alongside o' me, and says, 'Skipper,' says he, 'what wessel is she? Can you make her out?'

"Now I was looking hard at the other smack through the glass, and the mornin' mist liftin' a little, I'd just made her out when the mate asked the question.

"'Yes, mate,' says I, 'I've managed to fit a name to her, and I'm sorry to tell you as it's the *Queen of England,* with your uncle and your little brother Tommy aboard.'

"The poor chap was terribly hove aback when I

told him, and he clasped his hands together, and said, ' O skipper, do let's go an' save 'em.'

" ' With all my heart,' says I, ' only I'll go in the boat myself, and you must stay in charge of the wessel.'

" It was, if anythin', blowin' harder than in the night, and such a powerful sea runnin' as to make it almost impossible for a boat to live, if launched, but we ventured, and you may be sure the boat wasn't long a'bein' thrown out. She had no sooner touched the water than myself and the third and fourth hands jumped into her, and after some real hard work we fetched alongside the *Queen of England*, and scrambled up aboard of her.

" We found things in a funny old state. She was heeled over a good two planks, the ballast had shifted, and the smack was quite half full of water.

" The skipper, whom I knew very well, exclaimed ' Thank God you've found us alive, it's more'n I expected.' We at once got the crew into our boat, and the *Mizpah* bein' smartly handled by the mate, we were quickly aboard of her, and hoisted our boat in again safe an' sound, and with great gratitude to Almighty God for His preserving mercies. We determined not to leave the wreck, but remained by her about five hours, when the weather fined a little, and her skipper was anxious to go back and try to save his wessel. Both wind and sea havin' abated we again launched the boat, and the skipper and three of my crew went away in her.

" As they were leavin' I said, ' If you find it possible to save the wessel, hoist our boat in, and I'll then run down and take you in tow.'

" It wasn't many minutes before I could see 'em preparin' to get the boat on deck, and I at once made our arrangements for towin'.

" In about three hours from the time the boat went back they had her pumped dry and our rope aboard. As soon as everythin' was ready we made sail for Copenhagen; but the wind baffled me, so that I was forced to give in and make for Yarmouth, where we arrived safely with our prize the third day after."

These smacksmen seem to be acquainted with every inch of the great ocean floor above which their lives are spent; and indeed I have found many among the older skippers—born before the days of school boards—to whom the restless, toilsome life at sea has taught all the lessons they ever learned. Of course, educationally considered, the smacksman of to-day is much in advance of his predecessors; but for all practical purposes of business, the older men knew as much as they needed.

" I'm an old feller, sir, an' I've been up and down the North Sea fishin'-grounds all my life, till I could a'most find my way blindfolded."

So spake old B——, a grey-haired veteran of

some fifty-five winters, whom I met in one of the Grimsby vessels, and who bore the appearance of a man whose word could be trusted.

I laughed and said, " Well, skipper, I can quite understand your finding your way blindfolded provided you had some one standing by to explain the prickings on the chart, and the vessel's course by the compass."

" Bless yer heart, sir, I didn't mean that sort o' thing at all. Why, any man as understood navigation could do that as easy as winkin'; but I reckon it 'ud puzzle any salt-water sailor as wasn't a fisherman born an' bred to find his way about the North Sea with his *fingers*."

" It would indeed; but explain what you mean. I confess you have fairly puzzled me."

" You're not the first as has been puzzled, by a long way, sir; but it's as simple as A B C, for all it sounds so difficult. In fact I may say as it's simpler, for I knows lots o' fellers as, like myself, never larned their alphabet, an' yet they can find their way about the North Sea just as I've been a-tellin' yer."

" But you haven't been telling me, or at all events you haven't explained how it's done."

" Well, yer see, sir, the North Sea is all banks an' flats an' pits, an' after draggin' a trawl about astern of yer wessel pretty well every day for forty

M

odd years, a man must be uncommon stupid if he don't know the different sorts o' bottom. It 'ud take a long time to talk over the whole of it with yer, an' besides any one can see for theirselves on the chart; but just for example like, I may say as about the east'ard o' the tail end o' the Dawger we find light-coloured sand with small white shells, some of 'em so small as yer can hardly see 'em to be shells at all; a bit further east is what we calls the 'coffee soil,' close agin that comes red sand. Now, all that's a mighty fine spot for haddocks about the month o' September, an' it's a favourite trawlin' ground for the Humber smacks. There's one objection, an' that is there's such a strong eastern set o' tide thereabouts, that after only four hours' trawlin' you may have as much as six hours' hard sailin' to get back to the spot where yer started a-trawlin'; but it's well worth the trouble, for there's a power o' haddocks there at times. Well, as I was a-sayin', there's all sorts o' different bottoms; there's soft mud, an' a awful bad smell along of it; then there's shingle, an big rocks, as breaks yer nets all to shivers; an' there's miles an' miles, further to the south'ard, o' scruffy ground, where they gets lots o' oysters, but that agin is allus hard upon the nets.

"Now yer see, sir, there's nothin' in the world can be easier, when you've once larned yer lesson,

than to pick yer way about in the North Sea just
with nothin' else to guide yer than the depth o'
water an' the natur' o' the bottom. You've got
adrift from yer fleet, or maybe you've come out
o' the Humber or out o' Yarmouth or Lowestoft,
an' haven't found them, 'cause the admiral's shifted
his fishin'-grounds. Well, all you've got to do is jest
to take a cast o' the lead, being careful to put a
good lump o' toller [tallow] at the end of it. By
that dodge yer gets two things at once. The line
tells yer the depth o' water, an' the toller brings
up the sand, or the mud, or the shells, or the
shingle, or the weed as is down on the bottom, an'
all you've got to do is to put two an' two togither,
an' you've got all yer wants to know."

I have frequently since this conversation had
opportunities of practically verifying B——'s asser-
tions, and have invariably found his statements
amply corroborated. And I may here remark that
to an ardent naturalist there is much that is
interesting and instructive in the contents of the
trawl net, especially if there be an opportunity,
which I have myself frequently enjoyed, of passing
from fleet to fleet over a couple of hundred miles
or so of the different fishing-grounds, from the
Dutch Coast to the Silver Pits, the Dogger Bank,
and northward to the Great Fisher Bank.

Before me, as I write, lie specimens of the remains

of various antediluvian birds and mammals, such as horns, head of the femur of a mammoth, leg of a bird of the Dodo class, enormous vertebræ and thigh bones, with teeth of the hairy elephant, &c. &c. Besides these there are specimens of amber, of North-Sea coral and sponge, hermit crabs, king crabs, sand eggs, and several kinds of echinus; while on a shelf at my elbow are ranged lumps of coal, beer and wine bottles, and many other articles all more or less covered with barnacles, some of which are of very large size.

Then there are the painful relics of the dead, sad evidences of shipwreck, of brave men battling for life, and the greed of the cruel sea.

However, I am not going to worry my readers or make my own heart ache by needlessly pursuing *that* subject, so we will, if you please, return to the question of heroism.

Skipper J—— M——, to whom I have more than once referred as a patriarch amongst his fellows, related to me with many sighs the following sad narrative :—

" I was master of the smack *Willie.* We was laying-to under close-reefed canvas on the night of the 29th October 1880, when the fleet jibed round about eleven o'clock at night. My own son John had the watch, and after all was stowed and everything smart he came below, leaving two lads as look-out on the bow. He said to me, 'Father, it blows very hard, but we are laying comfortable, and not much to fear!' Hardly were the words out of his mouth, when, like a clap of thunder, a heavy sea struck the vessel, and we immediately found ourselves under water in the cabin. The smack was on her beam ends, and water pouring down through the cabin-door. After a short time (it seemed long to us) the vessel righted herself, and we found breathing space. The first thing I said was—

" ' Are all hands safe ? '

" The answer came ' Yes.'

" ' Who is on deck,' I asked.

" ' The two lads,' said my son.

" I then put my head up what I thought was the cabin-door, and exclaimed, 'Thank God, the vessel is all right,' but one of the lads shouted—

" ' No ! the mast is gone overboard, skipper.'

" I said, 'Now all keep quiet and we will get a light,' for when it was fine weather I had taken the precaution to seal up a ginger-beer bottle full of matches, and stowed it in a drawer right up under the deck [this is a precaution taken by every thoughtful skipper], and in the same drawer was some dry lamp cotton. Of course all fire and light had been put out by the rush of water.

" Before I had got a light, my son said from the deck, ' Hand me up the hatchet, father; our gear has gone overboard (the fishing-gear was lashed on the weather-side, and it was thrown completely overboard, over the other side of the vessel) and the rope is running out.'

" I put my hand into a locker, and the first thing I felt was the required hatchet, and gave it to the mate, saying, ' Here's the hatchet, Arthur ; hand it up to Jack ! '

" He shouted, ' Here you are, Jack ; here's the hatchet.'

" No answer.

" I said, ' Shout louder, he is forward, perhaps,' but still no answer.

" With that I went on deck myself with a lantern, and shouted—still no answer. I searched everywhere, and what was my dismay and sorrow to find that three hands were missing, *my own son being one of the number*.

" But spite of my crushing grief the circumstances made it necessary to keep to duty, so I next endeavoured to see the extent of damage, and found the companion was gone, level with the deck ; all the stanchions of the weather-side bulwark and gear was also gone level with the deck : mast, spars, sails, boat, all gone—in fact, vessel clean swept of everything. But one of the most marvellous things was the two lads in the bows was not touched by the heavy sea. We had to set to

work to bale the vessel out after we found buckets,
and we continued at that till daylight, as the vessel
at first was half full of water, and the pump-gear,
that was right at the time of calamity, was all
washed clean away. After daylight the next day—
the 30th of October—I found one pump-box, with a
stick tied across it, and managed to free the vessel
of water. We found every bit of food all spoilt.
Our water, what was not upset, was salt, and we
couldn't drink it.

" The sea was still raging, and there we lay helpless, with no vessels in sight, neither food nor water
to sustain life, three of our number snatched from
amongst us by the cruel waves, and not knowing
any moment but that our own turn might come.
Thank God, in the midst of such overwhelming
trouble the voice of the blessed Saviour, by the
Holy Spirit, spoke to my heart and kept me in
peace, though my heart was breaking for my poor
lost boy. Truly could we say, ' In my distress I
cried unto the Lord : and He heard me ; ' for
after many hours of waiting and watching, and
all of us wet to the skin, and shivering in the
bitter icy cold, we sighted a Hull smack, and,
the Lord be praised, they saw our drifting wreck
and bore down to us. Taking no heed to the
violence of the wind and waves, those brave fellows
no sooner took in our sad situation than they threw

out their small boat, supplied us with food, water,
and firing, and then made fast a warp and took
us in tow.

" After three days and nights of slow progress we
at last, by God's mercy, reached the mouth of the
Humber, and were towed into Grimsby Docks.
Though I have been a fisherman for forty years, I
never spent such a weary, wretched time at sea as
those four days from the time the gale burst on us
till at last we were once again safe on dry land."

Finally I give one very brief but sad story related
by Skipper Jones of the Mission-smack *Clulow*.

" Some years ago, when I was master of a fishing-
vessel, I sent the boat away with fish to the steamer
Progress. It was blowing a strong wind with a
biggish sea running, and while the boat was alongside of the steamer, they saw an accident occur to
another boat, and one of the men was struggling in
the water. Away went my three men instantly
to the rescue, and they pulled for the life of them.
Of course from where I stood on the deck of the
smack I didn't know what they were pulling out
to windward for, but I kept an eye on them, and
saw them all at once lay on their oars as if they
had said one to the other, ' It is no use, the man
has sunk,' then they turned to come back on board.
But alas ! they hadn't pulled many strokes before a
lump of a sea caught the boat under the quarter,

and over she went, and I saw my three shipmates
drowned before my eyes. There was no help at
hand, and when a fisherman once gets into the
water, it is ten chances to one whether he will ever
get out again, as his sea-boots and clothes are so
heavy and help to sink him."

Thus were three brave fellows lost in the futile
endeavour to save a brother fisherman, and scarcely
a week passes without some similar act of gallantry
—alas, too often with the same result—being
witnessed amongst these North-Sea heroes while
engaged in their hazardous occupation.

I close this chapter with this quotation from a
London paper :—

" How seldom do we ponder over the fact that
' the price of fish ' is too often ' lives o' men,' as
the Scotch ballad puts it ! That is truer than ever
in these stormy days. Let us not be guilty of
the black ingratitude of enjoying the fruits of their
perilous toil, while we take no heed of the dangers
of the deep to which these brave fellows are exposed,
and do nothing to counteract or alleviate them."

CHAPTER XIII.

ANSWERS TO PRAYER.

. . . "More things are wrought by prayer
Than this world dreams of. . . .
For what are men better than sheep or goats,
That nourish a blind life within the brain,
If, knowing God, they lift not hands of prayer,
Both for themselves and those who call them friend?
For so the whole round earth is every way
Bound by gold chains about the feet of God."

IT has been my lot to prove during the past six years, not in mere theory, but in a very practical manner, the truth of the passage (Ps. cxviii. 8), "It is better to trust in the Lord than to put confidence in man." This was especially the case with regard to the acquirement of vessels for the purposes of the Mission.

In 1882, when the *Ensign* was purchased, several smack-owners assured me that she would be able to maintain herself by trawling. The experience of the first year so far tallied with this statement that I felt justified in 1883–84 in first negotiating for, and subsequently accepting the loan of, three more vessels, the *Salem* (now the *Temple Tate*), the *Cholmondeley*, and the *Edward Auriol* (now the *Clulow*).

The first of these three was bought from a Hull smack-owner, the second and third were specially built at Bideford, and the whole were the property of several gentlemen, who each invested a certain sum, amounting in the aggregate to £4800, in the belief that the vessels would pay a reasonable rate of interest by the profit upon their fishing, and they entered into a deed of partnership, appointing me managing owner, and lending the vessels for mission purposes. Then began the decline of prosperity in the fishing trade which has continued ever since without intermission. One result—and a very unfortunate one—of the great International Fisheries Exhibition was to attract attention to the question of our national fish supply, and induce several capitalists to embark money in the trade, with a view to its development in the interests of the country generally, and especially of the poorer population.

The consequences, instead of proving advántageous, have been simply disastrous, not only to the new-comers, but also to the old-established firms. Upwards of 140 new trawling smacks were equipped from Yarmouth alone, and the trade became abnormally active, without producing any of the happy

results which had been so confidently anticipated.
To-day there are numbers of vessels laid up in
harbour, which for the past two years had been
working at a loss; hundreds of men are out of
work; and upwards of £30,000 is reported to have
been lost last year alone upon the Great Yarmouth
trawlers. Other towns have also suffered in proportion.

It will therefore be readily seen that I committed
a most unfortunate blunder in accepting the positive assurance of smack-owners in 1882–83 that it
would be impossible to lose money upon trawling.
It speedily became evident to me that those who
had invested money in the three vessels above-
mentioned would do well to realise their capital
without delay.

It was a time of deepest anxiety. On the one
hand, I was in dread lest these amateur smack-owners
should be heavy losers; on the other, I feared the
utter collapse of the Mission, upon the success of
which I had founded my fondest hopes. My first
duty was clearly to protect from loss those who
had placed their money in that particular and very
unusual form of investment, for the sole purpose of
benefiting the work I had brought under their notice.
I therefore approached the owners of fleets with a
view to their purchasing the Mission-ships, but
discovered at once that by this plan the vessels

THE FLEET.

P. 188.

would not realise one-half of the original purchase-money, while at the same time the Mission would be practically at an end.

One alternative project presented itself to my mind, the adoption of which would at one and the same time protect my friends from heavy loss, and guarantee a continuance of the work; but the risk to myself personally was very great, and my solicitor strongly urged me to abandon the idea, and let the six owners take their chance with other specu-lators.

This advice I felt bound in honour to reject, and so it came to pass that, within one year of the partnership deed having been executed, it was revoked, the partners conveying the three vessels to myself in exchange for a total cash payment of £4550, the money being raised in part privately, and the remainder by means of advances on mort-gage from the owners of the various fleets, who readily consented to such an arrangement rather than allow their employés to lose the benefit of the Mission service.

By this means I became, in October 1884, the sole registered owner of the *Temple Tate, Cholmondeley,* and *Clulow,* and shortly afterwards of the *Edward Birkbeck;* and I immediately executed a declaration of trust, and was joined at first by three friends, and subsequently, in 1886, by five more, in forming a Board for the purpose of carrying on the Mission upon a sounder basis than hitherto. An appeal was made to the public for funds—(a.) to pay off the mortgages; (b.) to provide for the efficient maintenance of the work; and one of the first pleasing results of this appeal was to enable the Mission to repay in full (with 4% interest) the friend who had originally advanced £1000 to purchase the *Ensign,* which vessel, after being lengthened and entirely refitted, at a further cost of £1100, was rechristened the *Thomas Gray,* in grateful recognition of many acts of generous kindness by my friend, the Head of the Board of Trade, Marine Department.

It now became necessary for me to relinquish one or two other occupations and sources of private income, as the increasing demands of the Mission necessitated close personal attention, literally night and day. But the results, by Divine Providence, amply justified the sacrifice, and were manifested in a more extended sphere of labour at sea, ever-deepening interest amongst all classes on shore—from Royalty to inmates of alms-houses—and a rapidly growing income. The strain was, however, at times almost unbearable, and the labour overwhelming; yet, during all that time of anxiety, the blessed promise never failed, "Thou wilt keep him in perfect peace whose mind is stayed on Thee, because he trusteth in Thee;" while at the same time God was graciously teaching that "they that trust in the Lord shall not want any *good* thing."

Monday, the 8th of February 1886, was one of the first days of real spring. It may be thought odd, but that morning, as I sat at an early and solitary breakfast (having to be in the City before nine o'clock), the very brightness of the weather made me feel depressed ; for I was reminded that the long weary winter was past, and the summer season quickly coming, when there would be the usual voluntary offers from the clergy and laymen to conduct missions in the North Sea. I was saddened by the recollection that the number of vessels at our disposal had not increased since the previous summer, when all five had been crowded by volunteers.

While brooding over this fact, one of my children, a girlie of six years old, came tripping downstairs and cried eagerly, " Father, would you like to hear my morning text ? "

" Yes, darling, certainly I should."

The child placed her head on my shoulder and whispered, " Oh, taste and see that the Lord is good ; blessed is the man that trusteth in Him."

To her it was her morning text and nothing more, and she was proud of being able to repeat it correctly ; to me it came as a message from the Lord. " Here am I," I thought, " cast down and depressed, forgetting that the Lord's arm is not shortened, and that He who has already done so much can easily provide all that we need." I thought over the incident as I finished breakfast, travelled to the City, and walked to my office; and when, according to custom, the clerks assembled in my room for prayer at nine o'clock, I told them the whole story.

That morning three North-Sea skippers were present, men who were eager to know how soon some more Mission-vessels would be sent out; so when I had related the incident of the text, I proposed that we should specially wait upon the Lord for additional ships, and our prayers were accordingly very definite.

On rising from my knees, I turned to the pile of letters on my table, and on opening the third, found it to be an inquiry by the Duchess of Gratton as to the cost of a completely equipped Mission-vessel. Here was an answer to our prayers! Scepticism might demonstrate it to be a mere co-incidence, inasmuch as the letter was written and posted twelve hours before our prayer was offered; but the obvious response is that God leads those who are humbly seeking to do His will and walk in His ways to ask for precisely those things which He in His wisdom is about to grant.

At all events, I sat down—I could not do other-wise—and wrote to her Grace the simple story of the morning—the little girl's text—the morning prayer in the office (why should not there be morning prayer in the City office as well as in the Christian home?), and giving her the desired information as to cost.

The Duchess replied by return of post, " I am much touched by the story, and trust it may be God's will that I should give a vessel to the Mission as a memorial of my late husband, and named after him." A few days later I was asked to call and communicate fuller details as to the work, and before leaving, the Duchess handed me a cheque for £2150, only stipulating that the vessel should be named the *Euston*.

This was the beginning of a new era with regard to vessels, and I cannot but feel, in retrospect, how far better it would have been to trust the Lord in 1883 than seek the loan of vessels which ultimately I was obliged to purchase, thereby saddling myself with a load of responsibility and worry, which, by the exercise of simple faith in the living God, might so easily have been avoided. However, " we *know* that all things work together for good to them that love God," even our own mistakes being made a blessing to us in teaching the lesson of having no confidence in the flesh.

In concluding this chapter, I may fairly introduce an instance of the great advantage accruing to God's

people from the habit of obeying that exhortation
of Holy Scripture, " *In all thy ways acknowledge
Him, and He shall direct thy paths.*"

In 1883 an introduction to Mr. Harrison Mudd,
smack-owner and fish merchant of Grimsby, and
chairman of the local Smack-owners' Association,
enabled me to select the Hull smack before referred
to.   Mr. Mudd was indefatigable in rendering
assistance, and his advice proved simply invaluable,
while the manner in which he, a busy man, devoted
his time to the service of the Mission, placed me
under a great obligation to him.

Having obtained a suitable vessel, it was clearly
of first importance to secure the right man as
skipper,—a man who could not only show a good
record in his proper sphere of labour as a smacksman, but also give full proof of his zeal and
ability as a fisher of men.   Naturally, this need
also was taken to the Throne of Grace, and having
asked for Divine guidance, I again had recourse to
the genial and kind-hearted fish-merchant before
mentioned.

" Mr. Mudd, you have helped me to select a ship ;
now can you tell me of an earnest Christian man
to command her ? "

" Well, I know several good men who might suit
you, but the one whom I could with the utmost
confidence recommend, as being beyond doubt the

very best man for the post, is, unfortunately, not available."

" Why not ? "

" For the best possible reason. He is at sea as mate on board his brother's smack, and is not expected in port for several days."

" What is his name ? "

" Cullington—Skipper Cullington. But really it is useless to discuss him, if, as you say, you want the vessel to go to sea at once."

" True. And yet I regret that this man's services cannot be obtained, since he is, by your account, so very suitable for the position. Now perhaps it is rather an unusual request to make, but would you and your friends mind kneeling down here in your office and joining me in prayer? The vessel is to be used in God's service, and it is most important, indeed essential, that the man who commands her should be God's servant too."

A ready assent was given to this suggestion, and we knelt together and asked for wisdom in the choice of a skipper, and that the Lord would graciously send the right man.

We had barely risen from our knees when a clerk, who had overheard the first portion of our conversation, opened the door hurriedly and exclaimed, " Here's Cullington's vessel warping into the dock ! "

The precise cause of her returning to port before

her time I do not now remember, nor is it needful
to ascertain it. What I *do* recollect is the blessed
answer to our prayer, and the confirmation to my
heart of the Divine promise, "In all thy ways
acknowledge *Him*, and *He shall* direct thy paths."

A very few moments' conversation with Cullington
convinced me that he was a man of God, anxious to
be useful in his Master's service, and, after careful
inquiry in various quarters with regard to his capa-
bilities, I engaged him as skipper of the "Bethel-
ship."

From the very beginning this work has been
associated with prayer. When the condition of the
smacksmen was first discovered, it was laid before
God in prayer, and now, as I look back, and see how
the blessed work has progressed, it suggests to my
mind that the Lord is coming very soon, since He
seems to be gathering in His own from the sea as
well as from the land. When He said, "Go ye
into all the world, and preach the Gospel to every
creature," He did not mean the land only, but the
sea.

Long the cry had been unheard, "Who shall go
over the sea for us?" Now the Lord has sent out
His servants from the shore, has provided vessels to
preach in, and is giving great blessing. Numbers of
men are "coming over on the Lord's side." So, by
means of the Mission-vessels, bodies are being healed

through the medical and surgical aid ; the curse of the _copers_ is being driven out ; the men are being cheered by means of books and papers to read, and warm, loving sympathy. But all these things are for the furtherance of the Gospel, and sinners are being saved. Whatever purpose a smacksman may have in coming to the Mission-ship, he is made to feel before he leaves that the primary object of the vessel's presence is that Christ should be preached.

.   .   .   .   .   .

And we are still praying constantly and earnestly as ever, waiting on the Lord day by day for the maintenance of the vessels now on service, for blessing on this work, and for more vessels, so that every man in the North-Sea fleets should hear the Gospel. " For how shall they believe in Him of whom they have not heard ? and how shall they hear without a preacher ? " And how shall we preach without Mission-vessels to carry the preacher and in which to preach ? Hence we are still waiting on God, and as He has heard and answered before, we are assured He will do so yet again.

CHAPTER XIV.

HOW TO COPE WITH THE "COPERS."

"Clear strong tones will oft bring sudden bloom
Of hope secure to him who lonely cries."

IT was now abundantly clear that there could be
no compromise between the opposing forces. The
man who, as they happily express it, "came over
on the Lord's side" must renounce the *coper* and
all his works. There was no middle course. The
new Mission-ship was God's Mission-ship—the old
one was the devil's. Those who ranged themselves
on the side of truth and righteousness, purity and
sobriety, of Christ for this present world, Christ for
the eternal glory—these were found on board the
new Mission-ship. The men who were content to
"serve divers lusts and pleasures," who drank and
gambled, and some of whom—now a very small
minority—would at a pinch even barter away their
employer's property,—those who, in a word, were
"led captive by the devil at his will," were the
men who habitually frequented the foreign *coper*.

But the more intimately I learned to know the fishermen, the more assured was I that, even apart from those who were distinctly "on the Lord's side," many of them were men full of good intentions and resolves, men who were desirous, for their own credit's sake and for the sake of their families ashore, to "go straight" and keep sober. But these men were smokers, and to obtain tobacco they must visit the *coper*.

One case which was brought under my notice will serve to illustrate the danger to which these men were exposed. The man in question was a skipper, who held the dual reputation of being the best fisherman and one of the hardest drinkers in the fleet with which he was stationed. He was a grand specimen of humanity, a fisherman of splendid physique, and, when sober, a warm-hearted, good-natured fellow, and withal a loving husband and father. I said he was good-natured. Alas! it was this very excellent trait in his character which, without the necessary ballast of a firm will and the courage to say "No" and adhere to his purpose, was the cause of all his backslidings and the sorrow he brought upon his poor wife and little ones. He visited the *coper* for his "Rising Hope" (what concealed irony in that title!), and was too good-natured to resist the wheedling persuasion of the smooth-spoken Belgian skipper who carried on the grog and tobacco business in that particular fleet; and so it invariably ended in his emptying his pockets into the coffers of the foreigner, and standing treat to his brother fishermen.

His employer told me that on one occasion this skipper drew from him no less than £30 in gold as his share of "poundage" on a very successful voyage, this being in addition to the weekly wage of fourteen shillings paid to his wife during his absence. Within one week that man came to the owner, and touching his cap, said, " Would you oblige me with the loan of half-a-sovereign, sir ? " Every penny of the £30 was gone—dissipated; and the next day that skipper sailed away to the fleet for another eight weeks' voyage, and left a wife and young family ill provided for.

Does the reader say, " What a brute ! he deserved to be punished " ? When that story was repeated to me, it made me feel very, very sad; and when left to myself that night I said, " O Lord Jesu Christ, Thou didst cast none away as 'too bad' when Thou wast on earth; now be pleased to bring that poor man under the power of Thine own great love, and let him find in Thyself infinitely greater pleasure than in his present evil courses."

I mentioned this case to others, and a few months later had the joy of hearing that this skipper had been induced to go on board the Mission-ship,

had listened to the Gospel message from the lips
of a clergyman who was out at the time, had returned from his voyage completely changed, having
renounced the *coper* and all his works; and when
chaffed by some of his old chums he replied, "No,
I won't join you; *I've walked in the dark long
enough, and now by God's grace I mean to walk with
Him.*"

But, be it remembered, both this man and many
more like him were smokers, and, so far as I was
concerned, I could not find it in my heart to deprive
the fisherman of his pipe.

Thus the *coper* became a standing menace to the
work of the new Mission-ship, retaining a firm grip
upon its regular customers, and being, moreover,
a constant source of danger to the new converts.
Perhaps, it may be said, "Ah! your Gospel didn't
go far enough; you should have warned the men
against the sin of smoking; then they would not
have had occasion to go to the grog-shop for
tobacco." My friend, I don't believe in such a
Gospel, and therefore could not preach it. The
Gospel, as I have learned it myself, is good news of
salvation from the guilt and power of *sin*. I would
not suffer my boy to smoke, but neither would I
let him drink a cup of strong tea. I would not
tolerate for a moment the egregious stupidity of the
youth who, placing a cigar or a pipe in his mouth,

struts about and fancies himself a man; but I have the strongest possible sympathy for the poor fellow who, exposed to the icy blasts of the North Sea, finds warmth and comfort in his pipe during the weary hours of the long winter's night. To those who condemn smoking, I cry, "Agreed, agreed!" so far as the prohibition applies to young people and to persons leading sedentary lives; but draw the line, if you please, at deep-sea smacksmen.

No? Well, then, come to me, and I will arrange for your visiting the northern edge of the Dogger Bank for a week or two—that will suffice, you need not make a longer stay—and we will resume the discussion on your return to England. Need you provide any special articles of clothing, do you inquire? Do as you think best. I can only say for your guidance, that on one occasion I spent a week in the same locality during the month of June, and could scarcely keep warm, though wearing flannel under-clothing covered by three waistcoats, four coats, and a suit of oil-skins. But then, you see, I was not a smoker. Do you decline to make the trial? Then pray don't say another word about the sin of smoking, so far as it concerns men with the conditions of whose life you are totally unacquainted.

Yes; this was the light in which I viewed the question. Tobacco is as much a necessity to these men, who are called to bear such a tremendous phy-

sical strain, as a cup of afternoon-tea is to myself
amid the daily pressure of close mental application.
Were I, instead of having it brought to my study,
compelled to obtain my cup of tea at a refreshment-
bar, where intoxicants in every form were paraded
to my view, the sight would be no temptation to
me ; but none the less I could feel pity and sympathy for my brethren at sea, to whom the odour of
spirits on board the *coper* is a deadly temptation.
Should I say, "Poor fools! I'm sorry they have no
more strength of character," and then leave them
to go their own way utterly to the bad—to the
devil? No, God forbid! In this matter, as in
others, I sought to remember, that though the primary object of the Mission was a spiritual one, it
was not by any means the only one. The Mission
was intended "as well for the body as the soul,"
and I saw no reason why the enemy should not be
combated with his own weapons—aye, and beaten
out of the field altogether. Already, as we have
seen, the steady progress of the Gospel had materially
diminished the custom formerly enjoyed by the grog-
shop, but so long as the *copers* held a monopoly in
supplying tobacco, so long would the trade in spirits
continue, to the detriment of the Mission, the serious
loss of the owners, the impoverishing of families on
shore, and the ruin, body and soul, of the smacksmen themselves.

"But," said a friend to whom I ventured to confide these views, "you surely don't mean to say you would sell tobacco on board the Mission-vessels?"

"Why not?"

"Oh! fancy turning the Gospel-ships into tobacconist's shops! How shocked people would be! You would be sure to lose a great many subscribers."

"No, I won't allow that the sale of tobacco on board a Mission-ship would turn her into anything at all. Her character would not be altered; it would only be developed. If the ships are *mission*-ships now, they would merely become more worthy of the title were this idea put into execution. As for losing subscribers, I believe we should gain immensely. For many people who do not support us now would be enamoured of this new departure in practical philanthropy, while existing friends would feel increased interest, and not even the most spiritually-minded Christian would withdraw support, but would, on the contrary—I say it in all reverence—feel that the sale of tobacco would turn out for the furtherance of the Gospel."

"How so?"

"In the most natural, simple manner; it is merely a question of arithmetic. The Mission-ship is now visited (1) by all who, as believers, value the opportunity afforded to 'assemble and meet together;'

(2) by those who wish for a supply of literature; (3) by purchasers of woollen clothing; and (4) by sufferers who need relief from the dispensary. But there the category stops, and yet there still remain a vast number who have neither desire nor excuse for coming on board. Let cheap tobacco be added to the existing inducements, and a net will have been provided in which all will be enclosed. And when it is remembered that no man ever steps on the deck of a Mission-vessel, whatever his motive in coming, without hearing of the Saviour, I am sure you must agree that the step now proposed would turn out for the furtherance of the Gospel."

A smack-owner, who had been, he informed me, plundered most shamefully by reason of the *coper* traffic in his fleet, and who would therefore naturally hail with delight a scheme the outcome of which must necessarily mean increased earnings on the vessels and a greatly diminished cost of maintenance, told me frankly that he had no faith in the success of my plan. I demanded his reason.

"Because, in my opinion, the men go to the *coper* for *drink;* they *will have* it, and if you give them their tobacco for *nothing,* they'll still deal with the *coper* as much as ever."

"I am glad to say I don't agree with you," I replied. "There may be—there are—black sheep among the smacksmen, as everywhere else; but, as a result of close personal observation, I am convinced that the vast majority simply and innocently go to the *coper* for tobacco, and, once on board, they are tempted to drink, and many of them, unfortunately, cannot resist the temptation."

"Well," said he, "I fear you will find yourself sadly mistaken in your estimate of the men, and you will only meet with disappointment."

"On the contrary, I feel absolutely assured of success. I cannot for a moment admit that smacksmen as a class are bad and unprincipled; in fact, after mingling with them in their vessels out at sea, and in their homes on shore, I say unhesitatingly they are a splendid race of men, to whom I am proud and thankful to be privileged to lend a helping hand. They have their faults, but they are conscious of them, and that is a long step towards reformation; and what is more, they are thoroughly capable of appreciating any efforts for their well-being. But, may I ask, have you ever visited your own fleet?"

"Visited my fleet! I should think not, indeed. Why, my men would pelt me with haddocks if they got me out there."

"That appears to me a very sad confession," I replied; "but what could you expect? You distrust your men; you not only regard them as drunkards, liars, and thieves, but you refuse to believe in the possibility of improvement. To you they are utter reprobates, outside the pale of salvation. Could you then be surprised if, accepting your own suggestion, they were to regard you as a target for haddocks? Now, finally, let me tell you I have been amongst these very men in your employ; I have with my own eyes seen them take some of your gear to a *coper*. It was a very small.quantity and very old, but I admit to you that all the same those men were *thieves*. I admit they would probably *lie* to you on their return, and tell you that gear was lost overboard. I admit that they were *drunkards*, and I will not yield to you in abhorrence of such conduct; but, having agreed thus far, I will show you where we are at issue. *You* say, 'These men are a bad lot, and if I can only detect them, they shall feel the power of the law. *I* say, on the other hand, '*If* they are a bad lot, *why* are they?' To my own mind the answer is perfectly simple. These men have had for years in their midst a source of temptation—temptation that to weak natures is irresistible—temptation to drink and gamble and squander away their earnings —temptation to rob their employers—to rob those on shore who are dependent upon them for support —to rob and ruin themselves, body and soul. The floating grog-shop has been indeed the devil's mission-ship. The *coper* has posed as the one friend

of the smacksmen while they are on the fishing-
ground. Think of the hardships of their life, the
harsh toil, the bitter cold, the absence of all cheering,
humanising, moral influences, and can you marvel
that numbers of these men have fallen lower and
lower, struggling for a time—maybe for years—
against the foe, cursing their folly when sober, yet
drinking harder than ever at the next opportunity?
'A bad lot,' indeed! What would you and I, and
scores of other respectable, moral folks have been,
had we been cut off, on the one hand, from all the
privileges and opportunities with which we have all
our lives been surrounded, while exposed, on the
other hand, to the same temptations as those poor
smacksmen? No, no; what has been needed all
these long fearful years, what is wanted now, and,
please God, shall in the future be very fully manifested, is a spirit, not of self-righteous cynicism, but,
of Christian love and sympathy."

Other smack-owners, with whom I conversed on
the subject, were quite of my opinion that the
issue of tobacco to the smacksmen at a price
defying foreign competition would effectually check-
mate the *copers*, and they begged that the Mission-
vessels might be employed in this crusade; while in
every case where I consulted the men themselves
there was a most emphatic verdict in favour of the
plan. One after another these smacksmen said to

me personally, "If you can only give us the bacca from the Mission-vessels, we won't trouble the *copers;*" while in several cases I received letters from sea earnestly petitioning that the Mission would take the matter up forthwith, and get rid, by one bold stroke, of the cause of incalculable misery and loss.

At Christmas 1884 the first sign was given in the publication of the following passage:—

"Is there no means whereby tobacco can be supplied free of duty without the baleful temptation of the *coper?* Is there such a way? There is, and it is simple enough. The objections are purely sentimental. Those who would not themselves use tobacco can surely feel that its supply by the Mission-vessels, which the men could visit without the dreadful besetment of temptation to drink fiery poison, would of itself be a judicious thing, besides the grand result that the *copers* would be banished from the fleets, and thus temptation be removed from the weakest and most self-indulgent. The boon this would prove to the smacksmen, only those of us who have lived amongst them can fully know."

In the spring of 1885 I appealed for assistance to Sir Edward Birkbeck, who had always nobly championed the cause of the fishermen in the House of Commons, and he very kindly under-

o

took to put a question to the Chancellor of the Exchequer. The question was asked, Would the Government allow the Mission-vessels to carry tobacco out of bond and sell it duty free to the smacksmen? The answer was a polite but firm negative. The Chancellor of the Exchequer "regretted that Her Majesty's Government could not see their way," &c. &c.

Then I was received by the Chairman and Deputy-Chairman of the Board of Customs. Sir Charles Du Cane was most courteous and kind; he expressed warm sympathy with the object in view; did not doubt the purity of the motive; was of opinion that the supply of tobacco in the way I suggested *would* have the effect of driving away the *copers;* but——

Alas! upon that terrible rock of red-tape all my hopes of official sanction and assistance were hopelessly shattered.

"Our regulations," said the Chairman, "will not admit of our doing this for you."

"Well," I replied, "you must not be very much surprised if we find some means of doing it for ourselves. This evil has too long disgraced our country, and if the Government will not, or cannot, move in the matter, I have no doubt private enterprise will both discover and apply a remedy."

Sir Charles gave me to understand that personally

he heartily wished success to any effort in the direction indicated, but that H.M. Commissioners of Customs could not grant facilities.

Leaving the Chairman, I went downstairs to the Long Room, and inquired minutely into the conditions under which English-manufactured tobacco is exported to the Continent. Having satisfied myself that there would be no risk of contravening either the statute law or the Customs regulations in shipping a cargo of tobacco to a foreign port for the purposes of the new scheme, and being assured also that the authorities, if they did not assist, would certainly not hinder, the execution of the project, I left the precincts of the Custom House in a far happier frame of mind than when I entered, and full of hope that the hour of the *coper's* doom was at last about to strike.

CHAPTER XV.

DRIVING NAILS IN THE "COPER'S" COFFIN.

> "Thus, with somewhat of the seer,
>   Must the moral pioneer
>   From the Future borrow :
>   Clothe the waste with dreams of grain,
>   And on midnight's sky of rain,
>   Paint the golden morrow ! "

THE preliminary inquiries at the Custom-House clearly proved that, although we were denied the privilege of shipping tobacco direct from this country to the fishing-grounds, there was no legal impediment to our obtaining all we needed by other means, though the plan would involve considerable circumlocution, vexatious delay, and an expenditure which I would gladly have avoided.

As fishing-vessels are not permitted to carry tobacco under any circumstances, I was advised in one quarter to remove all the trawling gear from one of the Mission-smacks, convert her into an ordinary trader under the Merchant Shipping Act, take a cargo of tobacco on board in the Thames, and then clear for a Continental port.

" But what advantage would accrue from such a proceeding ? " I inquired. " I don't want to send tobacco to the Continent, but to the trawling fleets."

" Of course you do," said my adviser, a person skilled in shipping matters, " and you would ' clear ' for, say Hamburg, and when once outside the territorial waters, you would simply go direct to the fleets and drop your cargo of tobacco there."

" In other words, you would have me make a false declaration. You advise me to state at the English Custom-House that my cargo of tobacco is going to Hamburg, while knowing that it will never reach that port."

" Oh, it is merely a matter of form ; such things are done constantly."

" They may be, but I will not take your advice ; it would be ' doing evil that good may come.' With regard to the affairs of this Mission, I have desired hitherto to remember the Divine precept, ' *In all thy ways acknowledge Him, and He shall direct thy paths,*' and I am not going to depart from that good rule simply because a difficulty confronts me. The adoption of your suggestion necessitates telling a distinct lie. How could I possibly seek God's blessing upon it ? "

Finally, after much anxious inquiry and investigation, both personally and through various agents, I found that the only way open to us was to

purchase tobacco in England, export it to the
Continent, clearing the Customs in the usual way,
and then sending a Mission-vessel to the foreign
port to take over the cargo. It would be necessary,
under these circumstances, to have an agent abroad,
and an introduction to M. Adolphe Bach, the German Consul at Ostend, speedily settled that difficulty,
M. Bach promptly consenting to receive a consign-
ment of English-manufactured tobacco, and to
superintend all the needful formalities to which the
Belgian Customs required us to conform.

On the 7th of October 1885, the first three tons
of tobacco were consigned by the General Steam
Navigation Company's steamer *Swallow* to M. Bach.
The same night I went over by the mail to Ostend,
found the Mission-vessel lying ready for her cargo,
the steamer ready to deliver it, and apparently everything working smoothly ; but—

> "The best-laid plans o' mice and men
>   Gang aft agley."

And presently, while I was standing on the quay
chatting with the German Consul, we were surprised
and alarmed to see Skipper Jones approaching us,
accompanied by the Consul's clerk and a couple of
douaniers, his usually smiling face—as one of the
men afterwards remarked—"as long as a handspike."

" Why, skipper, what's the matter ? " I said.

" Matter enough, sir ; they won't let us take the tobacco aboard."

" Why not, pray ? "

" 'Cause they say as it's contrary to Belgian law to let tobacco go aboard a fishing-smack."

" And can't you move them ? "

" Move them ! no, sir ; an' I don't think you will either ; they seem as firm as rocks.   But of course I've had to take it all second-hand, as I can't talk their lingo."

I looked inquiringly at M. Bach.

" I cannot understand it," he said.   " I was assured there would be no difficulty."

" Well," I replied, " I've not come all this way to be baulked at the outset without a remonstrance, and I'm not disposed to 'take things second-hand,' as the skipper says.   Give me your papers, skipper."

Jones handed me the parchments, and M. Bach and I thereupon entered the Custom-House, and after being passed up from one official to another, we were at length informed courteously, but very firmly, that the Mission-vessel could not be allowed to take over the tobacco, or, at all events, could not be permitted to leave the harbour with it on board.

" Est ce que vous pouvez parler anglais, monsieur ? " I inquired, in politest tones, of the official.

" Non, monsieur," he replied.

" Then," said I, in English, to M. Bach, " is this the final court of appeal ?   Can't we get behind this man ? "

" Yes ; we can see the chief; but it is use-less."

" Pardon me ! I'm not *au courant* with Belgian methods, but in England I've always found it best to go to the fountain-head."

" As you please," said my friend ; " you shall try if you like.   I can quite understand your not wish-ing to return to England without accomplishing your object."

The German Consul's name proved an open-sesame to the presence of the chief, and when M. Bach had introduced me and explained the nature and object of my errand, and the difficulty which had so unexpectedly presented itself, he very readily offered to do anything in his power to meet my wishes.

This was encouraging, but it was, alas ! only a momentary gleam of sunshine, for the dark cloud appeared more impenetrable than ever when the chief read to us the precise wording of the Belgian Act bearing upon the case.

But a happy thought struck me.   " How do you know, monsieur, that ours is a fishing-smack ? "

The chief looked amazed.   " How do I know ? "

he exclaimed. "I have but to step to this window and see with my own eyes the trawling gear on your decks."

"But if neither your own eyes nor the eyes of your subordinates could see that trawling gear, would not the case be altered?"

He laughed. "No," said he, "the case would *not* be altered; for you would still be called upon to produce your official papers, and all you could show would be your fishing license."

"Pardon, monsieur! That may be so with regard to Belgian craft, but each of these Mission-vessels carries a certificate of British registry under the Merchant Shipping Act."

"I was not aware of that fact," he replied, "but doubtless it is so."

"It is so, monsieur, and I have both the certificates in my pocket at this moment. Now, you have very kindly said you will serve me if it be in your power; therefore I produce for your inspection the certificate under the Merchant Shipping Act; the other one shall remain in my pocket."

"Yes, this certificate appears to be quite regular," said the chief; "it is that of an ordinary vessel."

"Quite so! Now, monsieur, you have with your own eyes seen that we are properly registered. Will you kindly give me one hour's delay, and if at the end of that time your *sous-officiers* are able to report to you that *their* eyes can detect no trace of fishing-gear on board the Mission-ship, will you then instruct them to place no impediment in the way of our taking the tobacco?"

The chief laughed again. " Ah!" said he, "I see your drift. Well, I said I would help you, and I will. This trade in spirits is most injurious in every way, and we do our utmost to stop it, though without much success. But your plan must succeed. Now it is quite clear that, whether you have the fishing certificate in your pocket or not, you cannot fish without the necessary gear. I will therefore agree to your proposal, and will send officers on board an hour hence."

Thanking my benefactor very warmly, I hastened down with M. Bach, told the skipper, to his huge delight, what had transpired in the Custom-House, and without a moment's delay set all hands to work to remove the trawl-beams, nets, &c., from the vessel. Long before the time agreed upon, the gear had disappeared from decks and hold, and it was subsequently placed on board the *Swallow* for conveyance to London.

In due course the official permit was received, the cases of tobacco were safely stowed below ; and when I came to reckon up the various bills and accounts, it appeared that, after adding all charges of transit, harbour dues, &c. &c., to the manufacturer's price, the tobacco had cost just one shilling per pound.

With her cargo of tobacco on board, the Mission-smack sailed from Ostend, and provided beforehand with the approximate position of the various fleets, she quickly made the round, distributing the cargo in so many hundredweights to each of her consorts, by whom in due course it was retailed to the smacks-men at the cost price of one shilling per pound. The *coper's* charge was eighteenpence, and he could not afford to sell for less, so the effect of the new departure began immediately to make itself felt in all the fleets with which Mission-vessels were stationed.

Then came a hitch. One could hardly expect to secure immediate success without encountering checks; but this was no ordinary difficulty, being nothing less than a strongly expressed opinion on the part of the men that our cut Cavendish tobacco was not equal in quality to the *coper's* " Rising Hope." What was to be done? We were already selling at cost price, and it appeared on inquiry and compari-son of samples, that the company whose tobacco we were then dispensing would charge several additional pence per pound for an article which could be regarded as safely challenging competition by the foreigners.

In this perplexity I turned instinctively to God

for guidance, and, as ever before, He graciously provided precisely what we required—"a friend in need," and when at last he came, he proved "a friend indeed."

One Sunday night, just at this juncture, I was lying awake, puzzling over the *coper* question, convinced that victory was only delayed, yet in doubt as to the next move. When on the point of dozing off, after again committing the whole matter to Him whose Word says, "*Except the Lord build the house, they labour in vain that build it,*" the name of Mr. W. H. Wills, M.P., flashed upon my mind. I was not personally acquainted with him, but had recently stayed in a house where he was known, and I had learned that he was wealthy, philanthropic, and, moreover, a partner in the well-known firm of W. D. & H. O. Wills of Bristol, the great importers and manufacturers of tobacco. Thinking of Mr. W. H. Wills, and wondering whether he could and would help me, I fell asleep. On the following morning the whole subject recurred to my mind while dressing, and I began to consider through whom I might obtain an introduction to Mr. Wills. At my office during the morning the matter still occupied my thoughts, until about three o'clock, when a most remarkable circumstance occurred. A clerk opened my door and announced "Mr. W. H. Wills, M.P. !"

As he entered Mr. Wills exclaimed—

"Well, Mr. Mather, you will wonder what has brought me to see you."

"No, I don't in the least," I replied, "and before you say a word about your errand, I'll explain why I say so."

"Well, that is certainly a most extraordinary coincidence," remarked my visitor, when the story was concluded, "and it only serves to quicken my interest in your matters; for the fact is, I was struck by the case you made out in your letter to the papers the other day, and it occurred to me that my firm at Bristol might possibly help you."

"If your firm is in the habit of exporting tobacco to the Continent, I have no doubt it is in their power to help," I replied. "But would they be willing to help? for it seems to me we shall need very exceptional terms if we become purchasers."

"Of course I cannot pledge them, but my impression is they will be prepared, in consideration of the object, to make a most liberal reduction on the usual prices; at any rate, I shall strongly urge them to do so."

After making many inquiries into the condition of the deep-sea fishermen, and eliciting information relative to the various methods adopted by the Mission with a view to sweetening the bitterness and rendering the hard life not quite so unbearable

as hitherto, Mr. Wills left me, promising that I
should hear very shortly from his firm at Bristol.

Within three days two of the partners, accompanied by their London manager, called upon me,
and expressed their willingness to furnish all the
tobacco we might require, *charging only the actual
cost of production.* Need I say how intensely
thankful I felt, and that this generous offer was
immediately accepted ?

Since then Messrs. Wills have supplied for consumption at sea upwards of £5000 worth of cut
and cake tobacco in consignments of three tons—
the former in half-pound packets, the latter in what
are termed " pocket-pieces."

The money received for tobacco is at once lodged
in an iron safe placed in the skipper's cabin for this
purpose, and of which the ship's-husband keeps the
key. The moment a Mission-vessel arrives in port,
it is the duty of the ship's-husband to count the
money, satisfy himself that it tallies with the
skipper's accounts, and then pay it into the bank at
Great Yarmouth for transmission to London. I
may note in passing, that before banking this
tobacco cash—which at times amounts to upwards
of £100 per voyage—the ship's-husband is obliged
to have the whole of it thoroughly washed in
boiling water. The bankers bore the infliction very
patiently for the first two voyages, but at length

even they were roused to resistance, and refused to handle such "filthy lucre."

Two years have elapsed since the first cargo of tobacco was shipped to Ostend, and the effect of the action then taken has been to neutralise completely the traffic of the floating grog-shops.

The owners have been unanimous in their warm thanks for the boon thus conferred, and I have before me, as I write, several letters expressive of gratitude and good-will ; *e.g.*, the managing owners of the " Red White " fleet say :—" We cannot adequately convey to you our sense of the great importance of the work you have undertaken in our fleet, nor our appreciation of the results already attained."

Mr. Burdett-Coutts, M.P., as owner of the large *Columbia* fleet, wrote to the daily press :—" The only effectual attempt that has been made to counteract the work of the *coper* has been carried on through the agency of the Mission-smacks. It is not, as a rule, easy to estimate how much or how little practical good is effected by missionary agencies, but here the case is clear. I gladly add my own testimony to that of others, and say that, at present, the Mission affords the only relief from the temptation, and the only remedy to the evils of the *copering* system. I have only to add that I hope some good will be done with regard to the matter at the forthcoming International Conference at the Hague."

The Conference here referred to was convened for the purpose, *inter alia*, of arriving at an understanding between the six Fishing Powers—England, France, Germany, Holland, Belgium, and Norway—as to some means of regulating the *coper* traffic. To my own mind it appeared that the traffic was so infamous as to demand not mere *regulation*, but no treatment at the hands of the Powers short of summary and total abolition.

However, while the eminent diplomatists of the Powers were busy arranging preliminaries, the *Mission to Deep-Sea Fishermen* was patiently and successfully pegging away with the sale of cheap tobacco, so that by the time (in June 1886) the Conference ultimately met, and solemnly proceeded to discuss the vital question of " regulating the *coper* traffic," the Mission had so far succeeded that there remained no traffic to " regulate " in those fleets where our vessels were cruising; the *copers* and their traffic had been—not *regulated*, but *relegated* to their native shores !

As the *Nautical Magazine* expressed it: " While no end of high personages are discussing this question, the Mission to Deep-Sea Fishermen has cut the knot, and smacksmen can now buy tobacco from the Mission-smacks, and therefore need not go to the *coper* any more. . . . Good thanks are due to the Mission. Make the *coper's* trade unprofitable, and unless he goes to sea for pastime, which is not likely, his presence and smack will cease to adorn the Dogger Bank."

The *copers* were driven out because the smacksmen by their conduct completely falsified the prediction, "They *will have* the drink, and if you give them their tobacco for *nothing*, they'll still go to the *coper* for grog." These much-maligned men have given abundant proof of an honest desire to do right and avoid temptation, and no one has more heartily rejoiced than the smacksmen themselves in the utter discomfiture, rout, and banishment of their *soi disant* friends.

There are, of course, several fleets where the foreign pest still holds undisputed sway, where the trade in gin and brandy is plied as briskly as ever. Since the opening sentences of this chapter were penned, I have heard of a fleet where three *copers* are now cruising, and where, to use the words of my informant, "they'll stay on to blast the lives of my brother-fishermen till you send a Mission-ship to drive 'em out."

That is a point which must be left to the readers of my narrative. It is for them to give the signal, and that done, the *copers* will vanish. But it cannot be too plainly stated that the Council of this Mission

P

can make no move in the direction indicated until
ample funds are placed at their disposal, not merely
to defray the prime cost of new vessels, but to cover
the expense of maintaining both the fabric of the
vessel and the various agencies for the spiritual,
moral, and physical benefit of the men in whose
fleets new ships have still to be stationed.

The pressing problem is how to increase our
annual income. Its solution is perfectly simple.
The necessary increase will be immediately forthcoming if all the readers of *Nor'ard of the Dogger*
pledge themselves to be annual subscribers, and to
use their influence with friends and neighbours
with a view to their following suit. If this were
done, if supporters of the Mission would set themselves earnestly to the task, and, risking rebuffs and
the cold shoulder, would plead for subscriptions, our
receipts would very speedily be *doubled*. Who will
assist to bring about a consummation so desirable ?

When once the great blue flag has been hoisted
in a fleet, the *coper's* day is over; and I long and
pray for the moment when this shall become a *fait
accompli*, for the glory of God, the benefit, soul
and body, of the smacksmen, and the gladdening
of many a poor woman's heart which to-day is
aching—aye, and must break, unless relief come
very soon.

.   .   .   .   .   .

Since the foregoing was in type a communication has reached me from the Board of Trade, which has also been published in the press, announcing that on the 16th of November 1887, the Convention above referred to was signed at the Hague, and that one of its provisions contemplates the absolute prohibition of the sale or barter of spirits in the North Sea. Of course this has still to be submitted to the respective Legislatures, but there can be little doubt as to its receiving Parliamentary sanction.

The adage, "Troubles never come singly," is being reversed, for the smacksmen are getting their good things in couples to-day! What was my delight to find upon my table an official letter marked "Customs," and commencing, "Sir, Her Majesty's Commissioners of Customs have reconsidered," &c. &c. There! I am not at liberty to quote the whole letter, but it amounts to this, that the experience of the past two years has convinced Her Majesty's Commissioners that the concession I sought in vain, as related in the previous chapter, would, if granted, prove a powerful lever in the hands of the authorities in the prevention of smuggling. Moreover, for the Mission it means a clear saving of the entire cost of employing one of the Mission-vessels solely as a tobacco carrier. For all this I devoutly thank God.

CHAPTER XVI.

"*FOR THE FURTHERANCE OF THE GOSPEL.*"

" How beautiful to us should seem the coming feet of such !
  Their garments of self-sacrifice have healing in their touch ;
  Their gospel-mission none may doubt, for they heed the
    Master's call,
  Who here walked with the multitude, and sat at meat with
    all ! "

As already mentioned, I had, in conversation with
an adverse critic, stated my belief that the sale
of tobacco by the Mission-smacks would not in
the slightest degree militate against their usefulness,
but would rather prove to be a highly advantageous
development of their legitimate mission character,
and would most certainly, in the language of Holy
Writ, " turn out for the furtherance of the Gospel."
Events have abundantly verified this forecast, and
served to justify the new departure of October
1885.

Even a cursory examination of the weekly sum-
maries furnished by the master of each Mission-
vessel, shows conclusively that great numbers of

men have visited the cruising Temperance Hall during the past two years with the object of obtaining tobacco, who but for that inducement would probably have found no sufficient attraction on board.

In glancing through the Reports, I notice such entries as " Forty this morning for tobacco," " Thirty-seven visitors for tobacco and books."

It must be observed that in the first of these cases fully two hundred and fifty men were represented, and a corresponding number in the second, for each purchase of the weed would be not for an individual merely, but for the entire crew of the smack in whose boat he came—the plan being, as already explained, to deliver fish to the carrier, and sub-sequently call alongside the Mission-vessel on the return journey.

It may be taken for granted that the actual callers would undoubtedly receive a word of counsel from any clergyman or lay missionary who might happen to be at hand, or, failing either, from the Mission-skipper or mate, but the effort would not end there. The recipient of good advice might or might not repeat it in the ears of his shipmates, but he would be certain to hand over to them a bag of books with which he might be intrusted.

It is therefore a standing though unwritten rule that the purchase of tobacco carries with it the pre-

scriptive right to become possessed of a supply of
literature, though alas! spite of incessant effort,
the stock with which we are able to furnish the
Mission-smacks from headquarters often runs lament-
ably short of satisfying the insatiable craving of
the fishing crews for " a bit o' reading."

On the principle that " a penny saved is a penny
gained," the empty tobacco cases, instead of being
broken up or tossed overboard, are brought into
Yarmouth at the close of each voyage and placed in
the care of the ship's-husband, by whom they are
forwarded to the offices when required.

An early-morning visitor to Bridge House—but
it would not do to be later than nine o'clock—would
be interested to notice a procession of men, each
of whom carries a heavy tobacco-case down the
steps to Blackfriars Pier, and presently a wherry is
observed putting off into the stream, rowed by a
couple of stout Thames watermen. If we follow
the boat through London Bridge we shall see her
pull alongside the tier of fish-carriers, when the
cases are hoisted out upon the steamer's decks and
transferred to the hold for conveyance to the various
fleets to which our agents are accredited. Two
days later they arrive at their destination, and are
transhipped in the small boat from steam-carrier
to Mission-smack. This process is not unobserved by
the crews of surrounding vessels. They scent the

BOOKS AND TOBACCO.

prey from afar, and presently swoop down in eager crowds upon the vessel bearing the "blue label." The tobacco cases are promptly burst open, and bags of books, bundles of unbound magazines, and illustrated papers are distributed amongst the numerous applicants. There is a brisk al fresco auction sale of woollen mufflers, mittens, and sea-boot stockings, and it not unfrequently happens that the cruising library is absolutely cleared out within an hour of the steamer's arrival. The moral of this story must be so obvious to all that it would be quite superfluous to attempt an application—*verbum sap !*

It will be apparent that even were the operations of the Mission confined to such labour as above depicted, a vast amount of humanising, elevating influence would be brought to bear upon the populations of those great deep-sea villages.

Here is a smacksman's opinion upon the matter, expressed in his own words :—" In the whole fleet there won't be no church, no gospel, no book to read, not a bit of help noway for the poor fellows —nothin' but the *coper*, leastways not unless one of the Mission-ships has joined the fleet. And if any of the lads get hurt or fall sick, there'll be neither doctor nor physic for him. If you'd been as long among trawlers as I've been, and knew their life as well, you'd wonder they weren't ten times coarser nor they be. No home, no church, no preacher, no

Bible—leastways not save the Christian men, and there are some good 'uns—no anything but the *coper*. That's what trawlers need, something better nor the *coper*. When they're home for a day or two for refitting they're so glad of a rest they don't take no heed; if you want to help the trawlers you must do it at the fleets."

Yes, that fisherman was right. The best time to reach the trawlers and to help them is when they are cut off from every other source of help, and the gratitude of the recipients is most touching to witness.

Out of hundreds of letters to the same effect which have reached me during the past two years, I give a few pointed extracts; *e.g.*, a Hull skipper writes :—" I, with many more, feel thankful, indeed, that your efforts have not been in vain in regard to the stopping of the traffic out here of the greatest curse of our nation, namely, drink. *Praise the Lord for that, I can solemnly declare that the six weeks I have been out, only one coper has been amongst us; he stayed about two hours.* I must confess he sold a few bottles of his poison—but *very few*—and went away, I feel certain, to return no more; and I, with hundreds, feel thankful to you, because we can get our smoke from the Bethel-ship, and clear from all temptation. The drink *must* be stopped by it; lives will be saved by it; and, glory to God, souls *will* and *are* being saved through the Mission work out here.

For my part I have great reason to rejoice, for *when we left Hull seven weeks since there were but two of us that feared God; but now, praise the Lord, O my soul, all the five of us are rejoicing in Him. Thank God for a praying crew!"*

And the following quotation from a letter dated Brixham, speaks for itself as to the opinion of the men of Devon, upon the advantages now enjoyed during their annual visits to the North-Sea fleets:—
"I now take the boldness, but pleasure, of writing you a line to let you know of the many blessings I, with many of my Brixham brother fishermen, have received through the instrumentality of the Mission-vessel *Cholmondeley* and her noble crew, while fishing with the Short Blue fleet in the North Sea the spring months of this year; and praise the Lord, that while myself, with so many others of the Lord's people, have had so many blessings to our own souls, we have been able to rejoice over many of the dear men, that have hitherto been living ungodly lives, coming out boldly for God. I have rejoiced many times when I have seen and proved the glorious work that is being done by God, through the Mission-vessels and their crews, for men that had hitherto been uncared for. *I find also that the copers that formerly used to be always with the fleets, and doing a good trade, now seldom show themselves. Praise the Lord for that!* Dear sir, please excuse my boldness

for writing this to you, but I thought that while so
many of us men that sail from this little port for the
North Sea every spring get such lifts heavenwards,
I could but write and express our gratitude to you
and the supporters of the Mission work, and pray
that God will bless you all with health, and strength,
and means, *that the time may soon arrive when we
shall see a Mission-vessel with every fleet in the North
Sea*, and also when the abundance of the sea shall
be converted to God."

Here again a fisherman testifies both as to the
prevalence of evil in former days and its happy
banishment by means of this new development of
missionary enterprise :—" I sailed in a vessel with
an ungodly skipper, and several times, when all our
money was gone and we wanted grog, we would
signal to the *coper* and tell him to lay by us until
it was dark.   He did so, and after dark we have
filled the boat with the ship's stores, and received,
in exchange, grog of about half the value of the
things which we gave him.   Since the Mission-
ships have been in the North Sea these *copers* have
not altogether been driven out—they show themselves sometimes—but when they see the Mission-
vessel with a flag on the stay, which means that she
has tobacco on board, they go somewhere else."

But alas ! those closing words, they go somewhere
else, does not mean that they return into port van-

quished. Disheartened they may be, for they feel
the circle of their nefarious operations gradually becoming smaller and smaller as the Mission-vessels
multiply, but they will not give up the fight so long
as there is a chance of prey in fleets where the blue
flag has not as yet been hoisted.

Here is another specimen:—"A *coper* sailed
through the fleet on Tuesday, and did not stop.
On Saturday another Dutch *coper* sailed through
the fleet, but he did not stop to sell his stuff here.
The Mission-vessel *Euston* seems in this fleet (the
Lowestoft steam fleet) to stop all progress of the
coper. Since she has been stationed here I have
only seen two *copers* stay with the fleet, and then it
has only been for a few hours."

Successful as the Mission had been in its earlier
stage, it is within the past two years that the work
has expanded with quite phenomenal rapidity, and
has, thank God, not merely been confined to the
fleets at sea, but has embraced the families on
shore.

Thus the skipper of the *Cholmondeley* writes:—
"A happy time this morning, twenty-three present;
forty-one present this afternoon, when nine signed
the temperance pledge. I was surprised to see the
old enemy the *coper* amongst our fleet to-day; the
devil means to have a try yet, but the Lord is
answering prayer in the Columbia fleet. He is

not only saving the men, but He is saving their wives too. *One man said that when he went home his wife could not make it out, to see him go on his knees by his bedside and pray; he said it made her cry like a child, and three days afterwards she gave her heart to the Lord. He said, 'Now, bless God, my home is like a little heaven.'*"

The skipper of the *Thomas Gray* reports, as evidencing how eagerly the opportunity afforded by the sale of tobacco is seized by the missionaries to reach the hearts of the men with the story of Divine love :—" While with the Columbia fleet, when we were surrounded with boats for tobacco, I noticed one man who seemed very restless. I went to him, and shook him by the hand, and said, ' Old friend, what is the matter ? ' He told me he was ill, and also how his sins troubled him, and I took him by the hand and led him down into the cabin. There I supplied him with some medicine for his bodily ailments, and then I pointed him to the Great Physician who was willing to heal the wounded spirit. He said, ' I have been such a great sinner that this Saviour you are talking about will not look at me.' I spoke of Jesus, and said, ' You must tell Him all your story, not the half; keep nothing back from Him, lay yourself at His feet, and tell Jesus you are sick of sin, and ask for forgiveness, and you will receive all that you need from the blessed Saviour. Now,' I said, 'we will tell the Lord all about it.' So we kneeled together in prayer. I asked the Lord to show him the plain way; but before I finished praying the Spirit of God had laid hold of his heart—the dumb spake, and the prayer went forth to God: 'My God, forgive me, for I am so wicked. Lord, wash my heart in Thy precious blood.'"

But, not content with merely disarming the *coper* and neutralising his power for evil, the agents of the Mission have not lost sight of the scriptural injunction, " If thine enemy hunger, feed him; if he thirst, give him drink; for in so doing thou shalt heap coals of fire on his head." A brief extract from one of Skipper Goodchild's letters, and which is but a sample of what has occurred elsewhere, shows that no opportunity was allowed to slip of proving to the foreigners the true motive actuating the conduct of the Mission.

Says the skipper:—" This morning, as we were lying astern of the fish-steamer, I noticed a boat going to the *coper*—which is named the *Swallow*— and I noticed that this particular boat after leaving the *coper* came rowing towards us. I looked over the side and said, ' Well, my lads, what is it you require ? ' One replied, ' If you please, can you give the mate of the *Swallow* some linseed, for he has poisoned his finger.' I hesitated a few moments. But I

remembered how kind you have been to us smacksmen, when my heart said, 'Surely you would have
given this poor fellow anything to have eased his
pain.' I thought, too, how mercifully God had
dealt with us, and blessed our Mission. So I
made him up a parcel containing linseed and salve,
and some lint, and some books, for we are taught,
'Bear ye one another's burdens, and so fulfil the
law of Christ.'" And I may add what the letter omits,
that no sooner had the boat pulled away, than earnest
petitions ascended from the cabin of the Mission-ship
that God would deign to bless the kindly deed.

Another skipper informs me :—" We sighted a
coper bearing down towards the fleet, but the old
fellow kept outside the greater part of the day, and,
as far we as could see, only one boat visited him. He
sailed past us towards evening, and we pointed signifi-
cantly to the Mission-flag flying at our masthead,
which he appeared to thoroughly understand."

Then we have two medical students, while spending their vacation on a Mission-ship, determining
to carry the battle into the heart of the enemy's
camp. They write :—" Having decided to give the
fishermen's enemy a call, we went on board his
vessel, and found him a most intelligent man, a
Belgian, acquainted with seven languages. He informed us that, owing to the action of the M.D.S.F.
in underselling the *copers*, trade was very bad, and

that this was his last voyage. He was going to give the business up, and engage in steam trawling for the future instead. We had some conversation with him as regards spiritual things, and he told us that two of his sons were priests, and he seemed quite familiar with the Gospel, although destitute of a saving knowledge of the truth."

Again, a skipper's report contains the following: —"In my last note I mentioned that another *coper* had just arrived. The next morning, while the boats were delivering the fish; he sailed boldly in and out amongst the vessels; but we were after him, following so closely that he was unable to do any business. I am glad to say that the next day, baffled and discomfited, he sailed away. We also sighted another one. In this case he came very close to the steamer, to entice the men on board; but he was disappointed. It seems as if the *copers* are making a determined effort just now to win back their trade, but the result, owing to the Mission-ships, is a complete failure. The only chance for the *copers* now is where there is no Mission-ship."

And once more:—" We have had several services during the week, and at each service ones and twos have come over boldly on the Lord's side. One *coper* arrived last week. He says the fishermen are all 'totes.' He stayed three days, and says he shall not come again. Another came and stayed two days. He tells me the fishermen have no money for him now. As I am writing another has come, but I am pretty sure he will soon have to go. They are going from fleet to fleet; but when they find there is a Mission-ship, they soon have to leave. Thank God! their day is over. May the time soon come when every fleet shall have its Mission-ship."

Yes, their day is indeed over, and all who have had the courage to peruse my story to this point will echo this good skipper's closing prayer.

Several times, at Ostend, at Rotterdam, and elsewhere, I have "come athwart" the *copers*—to use a nautical phrase—and on one occasion I had very good grounds for uneasiness as to the probability of being assaulted by the men whose designs upon the English smacksmen had been checkmated; however, they happily contented themselves with giving utterance to some very forcible curses, which would probably "come home to roost." Having had frequent opportunities of friendly intercourse with Belgian, Dutch, Danish, and German ports I have been kept *au courant* with the movements of the fishermen's wily foe, and the information has been turned to valuable account.

The decline of the *coper* traffic has been unquestionable, leaving no room for doubt that it only remained to station a Mission-vessel with every fleet in order finally to banish and destroy this floating pest. In this connection a friend recently told me the following story :—

A gentleman of his acquaintance, passing through Flushing, was interviewed by a local smack-owner, who offered him a very handsome yawl-rigged craft at a price so astoundingly low as to awaken suspicion of trickery. The English gentleman did not hesitate to express his surprise at such a small sum being asked.

"Oh," replied the owner, "zhe fact is, she was a ver goot *coper*, but those horrid Mission-ships have knocked our trade on zhe head, and she is of little use to me now."

Perhaps it was uncharitable, but my view was rather from the standpoint of the English wives and children than the foreigner's profits, and I confess to a feeling of unfeigned thankfulness on hearing this admission of defeat.

From what I have said as to the admiral's control over the movements of the fleet, it will be seen that should the admiral not be in sympathy it is in his power to render the task of the Mission-skipper a most difficult one. However, this matter, like all others connected with the work, has been carried to the Throne of heavenly Grace, and to-day four at least, if not more, of the admirals are as they themselves truly term it, "on the Lord's side."

Q

One admiral confessed, after he had come to the Saviour, that many times when he had kept the fleet sailing during the whole of Sunday, it was not, as he had pretended, because of the absolute necessity of changing the fishing-ground, but simply from a malicious pleasure in preventing the assembling of a congregation on board the Mission-ship. That admiral is to-day one of the most earnest and zealous Christians in the fleet, and delights to facilitate in every legitimate way the accomplishment of our object.

Another of these important officials lodged a formal complaint with the owners against the skipper of the Mission-ship in his fleet, and prayed that he might be removed. Now that skipper was a most excellent man, and when he came to me in great trouble seeking counsel, I simply said, " Let us kneel down and ask God to change his heart." We did so, and on rising, I added, " Now, skipper, see to it that, of all men in the fleet, you show to that admiral the greatest attention and kindness—just heap coals of fire on his head."

The method has proved marvellously successful, and recently, when there was a rumour of that skipper's removal to another fleet, the admiral was the first to propose " a testimonial of real affec-tion from all the men and lads to one who had shown them so much love and kindness."

When we on land desire to publicly announce our joy on the occasion of some crowning mercy, we set the bells ringing. This is not possible in the fleets, but the same object is achieved by the display of bunting, and the hoisting of numerous M.D.S.F. and other flags on the Lord's day is a distinguishing mark to-day of fleets where, years ago, the hours were too often spent in drinking and gambling.

In the light of the preceding remarks as to the admirals, there is an especial pleasure in reading the following brief but cheering statement :—

" May the Lord be praised for His love and mercy to us, for He has answered our prayers on behalf of our admiral, for we prayed that we might see a Bethel flag at his topmast head, and there it was last Sunday."

But here an admiral speaks for himself :—

" I beg to return you very many thanks for the presentation of the beautiful flag, and I assure you that my heart is full of joy at the thought that henceforth there will be no more floating grog-ships cruising among the fleets. Although I myself have never patronised them, I rejoice that our brave fishermen will not have the same temptation put in their way as hitherto. The tobacco we have been able to purchase at such a reduced price has been a very great boon to the fishermen, and I assure you that they are very grateful. In conclusion, my earnest prayer is—morn, noon, and night —that He that made the sea and all that therein is, may bless your labours with abundant success. Likewise I wish God-speed to all those good men and women that have so liberally contributed towards the spiritual and temporal welfare of the North Sea fishermen."

And another :—

" Concerning myself, I bless God that ever the Mission was brought in the North Sea. Though one of the vilest, I thank God I can testify that I am a sinner saved by God's grace, and that I am a living monument of His sparing mercy in answer to many prayers. Oh, may He help me to be a bright and shining light before my fellowmen ! " He adds :—" Now I must say a word concerning the great interest that is being taken in the fishermen, and of the great relief that is given daily from the dispensary. I have been an eye-witness of hundreds of men and boys getting relief from it, myself included, with a few words for the Master (what I call good seed sown by the wayside), and a bundle or bag of books into the bargain. God bless such grand work ! I can honestly say that our work here—I mean our daily occupation—is now carried on more steadily, soberly, and also honestly towards our employers. Drunkenness, as you well know, has been our chief obstacle in the way of salvation. I well remember the time myself when I visited the *coper* for drink, and saw the dear old *Cholmondeley* in the distance with the flag flying at the masthead to call sinners into God's service; but now, thank God! many of us can say, 'Old things have passed away, behold, all things have become new.' May the Great Jehovah bless you and yours while on this earth, is the earnest prayer of all my brother fishermen."

Yet one more admiral :—

"Excuse the liberty I take in sending these few lines to you on behalf of my fellow fishermen, to thank you and all helpers of the Mission for the gift of those scarfs and muffatees. We none of us mind the small trifle we have to pay for them, as that helps to extend the work in other ways. We are all very thankful to you for the medicine; I am sure it has been a great boon to all the fishermen of this fleet, for this winter the fishermen at large have had very severe colds,—in fact we do not know what we should do without a Mission-ship. I myself am very thankful that it was ever put into your heart to start the Mission, for it was by the presence of the Mission-ship and the kind missionaries that visit us in the summer, that I was led to see I was a lost sinner and that I needed a Saviour; and, thank God, I am like blind Bartimeus of old, once I 'was blind, but now I can see;' and

it is my earnest desire to see more of my fellow
fishermen converted unto Christ."

The skipper of the *Temple Tate*, Great Northern
fleet, writes : " Eight skippers came to our last
service, and in speaking to them personally, one
young skipper, who had merely come on board to
buy tobacco, and had been induced to remain for the
service, said, ' I have not been living as I ought, but
I will lead a new life.' I replied, ' Have you come
to Jesus ? '   ' No ; I cannot say I have.'   ' Then
why not come before this service is ended ? ' and I
pointed out to him the danger in delay : ' God says
now, my brother, *now* is the accepted time ; this is
the day of salvation.'   We sang the hymn—

> ' Sinner, how thy heart is troubled !
>   God is coming very near ;
> Do not hide thy deep emotion,
>   Do not check that falling tear.
> Oh, be saved ! His grace is free ;
> Oh, be saved ! He died for thee.'

At the close of the hymn he cried, ' Lord, have
mercy upon me, a poor sinner.'   Bless God for His
saving power !   Since I have been at home I have
received a letter from another Christian skipper,
stating that the vessel of which this dear young
man was skipper is missing, and all the crew.   The
vessel's boat has been found at sea with the skipper's
bag of clothes in it, and that is all that is known up

to the present. God speed on the Mission-vessels, for this is only one instance of the great good that is being done among the fishermen of the North Sea by the Mission-vessels. God grant that the time is not far distant when each fleet shall have its own Mission-vessel."

Here indeed are results calling for fervent thanksgiving from all Christian people—all who from their hearts offer the daily petition—

" Thy kingdom come ! "

And now, in closing this chapter of personal testimonies, let me refer to the important work carried on, each summer, with ever-increasing success, by the volunteer missioners who elect to spend their vacation among the trawlers. The first clergyman to visit the fleets in a Mission-vessel was struck, as I fully expected him to be, with the evident earnestness and fervour of the Christian men, and the eagerness with which the others listened to the Gospel message. Here are his own words:—" What perhaps impressed me most, was the fact that the ' returns ' vouchsafed to such work —if so we may venture to describe them—are so comparatively speedy and plain. In Christian work on shore, of almost all descriptions, this is only seldom the case. There the ' husbandman' has often to 'wait' in patience for the ' precious fruits of the earth.'

There, sowing and reaping have many weeks, if not many months even, between them. But it is far otherwise with those who seek to ingather the great 'harvest of the sea.' It is 'yes' or 'no' at once, as a general rule, with these sons of the sea when you tell them of the Gospel of Christ. And it is 'yes' or 'no,' also, in such a manner as not to leave you in much hesitation as to which of the two is intended. The man is either in tears, or else he is still in his sins. He is off on the right tack, or he keeps still on the wrong. To those who have to labour among settled congregations on shore, and very often, therefore, in a general atmosphere of mere acquiescence and semi-profession, the contrast is especially marked; and is likely, also, if I mistake not, to be of much use."

This opinion has often since been proved by other clergy to be sound and true.

Eleven clergymen were afloat in the Mission-ships in 1886, twelve in 1887, and their earnest, untiring labours were of the utmost value, the administration of the Lord's Supper on board being esteemed an especial privilege by the Christian fishermen. Where so many excellent clergy have devoted themselves to the work, it would be invidious to make selection. I therefore content myself with a few quotations, without mentioning names; *e.g.*, " I found no less than forty-six wait-

ing for the privilege of commemorating our Saviour's
dying love, and after a few words on 'This do, in
remembrance of Me,' I administered the sacred
memorials to as true-hearted a congregation as
perhaps I ever had around me. Most impressive it
was, on that far-off watery waste, in company with
fishermen such as formed the first-called disciples of
the Master Himself, thus to celebrate the central
act of all time."

This from a skipper's report:—"The Sabbath
morning came in beautifully fine, but we could not
expect much of a congregation because the fleet was
so small—only twenty vessels—the others all being
home for Lowestoft regatta. We mustered in all
fourteen souls, and a beautiful time we had of it.
The men enjoyed the Holy Communion service
greatly, saying how near it seemed to draw them to
the blessed Lord and His last supper on earth."

The master of another Mission-vessel writes:
—"I feel thankful to God for sending the Rev.
Mr. —— out here. The men are coming from far
and near to hear the blessed words which come from
God through His servant. Morning service, twenty
present; afternoon service, nineteen present; fifteen
stood and testified of the saving and keeping power
of Jesus Christ. Praise the dear Lord, two souls
came out for Christ! The men are very sorry to
lose the dear clergyman, for it seems as if He has

drawn their hearts towards him with sympathy and love."

Here is a picture of the intensity of earnest religious feeling which, thank God, is so manifest at sea:—"It was a sight ever to be remembered to see two large bunches of vessels all lashed alongside the *Temple Tate*, in the middle of the Hull fleet, and the *Thomas Gray* in the middle of the Grimsby fleet, both with their large Mission flags flying. I have never seen a sight like that myself before, and perhaps never may again. But I hope we shall, for it was grand, as all the crews could come to church, from the skipper to the cabin-boy. I wish some of our friends could have seen this sight; they would never doubt again as to the work done in reality by the Mission."

I have sought in this chapter to convey to the reader, as far as possible, the opinions and conclusions of others, and I cannot do better than close with the testimony of a dear friend who has several times left his parochial work on shore in order to spend a Sunday in the fleets.

After detailing the various ways in which the Gospel-ship has rendered herself essential to the fishermen, he adds:—"But, after all, it is as the scene of religious worship, and as the representative of that power that ministers to man's spiritual desires, that the Mission-smack is most appreciated.

It is the Sion of life to these men. Here influences work suited to quicken, to gratify, and to develop the mind and the heart.

"Frequently have fishermen told me that it was its connection with their spiritual nature that gave the Mission-smack its transcendent value in their estimation. It would, indeed, be difficult to convey to a cold-hearted churchgoer on land an adequate idea of the enthusiasm with which the men look forward to the services in this floating church. I can never forget my first Sunday on board. . . .

"On the following Sunday, after our daily intercourse during the week, the enthusiasm was, if possible, more intense. As I dwelt on the evidence, afforded in the order of things around us, and more especially in the gift of the world's Redeemer, that the Author of nature was fatherly, and desired our happiness, tears filled many eyes, and the offer of a free, full, and present salvation from the guilt and power of sin, through the atoning blood of Christ, was felt by them to be glad tidings of great joy. When the Holy Communion was celebrated at the close of my address, twenty-five seamen communicated. During this day nine men voluntarily signed the temperance pledge."

With the advent of fine weather, offers of assistance from clergy and laymen come by every post, and the smacksmen look forward eagerly to the

ministrations of the Gospel during each recurring
summer. We, who all the year round have the
church at our doors, can scarcely realise what it is
to these deep-sea fishermen to have amongst them,
out in the fleets, "the means of grace," the chance
to "assemble and meet together to hear His most
Holy Word," and, above all, the unspeakable privilege of receiving, on board the Mission-ship, the em-
blems "of His most meritorious Cross and Passion."

May we not heartily exclaim—

> " Praise to Thee for saved ones yearning
>   O'er the lost and wandering throng ;
> Praise for voices daily learning
>   To upraise the glad new song ;
> Praise to Thee for sick ones hasting
>   Now to touch Thy garment's hem ;
> Praise for souls believing, tasting
>   All Thy love has won for them."

CHAPTER XVII.

AN EXPEERIENCE MEETIN'.

"And, South or North, wherever hearts of prayer
Their woes and weakness to our Father bear,
Wherever fruits of Christian love are found
In holy lives, to me is holy ground."

ON one occasion I had the privilege of going amongst
the fishermen accompanied by two friends, a clergyman and a London editor, both of whom were anxious
to judge for themselves of the result of so much
evangelistic effort in a novel sphere. It was arranged
beforehand that we should as far as possible give the
rein to the smacksmen, and be ourselves listeners
and learners. I was exceedingly anxious that these
two gentlemen should hear direct testimony from the
lips of the men who had been benefited, and not be
content to draw their inferences from second-hand
information.

We reached our goal on Monday morning at
daybreak, and when the news spread through the
fleet that we were on board the Mission-ship, a
great number of skippers and men came off from

their vessels to join us, and by half-past ten our decks were filled by earnest, hearty, God-fearing men.

My *compagnons de voyage* had not been particularly happy physically, for the run out was made in the teeth of a strong wind, and Neptune had exacted his usual penalty. So it happened that, spite of the bright calm day, two of the party felt considerable disinclination to do aught but occupy a couple of deck-chairs, with their feet raised on an inverted fish-box.

Those fish-boxes were most useful. The skipper sent a couple of hands below, and speedily through the main hatchway empty fish-boxes were flying upwards and falling around on deck, until a sufficient number were provided to seat all our visitors.

Our devotions commenced by the singing of the well-known hymn, so dear to the fishermen—

> " All hail the power of Jesu's Name,
> Let angels prostrate fall ;
> Bring forth the royal diadem,
> And crown Him Lord of all."

This was followed by the General Confession, and an extempore petition suitable to the occasion, and then all present knelt upon the deck and joined reverently and devoutly in that wondrously comprehensive petition—the words, far, far better than any of our own—in which our Lord Himself taught

us to address the Almighty and Eternal One as
"Our Father which art in heaven." As we came
to the words "*Thy kingdom come*," my thoughts
flew back to the time long ago when, amongst
some of the very men now kneeling around me, I
had listened to words of blasphemy, and now, thank
God, they were as earnestly praying for the advent
of His kingdom as my friend Mr. Thompson and
I had done years before, when pained by the
utter carelessness and godlessness of the majority
around us.

After several more hymns and prayers, I gave a
brief address, and presently overheard the remark
from one of the congregation—a fisherman who
had merely come to the Mission-ship to oblige a
friend—"Jim, look at that 'ere loafin' parson!"
I instantly looked round, and was dismayed to see
one of my two companions fast asleep; so, closing
my Bible, I observed to a fine old skipper sitting
near—"My friends are very weary, and moreover
are not accustomed to these long services. Can't
we have some change?"

"By all manner o' means, sir; let's have an
expeerience meetin'."

"An experience meeting be it then," I replied,
and promptly woke up my slumbering friends to
listen to what proved to us landsmen by far the
happiest, most interesting part of the day's exercises.

It must not be assumed that what followed was self-glorification on the part of these men. The special charm to me was the distinctness and directness of the testimony borne by one after another to the love and power of our Lord and Saviour. It was not for one moment blowing their own trumpet or sounding their own praises, but in a very marked manner ascribing all honour and glory " to Him Who hath loved us and washed us from our sins in His own blood."

First rose the aged skipper to whom I had appealed, and in touching tones he said, " Bless the Lord, I've been on His side these forty years, and so I can't say as I owe my conversion to the Mission-ship ; but as I stand here to-day and look around me on this large congregation, gathered willingly and gladly together on the deck of this floating house of God, and then in my mind's eye look back to the time, not so very long ago, when there were only two besides myself in this great fleet who ' knew the joyful sound,' I am 'lost in wonder, love, and praise.' Friends, I'm an old man, and I've been a many long years at sea. The Lord in His grace has preserved me safely through gales and tempests, when those I knew and loved well have been suddenly snatched away, and I can say indeed ' Goodness and mercy shall follow (ay, and *have followed*) me all the days of my life,' and, the

Lord's Name be praised, I know that at my time of life it can be but a very little while before I shall be able to take up the rest of that beautiful verse, and say, 'I shall dwell in the house of the Lord for ever.' Friends, I feel as if I couldn't say much to you to-day, my heart's too full; but this I would say before you all, I rejoice that I've been spared to see this day, and I feel inclined to take up the words of Simeon and say, 'Now, Lord, lettest Thou Thy servant depart in peace, according to Thy word, for mine eyes have seen Thy salvation.' It seems at times almost too good to be true ; but then I look across from my own little smack, and see this noble vessel with her great flag flying to invite us all aboard ' to hear His most Holy Word,' and I say to myself, 'No, old fellow, it's no dream ; the prayers of all the long years of weariness and darkness have been answered at last.' And then, my friends, as I've looked on, and seen the wonderful gathering in of precious souls for Christ, seen God's dear servants coming out and staying aboard the Mission-vessel, and holding services, and visiting from smack to smack, I've praised the Lord again with all my heart, and said in the words of the Psalmist, ' *This is the day which the Lord hath made ; we will rejoice and be glad in it.*' Friends, this, as you know, is my la..t voyage amongst you. The way has been opened for me to cast anchor ashore

R

and end my days on dry land, and I can't say
I'm sorry; and if there's one thing that helps to
make me feel the parting less, it's the knowledge
that you've got this blessed vessel amongst you
to be a comfort and a help to you in so many
ways."

As this dear old patriarch resumed his seat, there
was not a dry eye in the assembly. He had borne
for very many years a faithful testimony amongst
them for his Saviour, and every one, even the most
depraved, had respected him for his quiet, consistent
piety. After a moment's pause, Skipper J——— burst
forth in a song of praise. The words were unknown
to my friends and myself, but the fishermen knew
them well, and joined with much fervour. It was
not a long hymn—only one verse and a chorus, but
it harmonised closely with the remarks to which we
had all been listening with so much interest, and
contained expressions of thanksgiving for Divine
mercy in the past and of trust for the future.

Then followed in quick succession testimony after
testimony to the good which had been wrought on
board the " Bethel-ship," as the majority preferred
to style the Mission-vessel; and indeed from what
was stated it was abundantly clear that the ship had
proved to many of them " none other than the house
of God and the gate of heaven." It was most encouraging to hear so many own the saving power

of the Gospel of Christ, and in most cases bear testimony to the fact that their conversion had resulted from the evangelistic efforts on board the Mission-vessel. In one case it was incidentally remarked—and I cite it in proof of the foregoing statement—that on the occasion of the Mission-smack leaving for home at the close of her voyage some months previously, nineteen skippers of vessels had attended the valedictory prayer-meeting, *seventeen of whom were men who had learned to trust the Saviour on board the " Bethel-ship."*

Another Christian skipper told how three years before, when Mr. S—— was out in the Mission-smack, he had insisted on boarding the Belgian *coper,* and after faithfully pointing out to the foreign captain the evil of his ways, he had asked and received permission to suspend a " Sailor's Scripture Text-Roll."

" The next year," continued the narrator, " Mr. S—— came amongst us again, and one of the first things he did on the Saturday afternoon was to have the boat out and pull away to the old *coper.* There was the text-roll still hanging in the cabin, turned down to the words, ' *Be not deceived ; neither . . . thieves, nor covetous, nor drunkards shall inherit the kingdom of God.'* Mr. S—— again spoke so solemnly to the Belgian skipper, that he seemed greatly affected ; and at last, when the

missioner urged him to come aboard the Bethel-ship
to the services of the following day, he said, ' No, sir,
I vill not come. It is true I might myself be vid you
at ze sarevice; but my vessel would be then, like
yours, right in ze middle of ze fleet, and that would
be a bad thing. Vat you haf said has make me vary
miserable, and I vill show you I am in earnest by
taking my vessel right away.' Sure enough, as we
were pulling to the seven-o'clock prayer-meeting next
morning, there was the *coper* full ten miles away in
the wind's eye, and there was neither grog nor 'bacca
sold in the fleet *that* day. Well, gentlemen, the first
thing on Monday morning the *coper* came back again,
and sailing round the Mission-ship, hailed for Mr.
S——. He was soon aboard, and he told us
afterwards as the foreign skipper was reg'lar broke
down, and says he, ' I vill not any more carry on
this trade; I vill go back to Ostend, and sell my
vessel and go fishing.' Well so he did, an' since
that time he's bin skipper o' a steam-trawler; but
there was plenty more of them fellers to come and
take the berth, though it didn't last long, for before
the winter the Mission-ship had begun to sell 'bacca
at a shilling a pound, and then the *copers* had to
put their helms hard over, an' let go their foresail,
and away to some fleet where there was no Mission-
ship. And now I say let's pray that God 'll tell some
more folks ashore to buy Mission-ships, till there's

one of 'em for every fleet, and then it'll be good-
bye for ever to the *copers*."

"Speaking of *copers*, I should like to tell you,
friends," said another skipper, " of an incident that
occurred one Saturday when I was in the Grimsby
fleet. Two Dutch *copers* hove in sight and bore down
to our fleet, and as I looked I thought of the times
when I have seen these floating gin-shops cause a
deal of trouble and sin and death ; and I could but
pray that it might not be so now. I expected the
crews of the vessels would board them as soon as
they reached us, but to my surprise and joy there
were but two or three as did. Admiral Dixon sailed
round them, and invited the captain of one of the
copers to come on board the *Temple Tate* for the
services next day. He replied, ' I know you are
right, and if there was anything worth stopping in
this fleet for, I would come to-morrow.' They lay-
to with the fleet about two hours, after which they
bore away in different directions to seek after another
shoal of human fish that would be more ready to
take their bait. Another skipper, who was standing near me as I watched their departure, exclaimed, 'I never saw it like that before ; praise
the Lord ! ' "

When this man had spoken, several others engaged in prayer, and afterwards there were some
most gratifying incidents related illustrative of the

immense benefit conferred by the dispensary. The Mission-skipper related how he had attended to no fewer than forty patients in one morning after a three-days' gale. Then came an old fisherman, whose weather-beaten visage fully endorsed his announcement of "six-and-thirty years at sea, gentlemen, an' that's a longish bit, you know."

"It is indeed," I observed. "For my own part, I think six-and-thirty *hours* of what you fellows call 'strong wind' would be quite enough for an average landsman."

"Six-and-thirty *hours!*" exclaimed my clerical friend; "I have been all over the world in big steamers, and so can lay claim to some experience; but I'd rather take a whole voyage, such as I have been accustomed to, with a long swell and generally equalised motion, than have six-and-thirty *minutes* in a smack with such a choppy sea as we had yesterday. It gave me the sensation of being violently jerked and shaken to pieces. I have hardly recovered yet, and am bruised from head to foot."

This statement caused much amusement to the men, and one big brawny fellow, who looked as though he, at all events, was not a candidate for treatment, remarked, " Well, sir, anyhow, if you was broke to bits, the skipper here 'ud be able to put you together agin down below, now he's so clever at chemistry. Why, I seed him myself only last week mendin' a fellow up as had got his arm broke. It's a fine thing is that chemistry, an' we're right proud of our fisherman-doctor, I can tell you."

"*Surgery,* you mean—not chemistry," quietly interposed the skipper.

"All right, old chap," replied the giant; "call it what yer likes, so long as you go ahead on the same tack as you've begun; for I reckon it's the biggest blessin' out is that there dispensary, as you call it."

"Ay, that it is," was the loudly expressed response from the crowd on the fish-trunks.

"Now, my old friend," said I, turning to the ancient mariner, who all this time was standing by my side patiently awaiting a chance to continue his remarks, "this interruption is all my fault, and I must apologise to you for being so rude. We had just heard your opening sentence about 'six-and-thirty years at sea.'"

"Please don't, sir, please don't 'pologise. I'm rather glad for what has bin said, for that talk about the dispensary an' the blessin's of to-day jist tuk my mind back to them old days when fust I went to sea—ay, and for many a long year arterwards, when there wern't no such blessin's at all, an' poor chaps had to bear their aches an' their pains till they got home; an' if they was so bad as they couldn't bear 'em no longer, why they was put aboard the cutter an' sent home along o' the fish. Not the *steam* cutter, you'll mind, gentlemen, for that was long afore the days o' steamboats carryin' the fish—but a sailin' cutter, as depended on the wind to get her into port. Why, it's been bad enough, God knows, this last twenty years to be shipmates wi' broken bones for full two days afore you could get alongside the doctor, but at the time I'm a-talkin' about, I've knowed a poor fisherman put aboard the cutter after the boom had fallen on him in a gale o' wind, an' smashed his arm an' his leg an' one or two ribs. Well, after that gale it come on calm weather, an' the cutter was five days afore she fetched her market."

As the old man paused, I thought he had finished, and asked—

" Well, what became of the injured man ? "

" What became of him ? Why, what could become of him ? He died, sir—he died ; an' lots more have died, as I can myself rekerlect, all because they had none o' these blessin's as you people ashore have got on all sides o' you. You thought I'd done just now 'cause I stopped sudden. No, sir ; I could go on for hours a-tellin' you o' things as 'ud make your flesh creep ; but what's the good ? I only stopped just now 'cause when I begins about these old days a bump comes in my throat like, an' I wants jist to get away in a corner, and weep for joy and thankfulness. Oh, gentlemen, I'm but a simple old fisherman, an' I never learned to read till arter I got to know the blessed Saviour, an' p'raps I can't put my ideas into proper words like you would; no, nor even like some o' my brother-fishermen who've had the advantage of a good edication. But I'll tell you, gentlemen, I've got a heart, an' I feels overflowin' with praise to God this day when I looks around me an' sees this fine ship all crowded with smacks-men, and I realise that it's our own ship— our very own—or p'raps I ought to say, the Blessed Lord's ship, where He invites us to come, an' where we can get food for the mind, an' healin' for the body, and warm things as the ladies sends."

"God bless the ladies!" interposed another old skipper, and the whole congregation, as with one voice, raised a mighty shout of "Ay, God bless 'em!"

I turned to my friends and observed, "How I wish all the ladies who are busily working for these men could hear that expression of genuine gratitude!"

"Well, gentlemen," resumed the speaker, "I was agoin' to say myself, 'God bless the ladies!' but my old friend here took the wind out o' my sails.

Howsomever, we all jined him, and we all mean it too. Then there's the other blessin' o' these Bethel-ships, an' that is, they've just knocked them old *copers* into the middle o' next week." ("I hope they're knocked a deal farther off than that, my friend," I exclaimed.) "Well, sir, it's only a way o' talkin', yer see, to say what I said, for I knows they're knocked clean to shivers. An' let me tell ye, gentlemen, it 'ud never a' been done but for that 'bacca." ("Hear, hear," from the congregation.) "If these 'ere ships had come out here just preachin', why you might a' preached yourselves black in the face (laughter); but you may believe me, the reason why you've won the hearts o' my brother fishermen is all along o' the way you've gone to work." ("That's it, Bill," struck in the admiral.) "Now, when the admiral put his oar in, I was jist agoin' to add as the Blessed Lord Himself must a' guided you." ("He has, bless Him!" shouted Skipper J——.) "He must a' guided you to do these things 'cause He loved the fishermen, an' sent these ships along to call the fishermen of the North Sea, jist as He did them other fishermen when He was on earth. Now, gentlemen, I ain't a parson, an' you must excuse me if I don't put it jist in order, but I've bin thinkin' a lot about it, an' lookin' at them chapters in the blessed Gospel as tells the whole story o' how the Lord won them fishermen, an' it seems to me—I'm not agoin' to preach to you, gentlemen; you can see it in your own Bibles, an' I make no doubt you have seen it a'ready—it seems to me as He didn't go to 'em, merely SAYIN', ' Now, you men, I love you,' but right from the very beginnin' an' on to the end He PROVED as He loved 'em. An' now He's jist the same lovin' Lord to-day as He was in them old days, an' He said to you, ' Go along there into the North Sea among them fellers as don't love Me a bit, jist 'cause they don't *know* Me, an' when you gets to 'em, jist patch 'em up when they're ill an' sick an' hurt, an' give 'em lots o' good things for their bodies, an' then, when you've done all this, an' got 'em round yer a-thankin' yer, why jist up an' tell 'em as I sent yer to do it 'cause I loves 'em an' died for 'em.' " (" That's just like Him," said Skipper J—— again.) " Now, gentlemen, I'm not agoin' to keep yer any longer, an 'p'raps you'll think I'm a rummy old feller to talk like this 'ere; but I'm so full o' joy, so full o 'praise to my Blessed Master for all His love to me an' my dear brother-fishermen, that I felt bound jist to say what I have, an' I hope as you'll go and tell all the Christian ladies and gentlemen on shore that the fishermen at sea are grateful to them, an' are prayin' for 'em, an' are lookin' forward to standin' with them afore the Throne, to sing for ever the praises of our Blessed Saviour. Amen, Amen ! "

At this point I interposed, saying, I want to read to you a short poem of three verses which a lady on shore has composed for you. She heard me mention, in a lecture, your hearty greeting of "What cheer—O? What cheer?" so she sat down at home afterwards and wrote these lines, to which she has given the title "The Song of the Gospel Smacksmen," though I am afraid we can't sing it until some other good friend composes a tune. Now listen :—

WHAT CHEER—O? WHAT CHEER?

(The usual form of greeting to a passing vessel.)

We have a treasure of worth untold,
  It was the gift of our Captain's love ;
Rarer than pearls, and richer than gold,
  And free as the winds above.
Our Captain won it in mortal strife,
  In pangs of horror that none e'er knew ;
It is the gift of Eternal Life !
  This is our treasure—what have you ?
                    What cheer—O ? What cheer ?

We have a precious freight aboard,
  Of comrades drawn from the depths of sin
In the Gospel net that we cast abroad ;
  By ones and twos we have brought them in.
And every day we try for more—
  Oft and again we catch them too !
And we mean to gather a glorious store.
  This is our cargo—what have you ?
                    What cheer—O ? What cheer ?

TEA AFTER SERVICE.

P. 268.

We have a haven in yonder skies ;
   The harbour lamps shine into the night
To cheer our hearts and gladden our eyes
   With their beauteous, clear. and golden light.
Our Captain will welcome us all at last
   To His own dear home on those peaceful shores,
Where wild nor'-easters all are past.
    There is our port—oh, where is yours ?
                What cheer—O ? What cheer ?

The hours had flown by. With the exception of a brief half-hour for refreshment on deck—when my friends had the opportunity of noting the remarkable aptitude of North-Sea smacksmen for stowing away mugful after mugful of tea—there had been a continuous succession of spiritual exercises since 10.30 A.M.

The evening was now drawing in, and the admiral intimated his intention of returning to his own vessel, as, should a breeze spring up after the calm day, he would not fail to " put to."

Before he left, however, we all gathered round the capstan, while the clergyman read a portion of Holy Scripture : " These things have I spoken unto you, that in Me ye might have peace. In the world ye shall have tribulation : but be of good cheer ; I have overcome the world."

Very impressively did he deal with the passage ; but the reader can easily supply what I have not space to recapitulate here. Suffice it to say, that the man who had made the insulting remark about the "loafin' parson"—a skipper who had been one of the *coper's* regular customers—sobbed forth, as I grasped his hand at parting, "Oh, sir, I wish I had that peace as the gentleman was talkin' about!" Thank God, not many days elapsed before that man was led to the Saviour for pardon, and obtained the peace he so sorely needed.

As the last of our guests departed the cabin clock struck seven, and my friend the editor exclaimed, "Well, never in my life before did I attend a service lasting eight hours and a half, and never before have I been so intensely interested, nor so struck with the evident reality of simple faith and trust which seems to characterise these men."

The steward now summoned us below to dinner, and we three afterwards paced the deck for several hours recalling the events of that most interesting day.

"I have many times, at missionary meetings, joined in the well-known hymn commencing ' Jesus shall reign where'er the sun,' " remarked one of my companions ; " but after to-day's experience the line, ' *His kingdom stretch from shore to shore,*' will ever have to my mind a new force and meaning, for it is not merely ' the kingdom ' being established *upon* the different shores, but upon the intervening sea also."

And thus, in the bright moonlight, we talked

together of the Lord we loved, " Who had loved us and given Himself for us," and to Whom we, and the smacksmen in whose company we had spent the day, and all His people everywhere, would soon be gathered home.

CHAPTER XVIII.

CRITICISMS AND OBJECTIONS.

" Who murmurs that in these dark days
His lot is cast?
God's hand within the shadow lays
The stones whereon His gates of praise
Shall rise at last."

NUMEROUS correspondents have addressed inquiries to me upon the burning question of the price charged for fish, and how much of it ever reaches the pocket of the smack-owner or smacksman. It would be quite impossible to deal exhaustively with such a subject in these pages, and I will content myself with the following contribution.

One of the largest Billingsgate auctioneers once told me, that although the West-End fishmongers purchase " prime " fish at high prices, the average result of a morning's sale in the wholesale market depended largely upon the costermongers. The reader will understand this when I quote the details of a summer-night's catch dispatched to market from one vessel, *e.g.* :— .

1 trunk soles.
1 turbot.
2 trunks plaice.
40   ,,   haddock.

In this case the "prime" fish is purchased by the well-to-do tradesman, whose establishment contains every modern appliance for cooling the atmosphere and preserving his stock from deterioration. Yet even he abstains from large transactions, both on account of the heat, and because the West End of the town is practically empty.

But let us turn to the "offal" fish. In the winter the plaice would realise 18s. per trunk, and the haddock 12s. On this particular morning they sell for 4s. 6d. and 1s., and some mornings there are no bids at all, as in one case where I myself saw seventy-five trunks of haddock, in splendid condition, ruthlessly condemned by the inspector because the morning's market was over; no one had offered to buy them, and they would not keep until the next day.

The reason for this is obvious. The coster-monger—that person of rough exterior and forcible if inelegant English, whose manners certainly "have not that repose which marks the caste of Vere de Vere"—is withal a shrewd, hard-headed, quick-witted man of business, having, moreover, that qualification which gives to any buyer an

S

immense advantage in the markets—the possession
of hard cash.

Individually, the costermonger has, of course, far
less capital than the purchaser of "prime;" but
since the owners of barrows stand towards the tenants
of showy and heavily rented shops in the proportion
of a hundred to one, and there are tons of "offal" fish
as compared with hundredweights of the more expensive kinds, it is clear that, as a man expressed it to
me, "It's the *many* agin the *money*, don't yer see,
sir? and when the *many* says, 'Blowed if I'll buy
fish to-day,' why that means as they *won't* buy it;
an' when they make up their minds as they *won't*, I
should jest like to see who's agoin' to compel 'em;
and so that makes a bad market for the catcher.
In corse we're all sorry as it should be so, but then
yer can't expect the costermonger to make a hass of
'isself an' lose his money all to please the fisherman
—t'aint likely."

The costermonger is wise in his generation, and
while trundling his barrow or driving his "moke"
towards Lower Thames Street at two o'clock on an
August morning, there may be dense mists rolling
upwards from the river, but no fog dims his clear
mental calculations. Jingling his coin, he turns
over in his mind the important question whether it
will pay him better that day to buy fish, which, as
he hawks it through the streets, must lie for hours

in the full blaze of the summer's sun, becoming each moment less saleable, or whether a barrow-load of St. Michael's pines or of tortoises would bring a larger return for his investment of ready cash. There can be but one answer; and as the same calculation is being made simultaneously by hundreds of men while converging from all parts of town on one common centre, and in every case with the same result, it comes to pass that, for that morning at all events, prices will range low in the fish-market, and the spirits of ·smack-owners and smacksmen will be depressed in proportion when the returns of the morning's business are communicated to them.

•　　　•　　　•　　　•　　　•

The constant applications I received relative to the " price of fish," as this term is generally understood, induced me to pen a short booklet bearing that title, which I rejoice to say has proved very useful to the Mission.

Its publication led, however, to a few amusing mistakes; as, for instance, the following.

"You have perpetrated an atrocious hoax," said a gentleman to me one day.

It struck me as scarcely " parliamentary " language, and I inquired his meaning.

" Why, you have written a pamphlet called ' *The* -

Price of Fish,' and when some one sent it to my wife, she naturally assumed it to be a treatise on some means of reducing the household expenditure. Imagine her annoyance when, on reading the first few lines, she discovered it to be another of the many dodges for extracting money."

" I cannot admit that the pamphlet is a dodge," I replied, " nor its title misleading ; but tell me, did your wife read on to the end ? "

" Certainly not," said my visitor ; " she threw the pamphlet in the waste-paper basket."

" Then here is another copy, and I ask as a great personal favour that you will take it home this evening and read it aloud to your wife from cover to cover."

He agreed, and a few days later I received a letter enclosing a £10 cheque " in part payment of our fish-bill."

   .   .   .   .   .

" Why do the smacksmen go to sea at all in the winter ? " inquired a lady.

" Madam, they go to sea in order that your dinner-table may be furnished with its second course."

Said another lady, " I have made you some woollen things for the fishermen, but on second thoughts I am giving them away in my own village, for of course the poor fellows are not out at this time of year."

Oh, the number of absurd inquiries and remarks which have been addressed to me upon this matter of winter-trawling! One friend, a most generous helper of all good works, spoke very strongly against the practice.

"Very well," I replied; "it is, after all, merely a question of philanthropy. You are a philanthropist; but philanthropy will have its cod, and sole, and turbot. Do you say you would dispense with fish for six months every year in order to avoid this shocking waste of human life? Very good. Now let us see what your philanthropy is prepared to do—the lengths you are willing to go. You think that a general abstention from fish between October and March would be a practical step in the right direction. You would do this as the only means of rendering the loss of life at sea during the winter months absolutely impossible. But please bear in mind that, during the whole of that period of enforced idleness you would be compelled to maintain not only the thousands of smacksmen, with the added thousands of wives and children, but your philanthropic action must extend to the crews of the carrying steamers and their families, the smack-owners, the fish merchants, and the fishmongers, besides the army of trades-

men—shipwrights, sailmakers, blockmakers, black-
smiths, porters, boys, &c. &c.—who depend for
their daily bread upon this great national industry.
No, no, my friend; we must make propositions
bearing some relation to common sense."

With regard to the loss of life by "boarding"
or "ferrying" fish from the catcher to the carrier,
I have spoken elsewhere of the possibility of providing suitable life-jackets as a safeguard against
accident, and have cited cases in which the use of
them has made all the difference between life and
death; but the question is an exceedingly difficult
one, and can perhaps best be settled by wise legislation.   Not what is known as "*panic* legislation,"
nor one-sided legislation, resulting from the action
of any particular clique, either of employers or
employed.   Speaking as an observer, and profoundly
impressed with the necessity of additionally safe-
guarding human life, I should recommend that
the admiral of each fleet have plenary powers with
regard to the delivery of fish.   Nominally he has
such powers now, but I am unaware of any penalty
attaching to disobedience.

Such an occurrence as that mentioned in Chapter
IX. ought to be impossible, and would be, were the
admiral legally authorised to order the steam-
carriers out of the fleet.   If that were so, and every
act of disobedience on the part of a skipper ren-

dered him liable to penal consequences, we should soon hear less of the terrible waste of life in the trawling fleets.

I have before mentioned how much these men are—like the rest of the world—governed by example. There has been a " smart fishing-breeze " during the night, resulting in a heavy catch, and all hands are rejoicing in the prospect of increased poundage; but while the crew have been engaged in cleaning the fish, the breeze has freshened into a strong wind, and the skipper · sees with deep regret his amount of poundage becoming smaller and smaller; for that fish will clearly not be worth as much in the market if kept on board till next day as it would if ferried at once to the carrier and iced down in the hold.

It is very tantalising. True, the admiral has hauled off clear of the carrier; but there lies the steamboat close at hand, her decks clearly visible as she rolls and wallows in the surging seas, and the skipper carefully calculates the chances of his boat's crew making the short journey safely, and when presently he sees another smack sending her boat away, he hesitates no longer, but immediately follows suit. Of course there is a chance of the rash venture succeeding, which in itself would be almost regrettable, as, emboldened by the success of the one experiment, there would be less hesitation on a future occasion ; but, on the other hand, there are ninety-nine chances of disaster, and I am disposed to say that the loss of life resulting therefrom would properly come under the category of " preventable " accident.

The poor fellows who are lost under such circumstances are clearly sacrificed to the greed for gain, the very meanest of human motives, and I should be glad to learn that such inexcusable conduct on the part of any skipper rendered him liable to the ordeal of a Board of Trade inquiry. And knowing how powerfully the incentive to obtain the highest possible market-price acts upon the minds of these men, I repeat that the admiral should, in the exercise of his discretion, be empowered to order the carrier to steam several—say ten—miles clear of the fleet in bad weather, and thus remove temptation from men whose anxiety to make a good voyage might result in some of them making their final voyage, and causing irreparable loss and sorrow in happy cottage-homes on shore.

.   o   .   .   .

The first essential of missionary effort upon the high seas is a Mission-*ship*. It is evident that neither clergy nor lay missionaries can deliver their message from the crest of a wave, nor can a doctor advantageously treat his patients unless he

have at all events a dispensary and, if possible, a
hospital.   But let us assume the case of a trawling
fleet perfectly provided with all that the most
approved type of Mission-vessel implies for the
spiritual, moral, and physical well-being of the men
—at once the church, chapel, hospital, dispensary,
library, club, temperance-hall, and school.   When
a vessel possessing all these qualifications has been
provided, the entire cost defrayed, and all the various
machinery for good is in full working order, there
remains this hard fact to be faced—and it is well
that supporters of this Mission should have it clearly
placed before them—that, given the most favourable
auspices, the conditions under which mission-work
is carried on at sea must always differ essentially
from those governing similar efforts on shore.   We
are all familiar with the routine incidental to the
formation of a new district from an existing parish.
The temporary iron church is in due time followed
by the more permanent and costly structure; and
when at last the lofty spire dominates the whole,
there is general jubilation, and vicar, church-
wardens, and parishioners congratulate themselves
upon being not merely out of debt, but having no
possible liabilities looming in the future.   There
stands the solid building, and there it will probably
remain to be used by future generations of wor-
shippers.

Now let us consider the case of the vessel which
bears all the titles enumerated on the preceding page.
A generous friend pays for the building and equip-
ment, and everything works smoothly for the first
fortnight of her voyage.   The men of the fleet are
rejoicing in their new-found privileges, wondering
how they could possibly have managed to go through
life so long without them, and what would happen
were they again deprived of them.   All goes merrily,
when lo! the barometer falls, the sky is overcast, a
gale bursts upon the fleet; the most careful seaman-
ship is powerless in the face of what marine insurance policies truly term "the act of God;" and
when the storm abates, and numbers of poor fellows
are eager to seize the first opportunity of boarding
the hospital-ship, what is their dismay on finding
that she has sustained such damage as to necessitate
her immediate return to port for repairs!   This has
already happened with one of our Mission-vessels;
the experience may be repeated in the very next
storm; and it is precisely this contingency which,
apart altogether from ordinary wear and tear of
sails and running gear, must always be present to
the minds of those who " have their occupation in
great waters."

.   .   .   .   .

Once—and I am thankful to say *only* once—was
it suggested to me that the results possible of

achievement were not commensurate with the cost of attaining them; that for the sake of succouring 12,000 men the expenditure of so many thousands of pounds was out of all reasonable proportion.

Miserable calculator! It cost the life of the Son of God to purchase your salvation, and would you reckon the value of a soul, let alone the enormous physical benefits conferred, at so many pounds sterling? Go to Christ and get your own soul purified!

" But," wrote another critic, " why must there be this risk and loss? Cannot you trust the Lord to take care of the vessels? Have you no faith in His protecting hand over His people?"

Yes, we can indeed trust the Lord, but the Lord is not going to make smooth seas for us because our vessels happen to be Mission-ships. You would not assert that those dear fellows have no faith who for years have been going to the Congo and dying off like flies in the unwholesome climate. They say, and say rightly, " We go in *spite* of the climate; we are ready, if needs be, even to die rather than leave the heathen without the knowledge of Christ." The Master's command was absolute—" Go ye into all the world." There was no saving clause, *"provided always that the climate suits you."*

And so with ourselves. If we go to sea,

especially in the winter-time, we go with our eyes open to the risk involved; and if we are not sufficiently enamoured of our Master's cause to be prepared to face all dangers in His service, why we had better stay comfortably at home and make room for truer men.

A timid friend asked one day, "Do you think it right to risk the lives of good men by sending these vessels to sea in the winter season? Would it not be wise to lay them up in port until the spring?"

Yes, it would no doubt be very wise indeed, with that worldly wisdom which teaches us to "take care of Number One,"—the wisdom which wraps itself round with a cloak of selfishness, which consults its own ease, and does not concern itself about the needs of others,—the wisdom which taught the priest and the Levite to pass by on the other side.

Keep the Mission-ships in port during the winter! Why, it is just then that they are most needed. True, evangelistic and other services cannot be held. The stormy seas, the brief hours of daylight, the incessant toil, all these are against any general gathering for religious purposes. But it is evident that for coughs, and colds, and fevers, sprains, bruises, gashes, contusions, and fractures, the winter is a veritable harvest-time. Poor fellows! poor fellows! I blush to contemplate such conduct towards them! To think of sending out Mission-vessels in the summer season—the *yachting* season—the very time when fair-weather sailors like nothing better than a cruise in the North Sea; and then, forsooth, because the gales blow and the seas break on board, and there is general discomfort and frequent danger, we will deprive the smacksmen of succour in the time of their greatest need! I venture to predict that when the Mission-ships put to sea again the following spring, they would be howled out of the fleets; and richly would such a reception be merited.

No; this Mission was undertaken to meet the needs of the "toilers of the deep," and it would be utterly unworthy of its title were its ministrations to cease when the demand for them is greatest and their results most valuable. Why is it that the Mission is to-day held in high esteem by the whole body of smacksmen? I believe nothing has conduced so much to this as the fact—proved to them again and again—that, blow fair, blow foul, its agents are always at their post, and always in earnest.

"What brings these 'ere Bethel-ships cruisin' around at this time o' year, Bill?" said a man who had shipped from another fleet not privileged to possess one.

"What brings 'em ? " said Bill. " Well, I'll tell yer first what *don't* bring 'em, old lad. You may be sure as they don't come cos they *likes* it, and they sartinly don't come for what they makes out o' it in the money way ; and as for what they *does* come for, why I guess yer'll find out for yerself if yer pisins yer 'and with a fish-bone, or gets the roomatics, or breaks yer leg, or wants a tooth tuk out ; for they'll jolly soon doctor yer up, an' charge yer nothin' for the job, instead o' you gettin' sent to Lunnon aboard the carrier. Now, man, what does they come for ? "

"Why, Bill, if it's all true as you say, it seems as if they come just for the pleasure o' doing good."

"You're right, old fellow ! you're right; that's just what they *does* come for, and I say God bless 'em for it ! "

The skippers, and as far as possible the crews, of the Mission-vessels are chosen for this service by reason of special aptitude. They are men selected from the class whose good we are seeking to promote, and they would be shocked indeed by the suggestion that they should quietly stay in port while their brother fishermen are in need of their presence and help.

Yes, we must admit that it is sad indeed—and I speak from bitter experience—to lose the lives of good men. But how infinitely more sad when those who are lost are not trusting in Christ as their Saviour, and have no thought or hope beyond this present life! I conceive it, therefore, to be of the highest importance that Christian men should prove to these toilers how intensely real and practical is true Christianity : that their very presence in the fleets should say, as it were, " Here we are amongst you, braving the same perils, sharing the same risks, exposed to the same dangers as yourselves, in order that, whenever occasion arises, we may bind up your wounds, minister to your necessities if you are ill and helpless, and, while nursing and tending you, whisper in your ear the story of His love who came to be the Great Physician of your souls, and for whose sake we ourselves have come to you."

Believe me, this is a more convincing, converting Gospel than any amount of mere oratory expended on deck upon a warm summer's afternoon.

CHAPTER XIX.

HOW TO HELP THE MISSION.

> " O Lord of heaven and earth and sea,
>   To Thee all praise and glory be ;
>   How shall we show our love to Thee,
>   Giver of all ?
>
> For souls redeemed, for sins forgiven,
>   For means of grace and hopes of heaven,
>   What can to Thee, O Lord, be given,
>   Who givest all ? "

THOSE English ladies and gentlemen

> . . . "Who sit at home at ease,"

may with advantage, both to themselves and others,
not merely

> . . . "Think upon
>   The *dangers* of the seas,"

but upon the *privations* of their less fortunate
countrymen who "do business in great waters."
Not necessarily the privations in respect of food,
and warmth, and shelter, and dry clothing, and the
thousand physical comforts to which we ourselves

SIGNALLING.

are so accustomed as almost to include them in the
necessaries of life, but the entire absence of everything in the nature of mental food or culture, the
utter dearth of good wholesome literature.

During the tedious dreary winter the smacksman's life is one prolonged battle with the raging
elements, and there is little time, amid the strife,
for aught but a hastily snatched meal, or a few brief.
hours of uneasy slumber—broken by the cry of the
watch on deck to " Rouse out ! rouse out, there ! "
That is a cry which the poor weary men, worn out
and harassed by the constant demands upon them,
would fain disregard ; but they know full well that
to sleep on at such a time would be the act of mad-
men, for the safety of the smack and her crew
depends upon their prompt and cheerful response
to the summons.

But all things have an end—even a North-Sea
winter ; and when the brighter, longer days come
round, it is piteous to witness the painful *ennui* of
the illiterate, and the unsatisfied cravings of those
who, though able to read, have never a book in the
ship, and cannot afford to buy any ; for example, I
have heard a smacksman say, that during one voyage
he read Old Moore's Almanac through a dozen times,
for want of anything better !

Let those ashore, whose " lines are fallen in pleasant places," set themselves fairly for five minutes to

T

meditate upon such a condition of things as is here described, and I shall be more than surprised if they do not rouse themselves and vow that, so far as in them lies, the old order shall promptly yield place to the new.

To many of us the cry of the watch, " Rouse out ! rouse out, there ! " needs but to be uttered once, and we shall awaken from our slumber, not of careless- ness, but of ignorance of the needs of our brethren at sea, and hie us away to the library to search the shelves from top to bottom, nor rest until we have cleared them of every volume, unbound magazine, or illustrated newspaper which it is not essential to retain for our own use, and which will prove a very mine of enjoyment to the smacksmen.

And here let me give one piece of advice. When making the selection, don't throw aside, as useless for the purpose, certain books as being " only fit for children." I have seen a grizzled old seaman fairly gloating over a nursery picture-book. And well he might, poor man ; he had seen no living thing for nine-tenths of his life but the fish he caught and the sea-fowl which hovered around his vessel, and that child's book revealed to his simple mind such a wealth of knowledge, such glimpses of the teeming animal life in this fair creation, as perfectly overwhelmed him with astonishment and delight. Poor old fellow ! from how much of the fruit of the tree of knowledge,

of the very rudiments of ordinary nursery educa-
tion, had he been severed during all the hard toilsome years! Ay, and as I watched his simple
pleasure, I fell into a brown study, and heard the
pattering of tens of thousands of tiny feet, and
watched a multitude of sweet wee bairns from thousands of English nurseries running to the rescue,
their little arms full of literary treasures, an offering
of childhood's unselfishness to the big children over
the sea.   It was but a vision, yet it might well be
realised.

And further, do not reject as unsuitable the
reports of religious and philanthropic institutions.
To you, surfeited with good things, they may be
"dry" reading; but the pages of *some* reports, *e.g.*,
the British and Foreign Bible Society, the Religious
Tract Society, the Church Missionary Society, the
China Inland Mission, and others, teem with thrilling
incidents which would profitably engage the attention
and cheer the heart of many a Christian fisherman.

But, on the other hand, please, *please* do not fall into
the error (which some of our kind friends, with the
best possible intentions, have committed) of sup-
posing that volumes of very old sermons, which you
would not dream of reading yourselves, are suitable
reading for fishermen.

From time to time parcels arrive at Bridge House
containing theological works of very ancient appear-

ance and date, which might with advantage have been sold for wastepaper, and the proceeds sent as a donation to the Mission. Some of these volumes bear date the beginning of the seventeenth century, and are scarcely of a nature to be even deciphered, much less read to profit.

It is astonishing how much can be accomplished under this head by systematic begging. There are many ladies who do not care to undertake the duties of a local collector of money, but who could amass an enormous amount of literature by letting it be known in the neighbourhood that contributions in kind, whether small or large, might be sent to her care.

I am persuaded that we lose terribly by neglecting to " gather up the fragments," and doubtless many kind-hearted people, who are aware of our crying need, fail to respond to it, because, forsooth, their parcel is " too small to be worth sending." But " Mony a little maks a muckle," and these small parcels, when multiplied and poured into one common crate or sack or packing case, would serve to gladden many hearts in those little cabins away on the wintry sea. And is not that an object worth attaining ?

There can be no doubt that drawing-room meetings have proved of the greatest possible value, and have probably been the means of producing a larger amount of practical help than any other of the numerous methods adopted for the furtherance of the work. Given a well-filled drawing-room, and a full hour for the address, there is an absolute certainty of success. And it is not a mere question of the amount contributed in the plate at the door; but if people have been interested, they go away and think over what has been stated, and the more they ponder, the more convinced are they of the worthiness of the object which has been presented to them.

This mental cogitation culminates in the remittance of subscriptions and donations through the post, accompanied by a request for more pamphlets, as those brought away from the meeting have been given to friends.

"Please send me 200 copies of 'The Price of Fish,'" wrote an enthusiastic helper; "I intend to inclose one in every private letter I write."

An English lady, travelling in Sweden, recently picked up one of the publications of the Mission in the reading-room of a Stockholm hotel. Through reading the pamphlet her interest was awakened, and she has become an earnest helper and ally. I trust this may meet the eye of the thoughtful friend who left this little book in the reading-room! Will others take the hint and do likewise?

Such help as this is of extreme importance; the circle of sympathy widens almost without apparent effort; the mere enclosure to a friend of a tiny purse calendar awakens interest in the work, and straightway in a new sphere there is much inquiry as to the objects and methods of the Mission, resulting in another drawing-room meeting or public lecture, and the whole process is repeated again and again, with the happiest possible effect upon the funds of the Institution.

My experiences at drawing-room meetings and public lectures have been very varied as regards the attendance, the chairman, and the results. Upon one point my mind was long ago made up, that it is the greatest mistake to allow free admission to Dissolving View lectures. The small boys, Dick, Tom, and Harry are there—they come in crowds—but the people whom one desires to interest, those who would very gladly pay for a comfortable seat, and contribute to a collection as well, are conspicuously absent. I speak deliberately upon this point, and have no hesitation in pronouncing against free admission. Quite recently four public meetings have been held in connection with this Institution, each of which has averaged a financial result of £50, and there were overflowing audiences notwithstanding the charge for admission and, in one case, in spite of most unpropitious weather.

Speaking of the weather, it is sometimes rather helpful than otherwise to have half a gale blowing

during a meeting! People are more likely to realise
the condition of those in peril on the sea, when
themselves put to a little extra trouble and incon-
venience. Further, although one naturally prefers
a crowded drawing-room or public hall, yet there
is always compensation in the knowledge that those
who have braved the elements in order to be present are true friends, whose interest and assistance
are indeed well worth possessing and retaining. I
recollect at the moment two typical gatherings where
this was particularly impressed upon my mind. In
one instance, at a drawing-room meeting, where
seventy-five guests were expected, torrents of rain
reduced the number to sixteen. In the other case,
and for the same reason, a lecture was attended
by 700 people, in a hall capable of seating 1500.
But I have very good cause to remember both those
meetings as having furnished occasion for the most
liberal display of very practical sympathy.

Just a word as to chairmen. There is the prosy,
hesitating speaker, who conscientiously reads up
the subject beforehand and attempts to tell the
lecturer's story for him. I have had several of
these, and fervently hope to escape any renewal
of acquaintance with the type. In one instance
nearly half the allotted time was consumed by what
the chairman informed us would be " a few prefatory
remarks."

There is the business-like chairman, who knows quite well that his function is to introduce the speaker, and, at the close, to clinch any nails which may have been driven home. This man speaks to the point, and does not inflict a long address upon the audience unless he has something to say distinctly calculated to help the cause.

The most interesting specimen of this style of chairman was at a large meeting in the Midlands, where the president, a church dignitary, simply rose and said, "Ladies and gentlemen, in the course of a very long life I have, I trust, learned one most important lesson, namely, that the primary duty of a chairman is to occupy the chair. I beg therefore to introduce the lecturer and to resume my seat!" It is right to add that, at the close of the lecture, he made one of the most forcible and touching appeals on behalf of the fishermen to which it has ever been my lot to listen.

Finally there is the facetious chairman, and he may or may not be a desirable acquisition, in proportion to the power or weakness of his sallies. A mere punster is an abomination; but on the other hand there are genuine wits who may materially aid the object in view.

I was much amused one evening when, in a West-End drawing-room, a well-known physician remarked with the utmost gravity at the close of my address, " Ladies and gentlemen, if after all you've listened to to-night you don't put a liberal contribution in the plate, I hope the next time you eat fish a bone will stick in your throat." Immediately adding by way of qualification—" Oh, I don't want to hurt you. I should merely like it to remain there long enough to remind you that you hadn't done your duty by the fishermen, and to send you flying off to find your cheque-book ! "

I have no intention of converting these pages into memoranda of detailed instructions for ladies' work, full particulars of which are published in the various pamphlets issued by the Mission, and can be obtained on application at Bridge House. I may, however, be allowed to utter a word of warning as to the necessity of closely following the printed rules, for neglect of this simple precaution by a few ladies has furnished me with some extraordinary monstrosities and oddities in the way of woollen clothing.

There are now lying before me a sea-boot stocking as long as one of my specimen skippers; a helmet which would fit a brewer's dray horse; a mitten into which Goliath could have comfortably inserted both hands; and finally, a cuff, so minute as to suggest that the lady worker must have sent for her baby from the nursery and tried it on his tiny wrist, in order to satisfy herself that it was

sufficiently small to fit one of that race of pigmies—
the deep-sea smacksmen.

Ladies' working-parties answer admirably, if
properly conducted, and rendered interesting and
attractive. It is always well to commence and close
with prayer, and, if possible, to sing one or more
of the Mission hymns, of which copies are obtain-
able at Bridge House. If these working-parties
be held in or near London, a real live North-Sea
skipper can attend from the offices, and his nautical
yarns about the smacksmen, their temptations
and perils, cannot but render the gathering more
attractive.

Not infrequently the audience may be themselves
helped and refreshed by the narration of the story,
as the following letter shows. It refers to addresses
recently delivered by three skippers.

"The evening meeting was deep and rich in
blessing. Don't be discouraged about the silver
and the gold, you are doing a higher work. It is
the message of the *sea to the land*. We talk of
learning and science serving the Gospel. True, they
do, but these despised little ones, for whom no
man has cared, may be in these days serving it
more. It was beautiful to notice the spirit of
gratitude with which all the skippers spoke. The
hymns on the sheet were evidently much enjoyed
by the audience. I feel increasingly with regard

to each recurring meeting that in the case of the dear skippers who plead the cause of their brother fishermen, it is not talent, but the full consecration of the heart, and personal holiness, which succeeds and brings down blessing. Excuse this long letter, but I knew you would like some detail of the meetings."

Should ladies be in doubt upon any point connected with their work, it is clearly always better to write and inquire than to continue in uncertainty. A lady recently sent a valuable parcel of woollen articles which she had made with the assistance of her family and servants, but she took the opportunity of explaining that she had knitted no scarlet mufflers, as a friend had informed her that they "frighten the fish!" It is evident that either the lady or her friend or both had been made the victims of a hoax. It is certainly a novel point in natural history that fishes, at a depth of perhaps twenty fathoms, can detect distinguishing points of colour in the clothing of their would-be captors.

The reference to ladies' working-parties opens up another and a very important subject—the question of "Sales of Work."

A sale of work on a large scale, conducted from headquarters, cannot fail to attract attention, but does not pay—or at all events, exemplifies the truth of the adage, that "gold may be bought too dear;"

but local sales, if wisely arranged and carried out, must certainly succeed, both socially and financially. There is this further advantage in the sale of work, it gives the charm of variety to the labour of the working-parties, and instead of the perpetual sameness of knitting sea-boot stockings, helmets, and mufflers, ladies are free to follow their own inclination, and to make any article, whether of clothing or otherwise, which is likely to have a remunerative sale.

Thus fans, screens, water-colour drawings, painted tables and milking stools, and the thousand and one articles, useful and ornamental, which owe their invention to the ingenuity, and their production to the untiring activity and skill of lady-workers, are forthcoming, and obtain a ready sale both in town and country districts. I cannot too strongly urge upon our numerous *clientèle* of the fairer sex the adoption of these local sales of work on behalf of the Mission. In every instance where the custom already obtains a distinct success has been scored, and those who have not tried the plan would find it well to do so without delay.

It will be seen that in many cases a combination drawing-room meeting and sale of work would be an advantage, as in a recent case in London, where, at an afternoon meeting, the collection in the plate was about £12, but was increased shortly afterwards to

£26 by the proceeds of a sale in the dining-room conducted by the children of the house, during the brief period the guests were taking their tea and coffee. In another instance, a painted work-table, placed before the chairman at a drawing-room meeting, was sold immediately afterwards for £2, 2s., while doubtless a dozen similar articles would have been readily purchased had they been at hand, in order to help the good work. And as I am writing, a cheque for £20 has come from Bournemouth, the proceeds of a sale of work in a private house.

I am constantly receiving letters from ladies in all parts of the country, expressive of great regret that they cannot personally afford to make larger contributions. Let all such friends forthwith take to heart this question of sales of work, and we shall, before another year closes, have to record a very appreciable increase of income.

During the time this Mission has been before the public I have been over and over again cheered—and not infrequently, when, by force of adverse circumstances, I specially needed cheering—by the evident depth of earnest feeling in the minds and hearts of many of its supporters. There have been several princely gifts to the funds of the Institution; but, on the other hand, one has frequently noticed the most touching instances of self-denial, in order that some contribution might be made in aid of the effort to bring temporal and spiritual blessing into the hearts and lives of the smacksmen. For example, a lady, in forwarding a sum of money collected, remarks: "One of the contributions making up the enclosed is 1s. 2d., which, I think, is worth more than all the rest, because given by one in our service who handed me the difference between a good pair of gloves she *would* have bought, and a common pair, which she eventually purchased, in order that she might send some help to the fishermen."

At another time an aged and infirm Christian woman, a pensioner, whose cup of tea was the one small extravagance in which she indulged, denied herself luxury and sent the money thus saved to the funds of the Mission.

Many similar cases could be cited, showing the goodness of the poor to the poor, and also numerous letters from dear wee children, telling of little gratifications which they had willingly foregone, in order to assist the work, not merely with mother's money, but with some amount which they had themselves fairly earned.

Again we have the gifts of those who, in weakness and pain, while on bed or sofa, find leisure and relief in working the various articles supplied to the smacksmen ; thus :—A parcel was forwarded to the offices by an old friend of the Mission, who had received it with this brief little missive,—" With Alice's love to dear Uncle John, for the deep-sea fishermen, to whom she feels very grateful just now, as for weeks again she has been too ill to digest anything more than fish."

Another invalid has sent bale after bale of gifts, some worked by her own fingers, others contributed by acquaintances whom she had urged to take up the cause. This dear friend wrote recently, saying if any special mercy or blessing comes into her lonely life she loves to feel it is the outcome of the prayers offered by the smacksmen away at sea on behalf of their many benefactors. A very happy thought, and knowing what I do of the smacksmen and their prayers, I am disposed to agree with her.

A lady writes:—" Last evening after I had given my men's Bible class an account of my visit to the deep sea, they insisted upon making a collection all round, there and then, for the Mission, and I have much pleasure in sending you £1, 3s. 4d. that they collected amongst themselves. They are nearly all labouring men, many with large families and small wages, some out of work, so that the money represents a great deal of real interest in God's work among the trawlers, and will, I know, be followed by many a prayer for them."

What real delight there is in the perusal of such communications! Often have I had to stop reading

for a moment, while I cried, "Lord Jesus, Thou who
didst take little children in Thine arms, Thou who
didst commend the poor woman who cast two mites
into the treasury, Thou who hast said that not even
the cup of cold water given in Thy Name shall lose
its reward, do Thou bless those who thus by their
love to others are proving how real is their appreciation of Thy great love to them."

We cannot allow the bugbear of Church or Dissent
to interfere with the progress of the work. It is
not a question of the Establishment or of Noncon-
formity, but rather "Are you a fish-eater?" If
so, the fishermen have a direct claim upon your
sympathy. Indeed, whether you eat fish or not,
they have a claim on you, because you belong to
Christ, and are pledged to devote your talents, your
money, your time, your influence, your heart to
the task of winning to Himself those for whom
He died.

The following suggestion can speak for itself:—
"I am greatly interested in the Deep-Sea Mission,
and have been suggesting to my friends (and carrying out in my own house) that *each* time fish is
served, at dinner or breakfast, 1d. should be put
aside for the fishermen. It may seem a small sum,
but if every one interested would lay it thus aside, it
would prove, I am sure, a help to your funds." No
doubt of it.

The good effected by the Mission has by no means been confined to the high seas.

There has been a wonderful awakening of interest and sympathy throughout the country,—ay, and it has extended to other countries too,—and this, not merely in the case of those already engaged in all good works, but we have it in evidence that many who had previously been living to themselves have been stirred up, and have learned to have

> " A heart at leisure from itself
> To soothe and sympathise."

In no fewer than twenty-four different countries there are to-day contributors to the Mission. Some give money—three have given each upwards of £2000 to pay for new vessels—others render help in various ways, each of which has its value, and is keenly, warmly appreciated. An earnest young Cambridge undergraduate, anxious to serve his Divine Master, listened with rapt attention to the deep-sea story told at a drawing-room meeting, and when a friend at his side chaffingly inquired, " Jack, what are you going to put in the plate ? " he replied very seriously, " I'll put *myself* in the plate ! " He kept his word, for the following vacation found him in the North Sea on board the *Thomas Gray*, where he spent six weeks with much profit to himself, and real help and blessing to the

U

men amongst whom he laboured earnestly, not only in the Mission-ship, but in visiting from smack to smack whenever the weather permitted.

The help accorded has been truly most encouraging, not only in respect of direct financial results, but as evidenced by the warmly sympathetic letters from correspondents in all grades of society—gentle and simple. One dear little girl sends the text: "*So Jotham became mighty because he prepared his ways before the Lord his God*," a passage of Holy Scripture which has frequently been in my mind during the past few years in connection with this work; and if, through the good hand of our God upon us, the Mission has become a mighty influence for the benefit of the smacksmen—body and soul—those who are intimate with its motives and methods will unhesitatingly attribute this result to the fact that we have sought, day by day, ever since that memorable prayer-meeting on June 12, 1882, to remember the exhortation: "In all thy ways acknowledge Him, and He shall direct thy paths." And one specially cheering feature of the current correspondence is the assurance occurring in letter after letter: "We always think of you in our morning prayer." Pray on, dear friends:

> "More things are wrought by prayer
> Than this world dreams of;"

and in the affairs of this Mission, at all events,

it has been made abundantly clear that we have
asked those things which are according to His will.

> " Work, for the night is coming ;
>   Work through the sunny noon ;
> Fill brightest hours with labour ;
>   Rest comes sure and soon.
> Give every flying minute
>   Something to keep in store ;
> Work, for the night is coming,
>   When man works no more.
>
> Work, for the night is coming,
>   Under the sunset skies ;
> While their bright tints are glowing,
>   Work, for daylight flies.
> Work, till the last beam fadeth,
>   Fadeth to shine no more :
> Work while the night is darkening,
>   When man's work is o'er. "

CHAPTER XX.

"*YOUR FATHER KNOWETH THAT YOU HAVE NEED OF THESE THINGS.*"

"Prayer pulls the rope, and the great bell rings above in the ears of God. Some scarcely move the bell, they pull so languidly; others give but an occasional pluck at the rope. But the man who wins with Heaven is he who grasps the rope firmly and pulls continuously with all his might."

ANSWERS to prayer, as in the case of the Duchess of Grafton's gift, have been constant, and such experiences cannot fail to encourage all the workers, while at the same time causing us to feel as it were in the very immediate presence of God.

It appears to me that His hand is evidently with us, and that He is stirring up His people on shore to provide the means for sending the message of His salvation to those thousands of poor smacksmen out at sea.

The following incidents may be cited as confirmatory of the foregoing statement. They are cases selected from many which have occurred within the ken of all the office staff, and they serve to illustrate the words of our Divine Master, "Your Heavenly Father knoweth that ye have need of these things before ye ask them."

At the beginning of January 1886 there were heavy accounts in connection with the maintenance of the vessels, amounting to upwards of £700. As before, prayer was offered. The Lord was pleased so to answer, that whereas in January 1885 the total amount received was £350, upwards of £1000 was sent in during January 1886. Thus each bill was met at the appointed time. ·Towards the end of the month, however, we had a still more definite answer to prayer. The last bill amounted to over £200, while on the day fixed we were just £70 short of the sum required. This naturally caused anxiety, and at the morning prayer-meeting it was specially mentioned. The text for the day on the Scripture-roll was read aloud, "*He will be very gracious unto thee at the voice of thy cry; when He shall hear it, He will answer thee.*" Cheered by this "exceeding great and precious promise," very definite prayer was made that funds should be sent to meet the bill due at three o'clock. The morning letters yielded an insignificant sum, and as the hours passed away without further receipts, I felt compelled at two o'clock to sit down and write a note to our banker asking him to permit a temporary overdraft of £70. As one of the clerks passed out with this note, the postman entered by another door with two letters, which were eagerly opened. The first contained a new annual subscription of two guineas; the second ran thus:— " DEAR SIR,—Will you allow me to hand you enclosed cheque for £100 as a thank-offering for special mercies? Please do not allow my name to appear." A second clerk was despatched to recall the first messenger, and instead of seeking an overdraft of £70, we paid into the bank £102.

Shortly after the gift of the *Euston*, a drawing-room meeting was held in the West End of London from which great things were expected. The lady of the house left no stone unturned to ensure success, yet in some respects the meeting was a *fiasco*. Two well-known philanthropists, who were expected, failed to put in an appearance at all, and the guests who attended lost the opportunity of contributing at the time through some misunderstanding as to a plate for the collection. The lady of the house was greatly disappointed and distressed, but I reminded her that, having done her utmost beforehand, the result must be left with Him whose work she had sought to aid, and who controls the hearts of His people. We mutually agreed to pray continually that God would awaken in those who had been present a desire to help the Mission of which they had heard, and several of the guests very kindly sent donations by post, though not to the amount we had hoped for. How true were Cowper's words !—

> " Blind unbelief is sure to err,
>   And scan His work in vain ;
> God is His own interpreter,
>   And He will make it plain."

Several months passed, and one day in August a gentleman called upon me whose face seemed familiar, and he explained that he was present at the drawing-room meeting above referred to.

I laughed, and said, " Oh, I remember that meeting ; there was no collection ! "

" If there had been," my visitor replied, " I should probably not have called on you to-day. I thought very much of what you told us as to the perils and needs of the smacksmen, and was especially interested in that story of the little girl's text and the Duchess of Grafton's gift of a Mission-ship. Now tell me how much such a vessel costs, for I would like to give one myself."

" Do you mean the cost of an ordinary smack, or a completely fitted Mission-vessel suited in every way to our requirements ? because the latter is much more expensive than the former."

" I mean the latter, decidedly."

We went carefully into estimates based on the cost of previous vessels, and before leaving we knelt together, and my new friend gave God thanks for the opportunity thus afforded of helping His work.

Three days later the following letter reached me :—

"MY DEAR SIR,—I now enclose cheque value £2300, in accordance with the estimate which you gave me as the cost of a mission-vessel completely equipped for sea. In doing so, I would repeat my earnest desire that arrangements of some kind should be made which should as far as possible guard against the possibility of this vessel ever getting into the hands of any who do not *hold* and preach the Gospel of a *full, free,* and *present* salvation through simple faith in the finished work of the Lord Jesus Christ. I also specially desire that *Christians* (*i.e.,* true believers in Jesus), lay and clerical, of all denominations, may be free to preach the Gospel in this vessel, so long as they do so without putting forward any views which may be called distinctly 'sectarian,' and avoid pro-selytising. The main object of the Mission being to win souls to *Christ,* and not merely to a section of His Church, I doubt not that there will be no difficulty in this respect.

"Now with regard to letting my name be known as the donor of this vessel, I would only ask you to bear in mind Matt. vi. 1—4, and to refrain from mentioning my name either in the press or on the platform; but in answer to *bonâ fide* private inquiries (not for publication) you may use your own discretion. The less I hear of it the better I shall be pleased.

" That God may bless you and the work in which you are engaged, and that He may be pleased to accept· this vessel as a thank-offering from one to whom He has shown so much undeserved goodness, is the earnest prayer of yours faithfully,

———————"

. . . . .

On one occasion when at Yarmouth with a friend, we attended the parish church on Sunday, and heard a powerful sermon from Canon Venables on the text, " And He spake a parable unto them, to this end, that men ought always to pray, and not to faint." The preacher's exposition of the reality of prayer was very lucid. On the way from church we talked over the sermon, remarking, " It was well worth coming all the way from London to hear." The next day I particularly wanted to issue a cheque for £120 for the work of the Mission, but I knew that on Saturday the balance in the bank was only £35. Mentioning the need to my friend, he said, "Don't you remember the sermon last night? Surely you might ask the Lord to send what is wanted."

We did so, as definitely and directly as we could.
In the afternoon I had occasion to telegraph to the
office, and in due course the answer arrived ; but,
in addition to the reply to my inquiry, there was
the further statement, " A gentleman has just called
with a cheque for £100, which has gone to the
bank." With a thankful heart I handed the tele-
gram across the table to my friend, remarking merely,
" Men ought always to pray, and not to faint." Our
prayer was answered, and the need met just at the
moment required.

.   .   .   .   .

The months of June and July 1886 were especially trying. The summer season is always a
time of great anxiety with regard to funds, but
during the summer of 1886 the strain was unusually
severe, owing doubtless in great measure to the
absorbing interest of the general election. The
daily morning prayer in the offices was, however,
maintained, and there upon our knees we poured
out our hearts before Him, and found indeed that
" God is a refuge for us." Repeatedly there were
incontestable proofs that our God was caring for the
needs of His own work ; e.g., one day in July, when
the funds sadly needed replenishing, a gentleman,
an entire •stranger, entered the clerks' office, and,
refusing to give his name, placed a £100 bank-note
on the counter.

On Wednesday, the 21st July 1886, payments to the amount of £420 were due; but, on the other hand, a sum considerably in excess of this liability had been promised, and was relied upon to meet the payments. To our dismay this money had not arrived up to Tuesday the 20th, and it was then found that some time would elapse before it could be received. On that day two singularly appropriate passages of Holy Scripture came before me in my usual reading, "Give us help from trouble, for vain is the help of man" (Ps. lx. 11), and "Blessed is the man that endureth temptation" (James i. 12), and our urgent need was carried to the Throne of Grace repeatedly in the course of the day. Amongst Wednesday morning's letters was one enclosing a donation of £30; another, from an entire stranger, said: "I take great interest in the Mission to Deep-Sea Fishermen, and have much pleasure in sending you a cheque for £400 for it. Please enter my donation as anonymous." Four hundred was a very unusual sum to give, but it was exactly the amount needed, and thus God sent it. Well may we exclaim, "Blessed be the Lord, who daily loadeth us with benefits, even the God of our salvation."

Here once again is a proof of "the loving-kindness of the Lord." A gentleman whose advance of £500 at 4 per cent. had assisted in acquiring the earlier vessels, wrote fifteen months later, saying,

" I enclose a cheque for £20 as a donation to your funds, and return you the receipt for £500 cancelled, as I give the money instead of lending it to the Institution."

The following further instance of Divine care and goodness may be mentioned for the encouragement of those who appreciate the privilege of waiting upon God for the supply of everyday needs, whether they be purely personal or connected with His own work.

" O God of our salvation, *who art the confidence* of the ends of the earth, and of them that are afar off upon the sea," was one of the texts before us at a morning gathering for prayer, and we took especial comfort from this in regard to a considerable sum of money which it was exceedingly desirable, though not absolutely necessary, should be paid that day. The morning letters only yielded one-fifth of the required amount, and the prospect of meeting the payment was remote indeed.   Still that one word *confidence* remained in my mind, and in the course of the day I called on the treasurer and told him of the need and the text; on which he replied, " There have been such remarkable answers to prayer in connection with this work that you have every ground for confidence." I had barely reached my room on returning to the offices, when the secretary entered with a smiling face, saying, " A donation has just been paid which more than covers the payment to ———."

Instinctively I turned to the text-roll upon the wall, and saw, what I had not observed before, that the closing verse of the day's portion was, "*Oh that men would praise the Lord for His goodness, and for His wonderful works to the children of men.*" How singularly appropriate!

.   .   .   .

In March last a petition reached us from the skippers and crews of seventy-three smacks in the Great Northern (Hull) fleet, and my heart ached while reading their earnest prayer for a Mission-vessel, knowing as I did how impossible it was to comply with their request. The petition was backed by a letter from a Christian skipper in another fleet, pleading thus for his fellow-fishermen:—" Sir,— Can *nothing* be done for these poor fellows? Are they to have a Mission-ship, or shall the *coper* continue to line his pockets and drag the souls of men down to perdition?" I used above the word "impossible," but merely in the sense that it is impossible to build a ship without the necessary funds. For the rest, Holy Scripture teaches (and many blessed experiences of Divine grace have served to engrave the lesson indelibly on my memory), "in everything by prayer and supplication, with thanksgiving, let your requests be made known unto God."

The smacksmen's petition was emphasised immediately afterwards, when, during a brief visit to Hull, I was repeatedly stopped, while passing along the quays, by men who betrayed the utmost anxiety to have a Mission-vessel cruising with the Great Northern fleet.

"You have sent a ship to the 'Red Cross' fleet; why don't you send us one?" exclaimed a big burly skipper.

"Why do you want one?" I asked.

"Why do we want one! We want one for the same reason as the seven fleets that have one already. We want the blessed Gospel; we want the dispensary; we want the warm woollen wraps that ladies make for smacksmen; we want books to read; and we want to be able to buy our bacca without going to the *coper*."

While this good man was so clearly expressing the various needs of his fellow-fishermen, quite a crowd had gathered round, and there was a general chorus of "Ay, that's what we want."

I replied, "My friends, I've heard the same tale before scores of times, and I have only the one answer for you which has served in other cases, '*God sends the Mission-vessels. God has sent them already in answer to prayer, and His arm is not shortened. Can you trust Him?*'"

Several of the group were Christian men, and we

parted after agreeing to pray without ceasing that God would incline the hearts of His people on shore to send help to their brethren on the high seas.

I duly kept my share of the compact, also relating the story at various meetings, particularly a drawing-room meeting at Leamington, where I mentioned a letter which had just reached me from sea, stating that a foreign *coper* was cruising with the Great Northern fleet, and causing trouble by reason of what the writer termed "a roaring trade in that cursed aniseed brandy." This news had pained me exceedingly, and petitions were offered at the Throne of Grace for speedy help.

On Friday the 11th March, our morning text was " *Thou wilt keep him in perfect peace whose mind is stayed on Thee, because he trusteth in Thee.*" When all were assembled in my room, I drew attention to this passage of God's Word, and, after praying for grace to trust Him implicitly as to all the exigencies of His work, I proceeded to examine the letters, and found one announcing the gift of £2300, to cover the cost of building an eighth vessel, from two ladies who had attended the Leamington meeting, and had heard the story of the smacksmen's need,—the new ship, when completed, to be called the *Sophia Wheatly.*

It is unnecessary to add that the next steamer leaving Billingsgate for the fleet took out the good news, and many a heart was gladdened by the announcement.

During a brief absence from town on the occasion of the launch of the *Sophia Wheatly,* a letter was forwarded to me from the secretary of the smack-owning company who held a mortgage of £1300 on one of the earlier vessels, asking for a remittance of £300 in reduction of the debt.

A friend sitting opposite to me asked, " What will you do about it ? "

" There are no funds this week from which to meet this unexpected demand," I replied ; " but on the other hand, we feel most grateful to the Grimsby people for helping the Mission during its infancy, and we ought to oblige them if possible. It is therefore a matter which may rightly be the subject of prayer."

We both offered prayer, asking the Lord to provide what was required. The very next post brought a letter from an old friend of the Mission, who was on the point of leaving England for the winter. He wrote, " I have just been reading ' An Outsider's Testimony (Past and Present),' and am glad to send you the enclosed cheque for £200." Another friend, on hearing the story, said, " And I will add £100." Thus within twenty-four hours the need was fully met. Again we must say, " Oh that men would praise the Lord for His goodness, and for His wonderful works to the children of men."

The summer season is invariably a period of anxiety as to ways and means. At the commencement of last summer the secretary informed me that unless there was a very speedy and unlooked-for increase of the daily receipts, it would be absolutely necessary to contract a new loan, and he suggested the desirability of obtaining £1000 upon one of the vessels.

The steady but appreciable reduction, during the previous two years and a half, of our indebtedness under the head of mortgages on the original vessels had been a source of very great satisfaction and thankfulness to me, and I naturally shrank from what appeared to be such evident retrogression.

"It will be really necessary to arrive at some decision upon the matter at next Friday's Finance Committee meeting," said the secretary.

"Very well," I replied. "If, when Friday comes, there has been no relief of the tension, I will myself move that £1000 be borrowed for three months on mortgage of one of the smacks; but meanwhile I ask you to join with me in prayer that help may be afforded. I confess I cannot see whence it will come; but this Mission is either of Divine origin or it is not. I prefer to believe that it is, and when we need silver and

x

gold, to ask them of Him to whom alone they belong."

The secretary joined with me in prayer that day, and the next, and the next. Friday was approaching, and with it the necessity for active measures; but Thursday morning's post brought a letter from a firm of solicitors announcing the payment to the treasurer of a legacy of £1000. Once more had our God sent the very sum required, at the moment when it was most needed, and, as in former cases, through a totally unlooked-for channel.

CHAPTER XXI.

"*AS WELL FOR THE BODY AS THE SOUL.*"

" The dear Lord's best interpreters
Are humble human souls ;
The gospel of a life like theirs
Is more than books or scrolls.

From scheme and creed the light goes out,
The saintly fact survives ;
The blessed Master none can doubt,
Revealed in holy lives."

THE Rev. Canon Venables, late Vicar of Great
Yarmouth, when presiding at a crowded meeting in
the Town Hall, remarked : " This Mission com-
mends itself to me because it so practically exemplifies the words which we are hearing constantly
in church when we 'ask those things which are
requisite and necessary, as well for the body as the
soul.' "

In an earlier chapter I told how, on her very
first voyage, the pioneer Mission-ship proved to the
smacksmen that the Gospel in its fullest sense was
to be preached to them.   Since then the preachers

themselves have become more skilled in their mission —in other words, every skipper in the employ of the Institution is fully qualified to minister to the physical needs of those in whose midst he is stationed.

We owe much in this matter to my old friend and quondam schoolfellow, Dr. Schofield, who, as Hon. Physician and Surgical Instructor, undertook the training of the candidates in the elements of simple surgery and medicine, and each skipper now holds the certificates of the St. John's Ambulance Association and of the National Health Society.

Let me also gratefully express my indebtedness to several other medical friends who have at various times faced the discomforts of North-Sea life in order to render service to the Mission, and through it to the smacksmen.

Long ago the medicine *chest* with which we started was superseded by a carefully fitted dispensary closet, opening out of the skipper's private cabin, where bottles of concentrated mixtures—a great improvement upon the old method of weighing and measuring drugs—are ranged on shelves, effecting a very appreciable saving both of time and labour.

This medical and surgical work is, next to the spiritual, the most important. Considered only from the philanthropic point of view, it is the greatest possible boon that could be conferred on the fishermen, and this is, I believe, generally recognised. Only the other day I received a handsome contribution towards the medical expenses from a Jewish gentleman, who otherwise cannot be expected to have much sympathy with a Christian Mission.

"Are you Church of England or unsectarian?" asked a caller at Bridge House.

"Pray do not raise the question," I replied. "Personally I am a Churchman, but I have repeatedly said to some of my friends, the East Coast clergy, 'If these fishermen are influenced and converted to God through the simple Gospel message they hear out at sea, it is your business to make your ministry so attractive and helpful to them when they come on shore, that they will prefer your church to any other place of worship.' If the clergy do not do so they will inevitably lose the converts. Further than this I would only say we are a mission—and, mark, a mission 'as well for the body as the soul,' and the less we hear of ecclesiastical dogmas and differences out at sea the better. The 'harvest of the sea' is not reaped for the tables of Church people alone, and we may fairly claim from every fish-eater in the land some measure of support for a work which ministers so fully to the spiritual, mental, and physical needs of the poor fellows whose lives are spent, and risked, and lost upon the seas."

" Do you receive much public recognition and support ? "

" Yes, I am thankful to say the public, after they had once begun to see how much there was to be done among this entirely neglected class of men, have supported the Mission generously, not only by subscriptions and donations, but also by supplying us with literature for distribution among the fleets ; while many fair hands have been busy working woollen sea-boot stockings, mittens, comforters, and helmets for the smacksmen. These knitted articles have proved a boon for which they do not know how to thank the givers enough. The mittens have saved their arms in winter from a very painful sore, known as sea-blister, caused through the wrists being scarified by the oilskin which the men are compelled to wear, and which, from the constant wetting with sea-water, becomes hard and rough. What the woollen helmets are to them, any man will tell you who has stood at the tiller when winter wind and snow and sleet were blowing into his face, and mufflers are almost as acceptable on those icy waters. We have received great help from ladies who have thus worked for the fishermen."

" And have you special missionaries who go

regularly out with the Mission-vessels to preach to
the fleet?" continued my interlocutor.

"We have three lay missionaries besides the skippers, and we constantly take clergymen and lay
preachers out for a short time in the summer. In the
winter the skippers continue the religious work, and
we select our skippers with a view to this. We have
two services on board on Sunday and several during
the week. Sometimes the skippers go aboard another
smack to conduct a service, and they seize every other
opportunity to put a grain of good seed into the
ground. Some of the men will only come to us when
they are hurt or ill, and at such times a pointed,
earnest word will frequently have a good effect upon
their after life. The fruits of the work are already
apparent: ask the wives, and parents and children of
the men; ask the smack-owners, and ask the men
themselves. With a single exception, there is only
one opinion about the Mission-vessels. That exception is the coper, who regards us with hatred."

Since the foregoing was in type I have received
a letter from the Chairman of the Grimsby Smack-
owner's Association, from which I quote the following:—

"I was delighted beyond measure a few days ago
on overhearing one fisherman reading to a number
of others a letter he had received from an old chum,
telling of the glorious change that had taken place

in his life through boarding one of the Mission-ships. My personal observation impresses me daily with the fact that there is an unmistakable improvement in the character, the conversation, and the appearance of our men and boys. Never have I heard one derogatory word as to the Mission; but I hear its praises *daily,* and blessings invoked upon it both by the good and the questionable of our people. Mr. W—— has had a great deal to do in finding people and shipping crews for our vessels, and he made my heart glad as he related to me the change that had taken place in the habits and ways of a large number of the smacksmen. The evidences are unmistakable and glorious. I said: 'How do you account for the great change?' He replied, 'It is the work of the Mission-ships. The kindness of people in sending them help has made them feel that Christianity must be a good thing to move unknown friends to such acts.' And then he said the simple way the Gospel and temperance are placed before them by those on board the Mission-ships has laid hold of their heart in a wonderful manner."

Official testimony such as this is of extreme value, but there is also the spontaneous expression of gratitude from the men and their families, with regard to which I cannot do better than cite several instances in their own words.

One grim old fisherman, grizzled and scarred by many a winter's buffeting, wept like a child, exclaiming, "To think that ladies and gentlemen 'ud a' cared for us sea-folk like this 'ere!"

Another, who, with his two sons, had benefited in soul and body by the Mission, wrote :—

"For some long time I have felt a desire to write, but not having the pleasure of being personally acquainted with you, I feared I might be taking too great a liberty; yet, I thought surely the testimony of one who has every reason to pray, *God bless the Mission-ships!* would in some small measure repay you for your labour of love. Well, dear sir, to begin, I must tell you I, like many more of my brother-fishermen, never knew a mother's love nor an earthly father's care; so at the early age of eleven years I was sent from the workhouse to sea in a fishing-smack belonging to Barking. At thirteen I was bound apprentice, to serve until I was twenty-one, and although under the care of an uncle, my pen would fail to describe the sufferings I underwent during those long eight years; but then, dear sir, we had no Mission-ships, no message of love and mercy had reached the hearts of our skippers. How changed are the times now! The boy leaves his home under the care of those who have heard on board of the Mission-ships that Jesus is their Saviour, and instead of kicks and rope's end, he is taught to bend his knee at the Throne of Grace and seek the Saviour of all mankind; and, bless the Lord! many have found Him. I am sure many of our dear friends would like to hear us sing, 'My Jesus, I love Thee, I know Thou art mine;' and I know that Jesus is mine. My dear boys, too, know Jesus is their Saviour; and although we may never know those dear friends who have interested themselves so much in us, we will earnestly pray that one day we may know them in heaven."

The next extract speaks for itself:—"The man's heart was so full of joy he hardly knew how he could tell enough about it. He told me he had to write home to his wife and tell her all about how the Lord had found him out, and I am sure he will not mind my telling you as near as I can the answer he got to his letter (for he read it to me): 'DEAR HUSBAND,—I received your most welcome letter, and it was the best letter I ever had from you. Me and our daughter sat and cried for joy. My dear husband, may the Lord help you! What a happy time that will be when we all kneel together at the throne of grace! May the Lord bless the Mission people! What a lot of good they are doing.'"

One remarks, "But for the medicine-chest, I'd never have come nigh the Mission-ship. I was slow to come, for I feared my sinful life might be rebuked. Howsomever, I did come, for I sorely wanted medicine; and when the skipper spoke so kind and straight to me, I laughed at him; but after I got back to my own ship, I thought on what he'd said. I tried to forget it, but 'twere no good. I was ill at ease, and I came back to the Mission-ship and heard, what I'd never heard afore, that Christ Jesus had died for me."

To see them come aboard bruised and bleeding, injured in so many ways, to notice the intense relief afforded by the application of the suitable remedy, is of itself rich reward for the cost and labour of sending out such means of help. "Why, sir, till you came here we never had such a thing. A man might die like a dog—there was no help for him." So said an old weather-beaten fisherman, and he was not far wrong.

Besides this, much welcome testimony is borne by clergy and others who have visited the fleets; as, for example, the Rev. Mr. Bathurst, Vicar of Holy Trinity, Eastbourne, who writes:—

"The Mission skippers have had a training fitting them for such ready doctoring as saves many a sufferer from serious consequences. When it is remembered that these hardy fishers are out on the wild North Sea the whole year round, with the exception of a week at home after eight weeks at sea, and that they are called upon to weather every storm, and face every danger of the deep, we see at once that the Mission-smacks are acting the good Samaritan to the men who ply their daily toil in catching our supply of fish."

Clergymen and laymen go out on the Mission-ships throughout the summer season to minister to the smacksmen; and we need the prayers of Christians on shore that God will give grace to these workers to bring Christ, our Blessed Lord, to the heart of every smacksman. Though we do a great deal besides preaching the Gospel, as the term Gospel is commonly understood, it is well known throughout the fleets that, whatever the errand on board a Mission-ship, no man is allowed to leave without hearing of Christ. If he comes to the dispensary, he hears of the Great Physician of the soul; if he comes for books to read, he is taught that the best book in the world is the "Record which God gave of His Son;" if he comes to buy tobacco, or for the warm woollen clothing, he hears of the Lord Jesus Christ, whose love will warm his heart: whatever his motive in coming, he finds that the motive of those who send out the Mission-ships is to bring him to the Saviour.

It is a regular practice in the fleet for boats to call at the Mission-smack either for medicines or library books or tobacco on their way back from the steam-carrier to their own vessels. As many as forty cases of accident and illness were recently treated in *one morning* on board a Mission-smack; and never does an injured man leave the dispensary without hearing of the Lord Jesus.

The following details are quoted from the voluminous Dispensary Reports which each Mission-skipper is bound to furnish weekly :—

" Skipper of *Flower of Dorset* came with contused hand through the engine; one of the small bones was broken; I put it in splints and bandaged and dressed it. The admiral praised God it was on board the *Temple Tate* he was brought to a knowledge of the truth. Thus closed our Sunday on the North Sea, about 360 miles from Yarmouth. Praise God for His works of mercy and love on the bosom of the great deep !

" While holding service on board the smack *Unity* a boat came for me to go on board the *Temple Tate* to a young man with a poisoned knee. Another case was of a young lad with a very bad poisoned hand, from a Great Grimsby smack. That is the good my fellow-fishermen are receiving from the Mission-ship; and not only are they receiving healing to the body, but, praise the Lord ! in this last week's services five precious souls have come to the Great Healer of body and soul, and now are rejoicing in a sin-pardoning God.

" Thank God, we have been blessed with very

fine weather for this time of year, and the services at sea have begun in earnest. The men seem to be hungering after Christian knowledge. Fourteen large cases of books I have given away from the *Edward Birkbeck* this last voyage, and we have had 180 boats call during the past month. This means 540 men and lads for books, woollens, &c.; 70 of them came for medical aid."

" Again eight came for medicine, and two with ulcerated feet, which I dressed ; lent ten book-bags.

" A man came with smashed fingers, and one with bruised foot, caused by the boat falling on it while launching. A *coper* from Schiedam joined us yesterday afternoon, and was with us this morning, but I only saw three boats go to him, and in a few hours he sailed away.

" Visited three smacks, and found on board the *King's Oak* a man with his head cut open, but I soon dressed it for him, with the help of two medical students who accompanied me from the Mission-ship. At about seven o'clock in the evening Skipper George came to us and asked us to go on board his vessel, as his cabin-boy had met with an accident. Messrs. Bird and Elliot again went with me, and we found the poor lad with his head cut open and a large gash on his cheek. We dressed his wounds, and told him of Jesus and His love.

" The weather has been too rough of late for

services at sea—not so with medical and surgical work. We have had a great number of cases to be medically treated, and two very bad cases of crushed fingers. One skipper got his hand in the engine, and I dressed it with carbolic oil, and it is doing favourably. The other case was more severe. It was a poor boy's first voyage at sea, and he got three of his fingers crushed very much.

" A stoker from ss. *Speedwell* came with a smashed toe. I often think that if the friends on shore only knew what good the Mission-ships are doing amongst the fishermen, we should not want long for a Mission-ship at every fleet. Oh may the Lord spread the news ashore, and stir up the people's hearts, that those who can may come forward and help this noble cause, so that before long no one will want to cry out, ' Why are we without a Mission-ship ? '

" A man came on board with a poisoned hand, and was in great pain ; but I soon eased him by lancing and dressing his wound.

" Another man came on board this morning with a poisoned hand. I find the lessons I learned from Dr. Schofield very useful in these cases. The poor fellow was in great pain, and as I dressed his hand I told him of the Great Physician of the soul."

" Since the Mission-ship has been in the Columbia fleet," writes the skipper of the *Cholmondeley*, " there are men who were a terror to the crews, and men who were terrors to their wives and families, but now, praise God, they have happy homes. At one time their little children used to run from them, but now they are glad to welcome their fathers home. Only in the last fortnight three precious souls have been brought to the Saviour; and I was talking to one of the men's wives the other day, and she said: 'Oh, what a change there is in my home now since my husband has given his heart to the Lord!' Last voyage a great deal of medical work was done in the fleet. In one case, a poor lad came on board who had been struck with a rope, which had made a terrible gash on his cheek, and he had, at the same time, fallen on a piece of iron and cut his head badly. We dressed his wounds, and by doing so the skipper was able to keep him at sea, for in a day or two he was well enough to be back at his work. If it had not been for the Mission-ship he would have come home, and also have suffered great pain.

" Smart breeze ; the fleet sailing all day, but after the fleet shot their trawls a boat came alongside with a cabin-boy from one of the smacks, *Prince of Peace*, whose foot had been badly scalded.

" A man was brought on board the *Albatross* with his ankle dislocated. I put the poor fellow's leg up, and sent him away to his own vessel much relieved, and very thankful for what we had done

BRINGING PATIENT ON BOARD.

P. 336.

for him. After No. 1 patient had left, another came with his wrist strained and greatly swollen; then a man came aboard with a poisoned hand; after dressing it, I spoke of the Lord Jesus Christ; three others came for medicine. One vessel sailed after us with a man who had scalded his feet through the kettle falling off the fire. Visited the man and dressed his wounds.

" I had one case brought on board with a hand so badly smashed that I could see the patient's bones. I dressed it, not letting him leave without telling him of the Lord Jesus. The next case happened last Sunday morning: they brought a lad from the smack *Challenger* with his arm broken. By the knowledge derived from Dr. Schofield, and by the help of God, I succeeded in putting his arm right with splints and bandage. The lad was in great pain, and I breathed a prayer to God to give him relief. After the arm was put right he was greatly relieved, and seemed happy. He left the fleet for Yarmouth this morning."

" I had an accident on the 14th," says the skipper of the *Thomas Gray;* " my foot slipped, and I fell with my whole weight on my arm across the blade of a knife, which happened to be edge upwards. It was a fearful sight to look at, as I was bleeding profusely, the veins being severed and the arm cut to the bone. I soon treated it, and it is

Y

looking a trifle better this evening. I don't mind
a wound when I am out speaking of the love of
my Jesus. We had one come out for Christ yesterday, who now is rejoicing in the love of his
Saviour. I had a real lift heavenward. I did not
mind my arm, for I was so happy in thanking God
for answering our prayers on behalf our fellow men."

One of these surgeon-skippers was called on a
rough morning to visit a fisherman on board his own
vessel, in one of the Hull fleets, as the man could
not be moved. To a hardy trawler this means
something serious indeed, for so long as there is
the faintest possibility of moving, he will crawl
about somehow. The skipper pulled alongside, and
found, groaning in agony, a poor fellow who had
sustained a compound fracture of the leg. His
shipmates could do nothing for him. They were
unable even to put him on board the steamer in his
then condition. Of course, had the Mission-smack
not been there, the suffering man must have been
transferred to the steamer, notwithstanding the probability of vital injury. The Mission-skipper soon
gave relief by putting the limb in splints and carefully bandaging it, so that as soon as the weather
moderated the transhipment to the steamer could be
effected without special pain or risk. In thirty-six
hours that man was in London, where one of the
hospital surgeons took his case in hand, examined

him, and found the leg successfully treated and doing well. In what state, however, would he have arrived in London but for the " first aid to the wounded," rendered by the Mission ?

When a man is suffering from a compound fracture of the leg, after his agonies have been relieved, and the skilful Mission-skipper has bound up the injured limb, put it in splints, and eased him of his suffering, then is the time—and no time so opportune—to whisper to him of the love of Christ, to tell him that the same Divine pity which gave the Saviour for him, has prompted the hearts of God's people on shore to send out the Mission-ships. No wonder that man in the Hull fleet exclaimed, when his injury had been attended to, " God bless those kind folks ashore who send out the Mission-ships ! "

I heard recently a new and very ingenious meaning attached to the initial letters of the title of this Mission, and the story as it reached me was this : A skipper in one of the East Coast fleets had been away from his wife and family, away from Christ, a man who had treated his family badly ; and the children, especially one young girl, had often listened to high words between their father and mother, and had heard the father being scolded by his wife for his selfishness and his bad treatment of her and the children. But through God's goodness the man was reached by the Mission, and when one day he appeared arrayed in a blue guernsey bearing the initials M.D.S.F., this sharp little girl said, ' I know what *that* means.' ' Why, what can it mean,' said her father, ' but Mission to Deep Sea Fishermen ? ' ' No, father, it doesn't ; it means, *Mother Doesn't Scold Father !* ' "   The tale amused me ; but what a grand testimony it bears to the reality of the work the Mission, by God's grace, is doing.   There are scores of cottage homes on the East Coast to-day where *Mother Doesn't Scold Father*, because father has been laid hold of and secured for Christ on board the Mission-ship.

Skipper Frank Macdonald writes : "I have just returned from sea for two days.   When I first reached the fleet with which I am stationed, the Mission-ship had just gone home.   On one occasion during my visit a young man had his head gashed.   I immediately sheered alongside and inquired what was the matter. He said that he was putting out the boat to go on board the cutter when the boom fell and cut him on the head, and in that state he would have had, under ordinary circumstances, either to go about his work or be sent home in the carrier.   In this case I applied warm water, and had the hair cut off, and plaistered and bound up the wound.   The young man then said to me, ' Are you a fisherman ? ' ' Yes, I'm a fisherman,' I said ; and he exclaimed, ' I did not know that we had any amongst us like you.' I replied, ' Yes, *and thank God we will have a lot more.*' A few days afterwards the skipper came in his boat and thanked me for what I had done.

"Last summer, before I entered the service of the Mission, I was one day lying on the floor of my vessel in great agony, and there I lay on Thursday, Friday, and Saturday, praying that the Lord would send a Mission-ship. On Saturday evening one of my men shouted down the cabin, ' Here is a Mission-ship coming, skipper!' and the next morning I was taken on board, and there I fell in with a doctor [Mr. Treves] from the London hospital. I shall never forget that dear doctor, for his skill and his great kindness were the means of saving my life. When I was out the other day visiting my old fleet we had a little meeting for praising God, and I told them the story about ' Mother Doesn't Scold Father,' and one of the men said, ' I think I can beat that. M.D.S.F. means " Mather's Doctor Saved Frank." My name is Frank, and I am a living monument of what the Mission has done.' Another young man received a severe scald on his foot, and he told me what struck him above all was that each morning the Mission-skipper came to see how the foot was getting on. ' I can understand,' said he, ' a doctor getting into his carriage and driving along a road on a cold morning, but when it comes to throwing out a boat on the North Sea, and rowing to another ship, when per-

haps they might be lost, that is a totally different
thing ; but, thanks be to God, these Mission-skippers
have peace in their hearts, and should they die they
will die in harness.'   When I told the men of the
fleet with which I was stationed that I should have
to come away, they seemed as if they would eat me
up.   I said to them, ' Pray on,' and what was the
prayer ?—*that the Lord shall send a Mission-ship.*
There were many fellows there, and I told them
to pray that a Mission-ship should come, and I
prayed with them."

Reference has been made to the prayers of fishermen on board the vessels.   " I cannot," writes a
recent visitor, " soon forget the expression in one
dear fellow's prayer.   He began by saying : ' *O
Lord, Thou knowest that we thank Thee for salvation on each side of the fireplace at home.*'   That was
a very touching reference to the blessed fact that
both husband and wife were steering the same
course to glory.   Not only are the fishermen grateful for the work of the Mission, but also the fishermen's wives and children.   When I went ashore I
visited eight or nine of the fishermen's wives, and it
gave me great pleasure to go in and say, ' Are you
John So-and-so's wife ? '   ' Yes,' was the answer,
with a little alarm ; ' have you seen my husband ? '
' Yes.'   ' How was he looking ? '   I told her I had
taken her address from her husband and promised

to go and see her and her children, and when
I told her that her husband was quite well, I was
asked in, and the wife dusted the big arm-chair,
and asked me to say how her husband was looking,
and all about the services at sea; and the Mission was blessed again and again. In five of these
families the mothers called in the bairns from the
door and said, ' Here is a gentleman who saw father
the other day,' and so they gathered round, and
we had a short prayer for father at sea. It was a
delightful time, and I felt it a privilege to bring
five minutes' blessing to those people. The women
prize this Mission-work immensely; they thankfully testify as to what the Mission has done for
their husbands and fathers."

Skipper William Briggs writes:—" I have seen
some bad cases since I have been skipper of one of
the steamers employed in carrying the fish from the
fleet to the London market. One poor man was
brought on board of us, who had been kept on his
smack for two days, as there was no steamer leaving
the fleet, and we did not leave before the next day;
so it was almost a week before we got him to
London. When we took him to the hospital, the
doctor found both his thighs broken. Another day
a man was brought on board of us from the
smack _P_——. The skipper, not knowing what
was the matter with the man, had kept him on

board for a week in the hope of his getting better.
I was afraid the poor fellow was going to die before
we could get him to the hospital. The doctor had
to open his eyes and mouth, and told us he was very
bad with typhus fever. Then one day last February,
a man came alongside of us, and asked me if I could
give him something to put on his finger, as he had
got the end jammed off, and I persuaded him to go
to the Mission-ship at once, as she was close to us
at the time. In fact, we hardly miss a trip without
seeing some such cases."

In the foregoing chapter it has been my design
to furnish the reader with the statements from sea
in the men's own language. It now remains for
me to add that this work of healing is as yet only
in its infancy. The opinion I formed years ago was
that a time must eventually come when both the
hearts and the pockets of Christians ashore would
be sufficiently reached to enable the Mission to
convert every one of its vessels into a cruising
hospital, on board of which a fully qualified medical
missionary should receive and succour all who might
seek his aid, the patients being retained on board in
specially provided cots, where they would receive
the full benefit of skilled and tender treatment and
careful nursing. This, and nothing short of it, is
what I hope yet to see in every fleet.

CHAPTER XXII.

"*IN PERIL ON THE SEA.*"

" Ocean exhibits, fathomless and broad,
    Much of the power and majesty of God.
    He swathes about the swelling of the deep,
    That shines, and rests, as infants smile and sleep ;
    Vast as it is, it answers, as it flows,
    The breathings of the lightest air that blows ;
    Curling and whitening over all the waste,
    The rising waves obey the increasing blast,
    Abrupt and horrid as the tempest roars,
    Thunder and flash upon the steadfast shores,
    Till He who rides the whirlwind checks the rein,
    Then all the world of waters sleeps again."

FROM early childhood I have enjoyed frequent
opportunities of displaying an inherent fondness
for everything nautical; but the sad experience of
the past six years has taught me to regard the
sea with totally different feelings from those in
which I had previously indulged.

Even in fairest weather, when scarcely a breath
of wind is stirring, nor a perceptible ripple disturbs
the glassy expanse, the thought suggests itself—
nay, forces itself upon me — " Alas ! how many

brave men lie sleeping their last sleep beneath that placid surface? for how much sorrow, for how many broken hearts is that smiling ocean responsible?" Such conjectures as these crowd upon me, and the beauteous scene at once loses half its charm.

But when the wind howls round my house at night, rattling the doors and windows, and swaying mighty branches to and fro until the creaking and the groans suggest the cries of shipwrecked men in mortal agony; when dense fogs put a stop to traffic in the towns, and thickly falling snow hides the face of Nature throughout the land, then indeed the time has come, if ever, to utter that hymn of prayer—

> " O hear us, when we cry to Thee,
> For those in peril on the sea."

As a child I knelt for hours together at my nursery window watching the slow mysterious descent of the feathery snowflakes, thinking they came straight from the hand of God, and were being scattered upon the earth to make it clean and pure.

Now, when the snow falls heavily, my thoughts travel away to the fleets, and my prayers ascend that my brother-fishermen may be preserved from one of the greatest dangers which can possibly threaten them.

"Is there any place on the face of the earth where a snowstorm is so objectionable as in London?" said a gentleman in my hearing the other day.

Perhaps not "on the face of the earth;" but it is infinitely worse at sea, and worst of all in the North Sea. *There* it is not merely regarded as "objectionable," but is dreaded more than any other visitation, and is, as a rule, more disastrous in its results. When a snowstorm bursts upon a fleet of from fifty to two hundred trawling-smacks, it strikes dismay in its advance, and leaves desolation in its wake, for collisions are inevitable, and involve sad loss of life.

As a rule, for a full fortnight after a snowstorm, every day brings its fresh tale of sorrow. Men who have been rescued from foundering vessels arrive in the Thames by the carriers; others, in twos and threes, are taken into the East Coast ports; yet alas, frequently there is not even the satisfaction of saving some lives, but whole crews go down with the vessels. If the storm occurs at night, the driving flakes quickly obscure the lights; if in the daytime, the vessels themselves are hidden by the blinding snow, and the first intimation of the proximity of another smack is the crash, which, as a rule, brings death to the whole ship's company. One cry of horror, one wild but utterly futile struggle amid the darkness, one agonised prayer, and the wintry sea closes over vessel and crew, bringing, in many cases, hopeless sorrow into women's hearts ashore.

These are the tragic events which fill my heart with unutterable longing, and each fresh case gives additional point and fervour to the prayer which ever, morning by morning, ascends to the Throne of Grace from the offices and depôts of the Mission ashore, and from its vessels at sea: "Lord, hasten the day when, by the generous gifts of Thy people, every trawling fleet shall have its Mission-ship, every smacksman know the blessed Saviour as his own." If Christians on shore realised more fully the privation and peril amid which the 12,000 North-Sea smacksmen are toiling to supply our tables with fish, I cannot think we should have much longer to wait for a full answer to the prayer.

Scarcely a week passes without my receiving letters full of expressions of gratitude to God, and to His people, from men who have received help and healing on board the Mission-ships. Thus, a fisherman says, "The month came in upon us with as fearful a snowstorm as I ever witnessed. How our people found the comfort of their mufflers and mittens! It did one's heart good to hear them bless the dear friends who sent them such comforts." And again, "We had a happy time, and felt the

Master's presence. Four P.M. it came on a dense
fog; you could hear steamboat whistles and fog-
horns all round. Thank God, every man got on
board his own ship all right: the fog lasted till
10 A.M. Monday. I am happy to hear from the
skippers of different smacks that ones and twos and
threes are coming over on the Lord's side." And
this, " We had a very thick fog last night. The
first thing I noticed this morning was a smack with
her flag half-mast high. I heard the sad news that
a smack named *Willie* had been run down in the
night, and that six hands were lost out of seven.
The master had a slight chance for life, but he went
down to try and get his child, a little boy he had
brought to sea for pleasure, and both were drowned.
We had twenty-two skippers on board to-day to
service, and two came out for Christ. *Oh, may God
speak by this loss of life to those that are left!* The
master leaves a widow and eight little children; the
rest, I believe, are single men."

But there are other letters which are laid aside
sadly, and with the ejaculation, " *Lord, how long?* "
for they are written by men in fleets as yet un-
supplied with this means of grace, and one's heart
aches on reading again for the hundredth time the
question, " Why mayn't *we* have a Mission-smack
in our fleet ? "

Before the close of her second voyage the pioneer

Mission-ship encountered, on the 24th October 1882, a terrific gale, during which three vessels went down with all hands in the fleet with which she was stationed, and thirty-one men were washed overboard from other smacks. But the Mission-skipper, in reporting the circumstance, said :—

"It blew a heavy gale of wind on the night of the 24th, but, thank God, the 23rd Psalm was a great comfort to me all through the night, and though the billows boiled around and broke in thunder aboard our little craft, I was able to realise the Master's presence in the midst of the storm, and to feel '*He leadeth me beside the still waters.*' The next day, when the weather fined a bit, seven other skippers came aboard, and we held a prayer-meeting and thanked God for our deliverance."

Amongst many other instances, the skipper of the *Thomas Gray* wrote :—

"This morning, as I pen this note, my heart is full of gratitude and love to Almighty God for His guiding care and His tender mercies during the past night. It came on to blow yesterday morning, and just at dusk last evening the wind came down with terrific force and with squalls of hailstones. All went well with us till nine o'clock (all hands trying to get a sleep if possible). I was just dozed off myself when I was aroused by a cry from the deck, 'Jump out here, all hands; a ship coming into us!'

We all jumped on deck, only to see a large barque
running right straight for us. As quick as lightning
our helm was put hard a-starboard, and we let go our
mizen-sheet; our vessel gathered way, and we just
drawed our stern clear of the bow of the barque as
she went tearing on her course. Sir, people talk
of being afraid when death stares them in the face.
I may say at the time the ship was coming towards
us I knew no fear. God took it away, and I had
a calm peace within, and the words came into my
mind, 'Absent from the body, present with the
Lord.' When I asked my mate about it he said he
had the same feeling. Surely Jesus stood by us
as He did by His disciples of old on the storm-tossed
lake. After we got our little vessel settled again
I went down below, and then I seemed broken up;
my heart was full, so I took it all to Jesus and
left it at His precious feet, and came away refreshed
and strengthened. Glory to His Name:—

> ' In every high and stormy gale
> My anchor holds within the vail.
> On Christ, the solid rock, I stand,
> All other ground is sinking sand.'

This morning at daylight we looked around and
could see several vessels with sails blown away, but
I am afraid that is not all. Nothing but the mighty
power of God could keep the little smacks right last
evening. I hope and trust all is well with the

crews of the other vessels. Our prayers are for
them, likewise for a good many more who are praying for us on shore."

And the following, from the skipper of the *Edward
Birkbeck*, will give some idea of the difficulties and
dangers of a trawler's life :—

"To-day is the first of seeing the fleet since we
hauled on the Dogger Bank at 4 A.M. last Thursday
morning, in ten fathoms of water, being a queer
place for a fleet of smacks, and in the face and eyes
of a heavy gale coming on. Barometer at 28–7
and thick of rain. We up trawl, and sailed away
to get off the bank before we had more wind. We
sailed till I thought everything was going off the
deck, and hands too. We had to hang on to the
weather-rail, the seas rolling along like mountains.
At last we had to get the foresail to windward, and
close reefed for a storm. We could only see one
smack. Our vessel blew round the lower end of
the Dogger Bank. The wind lulled at midnight, so
that we could set a little more sail. We went sailing
away up. Saw a fleet, which I thought was ours,
but it proved to be the Great Northern, belonging
to Hull. Came sailing away up. Fell in with the
ss. *Gannet*, of Grimsby, looking for her fleet. Sailing away all night. On Saturday at 12 noon I saw
a smack which had been with the fleet on Friday,
and delivered her fish and got adrift from them in the

night. He told me the fleet was going up to east
end of Pits. Away we went all day and night.
Never see any smacks. Sunday morning, while
laying, I saw a smack standing up with a flag up.
I ran down to her and spoke her. He told me he
had left the fleet that morning. I ran away down
again, and threw all my fish overboard. Sheared
out eastward. Came across two of our steamers,
the *Industry* and *Perseverance.* Skipper Pinero
told me he had been up and down the Bank end
in deep water, but could not find them. Went to
eastward at night, and could not see them. Monday,
got into lat. 58°—first chance for a week. Ran
down again thirty miles. Among the Great Nor-
therns again ; at 11 P.M. spoke ten of them. They
had not seen them. I ran up again twenty miles.
Tuesday, strong wind from E.S.E. Went to eastward into twenty-eight fathoms of water. Joined
them at 10 P.M. last night. Ten sail of smacks
adrift yet, and the two steamers."

The master of the smack *Semper Paratus,*
Lowestoft, says :—" On the night of the 17th of
February 1879, about half-past eleven, we had our
trawl down, the wind blowing very hard at the
time, when we were suddenly roused by the watch on
deck shouting out, 'There is a smell of fire in the
cabin !' We immediately turned out of our berths,
got a lot of water in buckets from the deck, and

began pouring it in the stove and the surrounding parts, thinking perhaps the fire was in that vicinity. After the water had been applied the smoke abated, and we thought all was right; and being satisfied that all was safe, we had supper, and then I ordered the watch to go to their berths. After all was quiet the smell of fire again coming in the cabin, I began searching about again, and not finding any signs of fire, I opened the door at the fore part of the cabin, and by so doing caused a draught of air to rush through the cabin, which, I thought, would probably clear the sulphur away which was still remaining. On turning round I was struck with amazement on finding that flames had burst out at the foot of the mizen-mast; I then called all hands, saying, 'Our vessel is still on fire!' We began at once to pour immense quantities of water on the flames, which seemed to make no impression whatever; the smoke coming out in great clouds, we could not stand it, so we had to make for the deck. Another chance was left to us in trying to quench the fire—that was by cutting through the decks. We cut through the decks and poured water down, but all our efforts to subdue the fire were in vain. Finding that the fire had gained the mastery over us, my next thought was to save life. We looked to the boat as our only succour, but found that the stern had been knocked in; so I told the mate to take two of the hands and take their scarfs and stockings and plug the holes up the best way they could. Praying to Almighty God to help us, I looked round and could only see one single light anywhere near, which turned out to be the *Louise*, but could not tell how to reach her, knowing that our little boat could not live long in such a leaky condition. After we were ready with the boat, I gave orders to swing round as close to the other vessel as possible, so as to give us time to get to her before the boat would sink with us. We reached her in about six or seven minutes. When we got alongside the other smack the skipper of her called out, ' Jump out quick, my men !' and as soon as we reached the deck the boat sank, and went under the vessel's bottom. Thanking God for His preserving care over us, we manned the *Louise's* capstan, got the gear up, and sailed up to the burning vessel, and put out the boat and boarded her, and found out that she had burnt as far as the fish-room hatch. Finding that we could do no more, we got into the boat, intending to return to the *Louise*, but, to our surprise, when we got clear of the burning wreck, it came on a dense fog, covering the sea as if a veil had been drawn over us. We looked for the other vessel, but could not discern her; so we were left in a dense fog in an open boat on a cold, bleak winter's morning, our only help being in our brawny muscles to ply our large and broad oars. For a while we laid on our oars, and I said, 'Let us all shout at once.' With our lungs well inflated, we gave shout after shout; then came a dead silence, then after a little time of suspense we heard a shout through the fog, and shortly after we saw the masthead light of the smack *Louise* coming towards us. We got on board, and arrived safe into Lowestoft. Praise the Lord for His goodness and mercy unto us."

Skipper Henry states another instance of the love and care of God :—" It was durin' the stormy month of October. I was skipper of the smack *Shannon* of Lowestoft, and was out trawlin' with a crew of five hands, two of them bein' my own sons, one of fifteen years, the other thirteen. I remember well on the night of the 19th of October bein' called by the watch on deck to draw my attention to the state of the weather. After I had gone below in the cabin it appears that the wind had increased a good deal; I called all hands to get the trawl up, and durin' the time we were gettin' the trawl the wind had increased to a gale. However, we managed to get the gear all right, and then went to work to reef our little wessel, snuggin' her down as much as possible, but we had scarcely got reefed when the gale came down with double fury, though, thank God, all went well till about half-past ten, when there was a sudden lull in the wind and then shiftin' from S.S.W. to N.N.W. I ordered the crew to batten down all hatches and skylights, knowin' full well we should have somethin' more than common, as is always the case when the wind has been blowin' from one quarter and shifts suddenly to the quarter in the opposite direction. About an hour after the lull the wind came down with such tremendous fury that I do not remember ever witnessin' such a gale before nor yet since. We had done all that could be done, both for the wessel and likewise the crew, so we all went below, leavin' one hand on deck to look out. The rest of us was down below, as I said before, and we were conversin' about the preparations for eternity, when we were suddenly startled by a heavy sea strikin' our little wessel on the port quarter; the effect the sea made on her caused her to knock round about on the opposite tack to that which we were layin' on when the sea struck us. I jumped up to make for the cabin door to see if all was right, when I ran against the third hand, who had been stationed on the look-out; I said to him, 'Harry, what's the matter? The answer he gave me was, ' O skipper, she is now goin' down.' I instantly jumped up the cabin door, and then I could see with half a glance

the situation we were placed in—the little wessel
seemed buried in the boilin' and seethin' waters. The
scene I then witnessed caused my thoughts to flow
heavenward to the eternal throne of God. I then
went down to my dear boys in the cabin. I thought
I had but the moment to bid them farewell, which I
did, leavin' them and the other members of the
crew in the hands of a merciful and lovin' Father,
thinkin' the words spoken to them would be
the last on earth. I well remember the look of
peace and calmness that shone on the faces of my
dear boys; thank the Lord He was in our
little cabin. Returnin' back to the deck I found
the mainsail was lyin' aback, and owin' to the
intense darkness of the night I hadn't noticed it
afore. I therefore crawled along the weather rail
and eased the main-boom over to the other side;
this bein' done, the wessel righted up at once. All
hands were soon on deck and pulled the stay foresail and mizen down, and this bein' done they
went below again. I then took the station on the
look-out in the cabin door. I had not been seated
there very long before I heard the sound of music
proceedin' from the cabin and the voices of my crew
singin' praises to God in the words of that lovely
hymn,

> ' Praise God for what He has done for us,
> He has caused our hearts to praise him thus.'

Those words I shall ever remember, for they sounded like the sweet music of heaven. Nothin' more occurred to us, although the gale raged for two days longer. Thank God, many have been the storms since, but those dear boys still live to praise the Lord, havin' fully showed that the religion of Jesus Christ was able to give solid comfort when called to die, and also shows by their lives that it can also supply solid happiness while we live. On returnin' to our home their mother remarked how sad it would have been for all three of us to have been taken away; the eldest one said, 'Ah, mother, we should now have been in glory.' May God bless and keep them!"

Skipper F——— writes :—

"When we have spent two months toiling upon the North Sea, battling with wind and waves, we begin to dream of the happy times we shall have on shore with those that are near and dear to us. The time comes for us to hard up the helm for port, but to our dismay, after fighting with a westerly wind for four or five days, we at last draw in sight of the lights along the shore; but now the wind, as it were, is let loose from the heavens, and we have to scramble all hands on deck to scratch the canvas in as quick as possible. All the time we are thus engaged the wind is freshening and doubts begin to rise whether we can take the river, but our home comes afresh into our minds, and we risk it. All goes well till we are within a stone's throw of dock. Land is on both sides of us, but the night is one of the darkest nights we have ever seen ; neither moon nor stars are visible. Suddenly the cry of 'Lee, oh!' comes from the man aft at the helm. The wind is at its highest, and instead of the vessel coming round, she is dashed on the shore to leeward. All is excitement ; our little craft that has weathered the storms for the last two months and is so near home is almost falling to pieces ; water is flowing in upon us all round, the pumps are at work, but to no effect ; the boat is taken off the deck by the force of the sea breaking over us, and the vessel is beginning to sink. The only thing left for us to do is to take to the rigging, and owing to the wild sea that is running no one dares to approach us with assistance, and, although so near to land, we are kept in the rigging seventeen hours before help arrives."

Skipper Jones of the *Clulow* thus states his experience of a winter's gale :—

" I was bound home and the wind was dead against us. Presently the wind veered round easterly, and it looked like a dirty night, and we were in hopes of getting in early in the morning ; but at two o'clock in the morning called all hands to close reef. It was blowing very hard. Many in London and other

parts of England have reason to remember that
day; it was the 18th of January 1882, better
known as the Black Tuesday. After we had reefed
I knew it would not do for us to venture in on a
dead lee-shore, blowing as it did then. Just at
daylight the mate ran to the cabin door, called me
on deck, and I shall never forget that man's face as
he cried, 'O skipper! we have not got any water;
we are in breakers;' and so we were. The roar of
them breakers I shall never forget; it was terri-
fying. The only thing we could do was to run
through them, and we came out without damage.
It was a small sand called ' *Smith's Knoll*,' lying
about twenty miles off Yarmouth. Then the gale
came on with more force, and we were blowing
nearer to several sands, and it snowed so hard that
we could not see any distance. Knowing that we
had sands to leeward of us, and that we soon must
blow on to one of them if the gale continued in its
force, I stood in the rigging praying to God to
make the way clear for us, and, bless His name, He
did. Well we sighted one of the sands about three
in the afternoon. It proved to be Winterton
Ridge. We ran round it, and then it was dark.
Knowing my position, I could see no way of escape
in such weather; so we let go the anchor, and with
120 fathoms of trawl warp, we rode out the gale.
It was Tuesday afternoon when we let go the

anchor, and it was Thursday morning when we got on the way for Yarmouth, thankful for our deliverance. In making for the land, we saw a great deal of wreckage, and from Winterton to Yarmouth we counted seven ships ashore, many having broken up."

The perils incidental to boarding fish in the open sea are peculiar to smacksmen alone. The ordinary sailor may go for many months without having occasion to put out his boat, except in port, and from personal knowledge I fully indorse the following statement by one of the ablest of modern nautical writers:—" One journey in a smack is enough for a lifetime, and the recollection of it makes me declare—and I am sure there is not a sailor living who will contradict me—that of all the several forms of seafaring life there is absolutely none comparable in severity, exposure, hardship, and stern peril to that of the smacksman." It is distressing to hear in a single morning of no fewer than eight lives being sacrificed in one fleet alone, in the process of ferrying the fish to the carrying steamers; and this continues day after day, week after week, through the long, dreary winter season. May the God of all consolation hear the cry of the widow and the fatherless, bind up the broken in heart, and raise up many new friends for these brave but unfortunate fisher-folk !

How often, when the howling wind keeps me awake on a dismal winter's night, do I wish that every heart throughout the land could beat in sympathy with the thousands of storm-tossed smacksmen!

Repeatedly during the past five years I have pointed out, both in the press and at public meetings, that mission work on the high seas is, and ever must be, attended with risk. There are dangers of the smacksman's life from which no care or forethought can render him secure. The wisest possible precautions are valueless under certain conditions, and although the vessel may be well found and admirably handled, yet immunity from disaster can never be guaranteed.

During 1885 three valuable lives were lost from Mission-smacks. Surely no one would say, "Hold your hand; do not persist in a work which entails such sacrifice." There is a ready answer to such a protest. Those three bright young Christians were prepared to go to their Master's presence. But every winter there are broken hearts and desolate homes on the East Coast, because husbands, fathers, brothers, sons, will never return from the trawling grounds; and alas! in many instances the sorrow is unrelieved by the Christian's hope of meeting again to be forever with the Lord.

It is this sad knowledge which makes us give
an emphatic refusal to the timid counsel to stop
at home during the winter season. When the
Lord Jesus sent His disciples forth to preach the
advent of His kingdom, He bade them first "heal
the sick." This command we are seeking to obey
on the North Sea; and my readers will readily
grasp the fact that amid the wild winter gales, when
spars, tackle, and gear are constantly giving way,
there is far greater necessity for the presence of a
Mission-vessel, with its well-stored dispensary, than
in the calm nights and sunny days between May
and September.

In 1886 men were on two occasions washed
overboard, but were happily rescued. Now, in
1887, has come the heaviest blow.

The yacht *Breeze*, generously given to the Mission,
left Fowey on Friday the 15th of April for Great
Yarmouth, in charge of Skipper Smith, with Colpor-
teur William Field as mate, and Sheridan and White
as able seamen; Charles Pannell, senior clerk in
the publication department, being on board as a
passenger. Had all gone well the yacht would
have reached Yarmouth on the following Monday
evening, but alas! she was run down when some
miles off Beachy Head by the steamer *Australia*,
of and from Bremen for Cardiff, and Pannell, Smith,
Sheridan, and Field were drowned, the three first

mentioned being asleep in the cabin when the disaster occurred, shortly before midnight on Sunday.

The mate was at the tiller, and White had just gone below to put the kettle on before calling the skipper's watch, when a startled cry from the mate caused him to rush quickly on deck, to find the steamer tearing towards them at full speed, and a collision already inevitable. Indeed, he had barely time to seize a life-belt before the bows of the steamship crashed into the yacht on the port side, crushing the little vessel under the waves, and in another moment the huge bulk had rushed on into the darkness. There was, of course, not the faintest chance for the three sleepers in the cabin, and they were mercifully spared the agonies of a prolonged struggle; but White reports that though the intense gloom, and the fact that he was surrounded by floating wreckage, prevented his seeing the mate, he twice heard his hail of "Steamer ahoy!" and he swam in the direction of the voice, in order to share his life-belt with the drowning man, but only to hear, with terrible distinctness, the piteous prayer, "*O Heavenly Father, don't let me be drowned!*" and then all was silent. A boat having been lowered from the steamer, White was picked up, and was landed at Cardiff two days later.

Such is the story: but the sequel is painful .

indeed, for four happy homes have been blighted, and fifteen dependent relatives robbed of the bread-winner. It is for us—for all of us who are interested in this Mission to Deep Sea Fishermen, and who, by our prayers or our money, have contributed to its success and to the support of the workers—it is for us now to say, "These Christian men are gone to Christ, and we, for Christ's sake, and as a becoming tribute to their memory, will not suffer their loved ones to feel the bitterness of grinding poverty in addition to their already overwhelming sorrow."

For my own part, I could not rest until a special meeting of my colleagues had been called to discuss this pressing question, and there was not only perfect unanimity as to the absolute duty of endeavouring to minister some relief to the temporal necessities of the mourners, but a resolution was unhesitatingly passed, affirming the desirability of at once taking steps to develop the " *Widow and Orphan and Superannuation Fund*," in order both to meet the demand thus morally made upon us, and with a view to encouraging a spirit of self-help amongst the employés of the Mission, by assisting in the payment of life-assurance premiums. The importance and wisdom of this decision will be better understood when it is borne in mind that there are now upwards of sixty men in the service of the Mission, who are constantly afloat.

.   .   .   .   .   .

That last despairing cry of poor Field has rung in my ears night and day since I listened to the tale, and I am intensely thankful that his "heavenly Father" permitted that prayer to be overheard, although in His perfect wisdom He saw fit not to answer it, but rather to take His child home to the Father's house. Though perhaps it is wrong to say the prayer was not answered, for what saith the Scripture? "He asked life of Thee, and Thou gavest it him, even length of days for ever and ever."

God grant that as the story passes from lip to lip many minds may picture that midnight scene, may attempt to gauge the anguish of that dying man as thoughts of his tenderly loved wife and little ones crowded upon his mind. God grant that many hearts may respond in truest sympathy to the appeal I make on behalf of the helpless and broken-hearted, and thus, by means of succour nobly and promptly given,

"*Some* tears of the poor widow may be wiped away, and *some* cries of the fatherless be hushed."

When the Widow and Orphan Fund was inaugurated, we little thought that very soon another of the staff would be snatched away. Yet so it has proved; for since the earlier pages of this book have been in the press, the second mate of the *Cholmondeley*—Alfred Goffin—has been washed overboard in a heavy gale, and has left an aged mother to mourn the loss of her only son and sole supporter. In this case, however, I rejoice to say the sum of £100 has been paid to the widowed mother, the result of Goffin's insurance under the scheme above mentioned.

In an earlier chapter I referred to the "great March gale," which proved so fatal in the Humber fleets. One of the specially remembered disasters, so far as Yarmouth and Lowestoft were concerned, was the gale of December 3rd, 1863, when 165 smacksmen were lost from Yarmouth alone. And who shall dare to prophesy that this winter will pass without a repetition of the tragedy?

> " The fishing fleet is driven to and fro,
>   Their sails are torn to ribbons by a blast
>   Which smites the trembling vessel on the bow,
>   And lays upon the deck the falling mast.
>
>   O wives, who wait at home, and wait in vain,
>   For son and husband gone to win your bread,
>   Never to *your* arms will they come again ;
>   Far down they lie on ocean's shell-strewn bed !
>
>   Amidst the roar of winds and crash of waves,
>   Swept by the billows' fury from the deck,
>   The trawlers sink to deep, unfathomed graves,
>   While drifts their boat, a storm-tossed, helpless wreck."

P. 368.

FISHING THE TRAWL.

May God give to us all a truer estimate of our
personal indebtedness to these brave fellows, whose
lives are spent and lost in ministering to our
sustenance ; a truer sense of our responsibility to
place at their disposal the means of relief from
physical suffering, such of the comforts of life as are
possible in their circumstances, and, above all, the
opportunity of hearing of the precious Saviour's
love, and of gathering together without restriction
to worship God.

CHAPTER XXIII.

CONCLUSION.

" Hast thou not, on some week of storm,
  Seen the sweet Sabbath breaking fair,
And cloud and shadow, sunlit, form
  The curtains of its tent of prayer?

So, haply, when thy task shall end,
  The wrong shall lose itself in right,
And all thy week-day darkness blend
  With the long Sabbath of the light ! "

IT has been my endeavour to present in this volume the leading features of the work, while retaining the form of a consecutive story.

I have adopted this style in deference to the expressed wish of numerous friends who were anxious that a personal narrative should be placed before the public, and it is a distinct departure from the rule I had invariably laid down, that all published testimony concerning the Mission should emanate from independent observers, to whom facilities have ever been afforded for drawing their own unbiassed conclusions.

As a postscript to the chapters dealing with

the foreign drink traffic, I mentioned that the long-wished-for Convention between the six fishing Powers had at last been signed, and only awaits ratification. Also, that H.M. Commissioners of Customs have decided to grant to this Mission all the facilities which they withheld in 1885.

Now, as the final batch of MS. was on the point of going to press, I am under the pleasing necessity of cancelling several pages, in order to find room for some most gratifying communications.

Her Royal Highness Princess Christian has in many ways proved her deep interest in this truly national work, and recently, during her stay at Balmoral, she kindly seized the opportunity of bringing it under the notice of her Royal Mother. The result of this gracious action of the Princess is best made known by the following letters :—

CUMBERLAND LODGE, WINDSOR PARK,
November 13, 1887.

DEAR MR. MATHER,—I am delighted to be able to wish you joy of having succeeded in obtaining what you sought.

I enclose you, by desire of H.R.H. Princess Christian, this letter from Sir Henry Ponsonby, giving the Queen's consent to having the hospital ship named after Her Majesty. Will you write straight to Sir. H. Ponsonby as well, to acknowledge the receipt of this communication. Princess Christian is very pleased about it.—I remain, yours truly, EMILY E. LOCH.

[ENCLOSURE.]

BALMORAL, *November* 9, 1887.

MADAM,—The Queen has read with much interest the book relating to the Deep Sea Fishermen's Mission which your Royal Highness left with her Majesty.

And, in accordance with your Royal Highness's request, is most ready to express her approval of the work.

The Queen will give her permission to the hospital ship being named after Her Majesty, and intends to send £50 to the funds of the Mission.—I have the honour to be, madam, your Royal Highness's obedient, humble servant,

HENRY F. PONSONBY.

BALMORAL, *November* 12, 1887.

SIR,—You will have heard from Princess Christian that the Queen approves of the object of your work, and has commanded me to send you £50 to the funds of the Mission to Deep Sea Fishermen.—I have the honour to be, sir, your obedient servant,

HENRY F. PONSONBY.

E. J. MATHER, Esq.

BALMORAL, *November* 21, 1887.

SIR,—I am commanded by the Queen to inform you that Her Majesty will be happy to become Patron of the Mission to Deep Sea Fishermen. You are aware, of course, that this does not carry with it the right of calling the Society Royal.

Her Majesty desires me to add that she will accept the

dedication of your history of the Mission.—I have the honour to be, sir, your obedient servant,

HENRY F. PONSONBY.

E. J. MATHER, ESQ.

For this proof of Royal sympathy we are, I need hardly say, deeply thankful. I rejoice in it, not merely *per se*, but because of its undoubted effect upon the public mind, in quickening existing interest and awakening inquiry in quarters where the Mission to Deep Sea Fishermen is at present unknown.

Thus Her Majesty's gracious favour will prove a powerful incentive to redoubled activity in this blessed cause, which is truly not the cause of any one person or society, but of Him "*who went about doing good, and healing.*"

As to the smacksmen, they are true and loyal subjects already, but their devotion will indeed be increased on learning that their Queen is not content with governing them and claiming their allegiance, but that she feels for them in their trials and perils, and thus practically demonstrates the sincerity of her sympathy.

With regard to the proposed hospital-ship it must be conceded that the constant presence of a surgeon in the fleets, combined with increased facilities for the treatment of serious cases of illness and accident on board the Mission-vessel, and the retention there of the patients in cots provided for their reception, would prove of the utmost advantage to the thousands of poor fellows who are gashed, bruised, battered, and frequently suffering from severe illness, while occupied in reaping the harvest of the sea for our tables.

The whole matter rests now with the public. The sole hindrance is the financial difficulty, and this I am assured can—and will—be promptly surmounted when the facts are fully appreciated.

The period covered by this narrative has not only been marked by abundant evidence of widespread and daily increasing interest in the men whose cause I have humbly endeavoured to espouse, but the constantly recurring proofs of Divine favour and blessing have filled my heart with joy and praise. On the other hand, the severe mental and physical strain has often proved well nigh unbearable. The zeal and devotion displayed by the whole Mission staff, from the secretary downwards, was, however, beyond praise, and a constant comfort to me.

It is therefore with genuine thankfulness, and as a fitting close to my book, that I mention how, through the kindness of several true friends who have rallied round me during 1887, the desire of years has at last become a *fait accompli*, and the Mission to Deep Sea Fishermen is duly recognised, registered, and certificated by the Board of Trade, with a council of fifteen members, and various sub-committees.

The relief to myself personally can scarcely be expressed, but beyond this I rejoice to know that the permanence of the work is now practically guaranteed, and no longer depends upon the life or health of an individual. Thus the fishermen may continue to reap the full benefit of the active ministrations of the Institution after it has pleased God to remove me from the post of earthly duty to that blessed scene of heavenly service upon which our hopes are fixed.

In conclusion may I be allowed to say just a few words upon the point dealt with in Chapter X. I would most emphatically repeat that, for my own part, I regard this work as GOD'S work, and resulting from the unceasing petitions of the godly fishermen who waited upon Him for a blessing, which, though long delayed, has now been abundantly bestowed.

Sooner or later we all must learn that what God blesses most—indeed I know of nought else that He *can* bless—is loyal and true-hearted service which makes everything of Christ and His work, seeks to follow His leading, and ever gives precedence to His claims, while keeping the instrument in the background.

And now, finally, I would beg my readers, by

every consideration of national sentiment and of Christian love, to respond so far as lies in their power to the fishermen's cry for help, for although there are to-day eight Mission-ships on active service, yet last summer there were nineteen fleets.

But let it be remembered that, after all is done, there still remain conditions of the smacksmen's life which no philanthropic effort can alter. The fierce gales which rage on that wild sea claim annually their roll of victims, and all that the philanthropist can do is to minister to the poor broken-hearted widow and her babes. But it is our privilege— yours and mine—nay, our bounden duty to say, " God helping us, these men in the intervals of their toil shall hear of His salvation, so that, come what will, their feet may be firmly planted within that Ark of refuge from which no storm can ever remove or cast them away."

THE END.

It is 125 years since the Royal National Mission to Deep Sea Fisherme
began its pioneering work in the North Sea Nor'ard of the Dogger Bank fi
grounds. The Mission's small sailing trawlers with their Skippers and crews b
practical Christian care to the thousands of fishermen toiling the dee

Since 1881 when Ebenezer Mather saw for himself the plight of the fishe
and the conditions under which they lived and worked, the Mission has sou
bring spiritual care and welfare provision to all those who bring in the Har
the Sea

This work continues, 'regardless of creed, colour or nationality"
around the coast of the United Kingdom, a work recognised by Fisherm
Government, Civic and Industry Leaders as well as our colleagues and frie
other Maritime Ministries throughout the world.

As we celebrate the unique work of the Fishermen's Mission, our founder's
first published in 1887 continue to inspire us to provide dedicated servic
fishermen, their wives, widows and children both now and into the futu

Brian Miles, CBE,RD
Chairman of the Mission Council

ISBN 1-905200-14-5

9 781905 200146